PEARSON CUSTOM SOCIOLOGY
WITH READINGS FROM THE INTERSECTIONS COLLECTION

Formerly published as Intersections, Crossroads & Inequalities

EDITORS

KATHLEEN A. TIEMANN
University of North Dakota
Introduction to Sociology, Social Problems & Issues, Inequalities & Diversity

RALPH B. MCNEAL, JR.
University of Connecticut
Introduction to Sociology

BETSY LUCAL
Indiana University South Bend
Inequalities & Diversity

MORTEN G. ENDER
United States Military Academy, West Point
Inequalities & Diversity

COMPILED BY:

WESTMORELAND COUNTY COMMUNITY COLLEGE
SOC 155 -PRINCIPLES OF SOCIOLOGY

PEARSON

ISBN 10: 1-269-68259-8
ISBN 13: 978-1-269-68259-6

Table of Contents

Invitation to Sociology

Peter L. Berger

In this classic essay, Peter Berger gives us a peek at the kinds of people who become sociologists and the things that interest them. He argues that the "fascination of sociology lies in the fact that its perspective makes us see in a new light the very world in which we have lived all our lives." While looking at familiar things in an unfamiliar way is exciting, it can also make us uncomfortable, because it calls into question our previous understandings of the world. Berger's "Invitation to Sociology" reflects a well-known sociologist's passion for the discipline.

. . . *T*he sociologist . . . is a person intensively, endlessly, shamelessly interested in the doings of men. His natural habitat is all the human gathering places of the world, wherever men come together. The sociologist may be interested in many other things. But his consuming interest remains in the world of men, their institutions, their history, their passions. And since he is interested in men, nothing that men do can be altogether tedious for him. He will naturally be interested in the events that engage men's ultimate beliefs, their moments of tragedy and grandeur and ecstasy. But he will also be fascinated by the commonplace, the everyday. He will know reverence, but this reverence will not prevent him from wanting to see and to understand. He may sometimes feel revulsion or contempt. But this also will not deter him from wanting to have his questions answered. The sociologist, in his quest for understanding, moves through the world of men without respect for the usual lines of demarcation. Nobility and

"Invitation to Sociology," by Peter L. Berger, reprinted from *Invitation to Sociology*, 1963, Anchor Books/Doubleday & Company, Inc. Copyright © by Peter L. Berger. pp.1-24. www.randomhouse.com

degradation, power and obscurity, intelligence and folly—these are equally *interesting* to him, however unequal they may be in his personal values or tastes. Thus his questions may lead him to all possible levels of society, the best and the least known places, the most respected and the most despised. And, if he is a good sociologist, he will find himself in all these places because his own questions have so taken possession of him that he has little choice but to seek for answers.

. . . We could say that the sociologist, but for the grace of his academic title, is the man who must listen to gossip despite himself, who is tempted to look through keyholes, to read other people's mail, to open closed cabinets. Before some otherwise unoccupied psychologist sets out now to construct an aptitude test for sociologists on the basis of sublimated voyeurism, let us quickly say that we are speaking merely by way of analogy. Perhaps some little boys consumed with curiosity to watch their maiden aunts in the bathroom later become inveterate sociologists. This is quite uninteresting. What interests us is the curiosity that grips any sociologist in front of a closed door behind which there are human voices. If he is a good sociologist, he will want to open that door, to understand these voices. Behind each closed door he will anticipate some new facet of human life not yet perceived and understood.

The sociologist will occupy himself with matters that others regard as too sacred or as too distasteful for dispassionate investigation. He will find rewarding the company of priests or of prostitutes, depending not on his personal preferences but on the questions he happens to be asking at the moment. He will also concern himself with matters that others may find much too boring. He will be interested in the human interaction that goes with warfare or with great intellectual discoveries, but also in the relations between people employed in a restaurant or between a group of little girls playing with their dolls. His main focus of attention is not the ultimate significance of what men do, but the action in itself, as another example of the infinite richness of human conduct. . . .

In these journeys through the world of men the sociologist will inevitably encounter other professional Peeping Toms. Sometimes

these will resent his presence, feeling that he is poaching on their pre-
serves. In some places the sociologist will meet up with the economist, in others with the political scientist, in yet others with the psychologist or the ethnologist. Yet chances are that the questions that
have brought him to these same places are different from the ones
that propelled his fellow-trespassers. The sociologist's questions
always remain essentially the same: "What are people doing with each
other here?" "What are their relationships to each other?" "How are
these relationships organized in institutions?" "What are the collective
ideas that move men and institutions?" In trying to answer these
questions in specific instances, the sociologist will, of course, have to
deal with economic or political matters, but he will do so in a way
rather different from that of the economist or the political scientist.
The scene that he contemplates is the same human scene that these
other scientists concern themselves with. But the sociologist's angle of
vision is different. When this is understood, it becomes clear that it
makes little sense to try to stake out a special enclave within which
the sociologist will carry on business in his own right. . . . There is,
however, one traveler whose path the sociologist will cross more often
than anyone else's on his journeys. This is the historian. Indeed, as
soon as the sociologist turns from the present to the past, his preoc-
cupations are very hard indeed to distinguish from those of the historian. However, we shall leave this relationship to the later part of
our considerations. Suffice it to say here that the sociological journey
will be much impoverished unless it is punctuated frequently by conversation with that other particular traveler.

Any intellectual activity derives excitement from the moment it
becomes a trail of discovery. In some fields of learning this is the discovery of worlds previously unthought and unthinkable. . . . The
excitement of sociology is usually of a different sort. Sometimes, it is
true, the sociologist penetrates into worlds that had previously been
quite unknown to him—for instance, the world of crime, or the
world of some bizarre religious sect, or the world fashioned by the
exclusive concerns of some group such as medical specialists or military leaders or advertising executives. However, much of the time the

sociologist moves in sectors of experience that are familiar to him and to most people in his society. He investigates communities, institutions and activities that one can read about every day in the newspapers. Yet there is another excitement of discovery beckoning in his investigations. It is not the excitement of coming upon the totally unfamiliar, but rather the excitement of finding the familiar becoming transformed in its meaning. The fascination of sociology lies in the fact that its perspective makes us see in a new light the very world in which we have lived all our lives. This also constitutes a transformation of consciousness. Moreover, this transformation is more relevant existentially than that of many other intellectual disciplines, because it is more difficult to segregate in some special compartment of the mind. The astronomer does not live in the remote galaxies, and the nuclear physicist can, outside his laboratory, eat and laugh and marry and vote without thinking about the insides of the atom. The geologist looks at rocks only at appropriate times, and the linguist speaks English with his wife. The sociologist lives in society, on the job and off it. His own life, inevitably, is part of his subject matter. Men being what they are, sociologists too manage to segregate their professional insights from their everyday affairs. But it is a rather difficult feat to perform in good faith.

The sociologist moves in the common world of men, close to what most of them would call real. The categories he employs in his analyses are only refinements of the categories by which other men live—power, class, status, race, ethnicity. As a result, there is a deceptive simplicity and obviousness about some sociological investigations. One reads them, nods at the familiar scene, remarks that one has heard all this before and don't people have better things to do than to waste their time on truisms—until one is suddenly brought up against an insight that radically questions everything one had previously assumed about this familiar scene. This is the point at which one begins to sense the excitement of sociology.

Let us take a specific example. Imagine a sociology class in a Southern college where almost all the students are white Southerners. Imagine a lecture on the subject of the racial system of the South. The lecturer is talking here of matters that have been familiar to his students from the time of their infancy. Indeed, it may be that they are much more familiar with the minutiae of this system than he is. They are quite bored as a result. It seems to them that he is only using more pretentious words to describe what they already know. Thus he may use the term "caste," only commonly used now by American sociologists to describe the Southern racial system. But in explaining the term he shifts to traditional Hindu society, to make it clearer. He then goes on to analyze the magical beliefs inherent in caste tabus, the social dynamics of commensalism and connubium, the economic interests concealed within the system, the way in which religious beliefs relate to the tabus, the effects of the caste system upon the industrial development of the society and vice versa—all in India. But suddenly India is not very far away at all. The lecture then goes back to its Southern theme. The familiar now seems not quite so familiar any more. Questions are raised that are new, perhaps raised angrily, but raised all the same. And at least some of the students have begun to understand that there are functions involved in this business of race that they have not read about in the newspapers (at least not those in their hometowns) and that their parents have not told them—partly, at least, because neither the newspapers nor the parents knew about them.

It can be said that the first wisdom of sociology is this—things are not what they seem. This too is a deceptively simple statement. It ceases to be simple after a while. Social reality turns out to have many layers of meaning. The discovery of each new layer changes the perception of the whole.

Anthropologists use the term "culture shock" to describe the impact of a totally new culture upon a newcomer. In an extreme instance such shock will be experienced by the Western explorer who is told, halfway through dinner, that he is eating the nice old lady he had been chatting with the previous day—a shock with predictable physiological if not moral consequences. Most explorers no longer encounter cannibalism in their travels today. However, the first encounters with polygamy or with puberty rites or even with the way some nations drive their automobiles can be quite a shock to an American visitor. With the shock may go not only disapproval or disgust but a sense of excitement that things can *really* be that different from what they are at home. To some extent, at least, this is the excitement of any first travel abroad. The experience of sociological discovery could be described as "culture shock" minus geographical displacement. In other words, the sociologist travels at home—with shocking results. He is unlikely to find that he is eating a nice old lady for dinner. But the discovery, for instance, that his own church has considerable money invested in the missile industry or that a few blocks from his home there are people who engage in cultic orgies may not be drastically different in emotional impact. Yet we would not want to imply that sociological discoveries are always or even usually outrageous to moral sentiment. Not at all. What they have in common with exploration in distant lands, however, is the sudden illumination of new and unsuspected facets of human existence in society. . . .

People who like to avoid shocking discoveries, who prefer to believe that society is just what they were taught in Sunday School, who like the safety of the rules and the maxims of what Alfred Schuetz has called the "world-taken-for-granted," should stay away from sociology. People who feel no temptation before closed doors, who have no curiosity about human beings, who are content to admire scenery without wondering about the people who live in those houses on the other side of that river, should probably also stay away from sociology. They will find it unpleasant or, at any rate, unrewarding. People who are interested in human beings only if they can change, convert or reform them should also be warned, for they will find sociology much less useful than they hoped. And people whose interest is mainly in their own conceptual constructions will do just as well to turn to the study of little white mice. Sociology will be satisfying, in the long run, only to those who can think of nothing more entrancing than to watch men and to understand things human.

. . . To be sure, sociology is an individual pastime in the sense that it interests some men and bores others. Some like to observe human beings, others to experiment with mice. The world is big enough to hold all kinds and there is no logical priority for one interest as against another. But the word "pastime" is weak in describing what we mean. Sociology is more like a passion. The sociological perspective is more like a demon that possesses one, that drives one compellingly, again and again, to the questions that are its own. An introduction to sociology is, therefore, an invitation to a very special kind of passion. . . .

☺ ☺ ☺

Questions

1. According to Berger, what is the role of curiosity in sociological studies?

2. What do sociologists study?

3. Why did Berger argue that sociology can be dangerous? If sociology can be viewed as dangerous, to what extent might sociologists also be viewed as dangerous?

4. What does Berger mean when he says that "things are not what they seem. . . . Social reality turns out to have many layers of meaning. The discovery of each new layer changes the perception of the whole." Provide an example to illustrate Berger's statement.

Body Ritual Among the Nacirema

HORACE MINER
University of Michigan

As many sociologists will tell you, cross-cultural research is difficult but exciting. Not only might you encounter unusual or disturbing behavior during your research, but you may also find yourself in danger or face-to-face with ethnocentrism— your own, that is. It is easy to judge the rituals, behavior, and general way of life of other peoples as bizarre, strange, or inferior compared to our own. In this reading, Horace Miner lets us confront these issues by allowing us a peek into the lives of the mysterious Nacirema tribe. As you read, note the way the tribe members live, the things that are important to them, and the ways in which they get others to conform to socially approved, but rather odd, behaviors. Would you want to live among the Nacirema?

The anthropologist has become so familiar with the diversity of ways in which different peoples behave in similar situations that he is not apt to be surprised by even the most exotic customs. In fact, if all of the logically possible combinations of behavior have not been found somewhere in the world, he is apt to suspect that they must be present in some yet undescribed tribe. This point has, in fact, been expressed with respect to clan organization by Murdock (1949:71). In this light, the magical beliefs and practices of the Nacirema present such unusual aspects that it seems desirable to

"Body Ritual Among the Nacirema," by Horace Miner, reprinted from *American Anthropologist*, Vol. 58, No. 3, June 1956. pp. 503–507.

describe them as an example of the extremes to which human behavior can go.

Professor Linton first brought the ritual of the Nacirema to the attention of anthropologists twenty years ago (1936:326), but the culture of this people is still very poorly understood. They are a North American group living in the territory between the Canadian Cree, the Yaqui and Tarahumare of Mexico, and the Carib and Arawak of the Antilles. Little is known of their origin, although tradition states that they came from the east. According to Nacirema mythology, their nation was originated by a culture hero, Notgnihsaw, who is otherwise known for two great feats of strength—the throwing of a piece of wampum across the river Po-To-Mac and the chopping down of a cherry tree in which the Spirit of Truth resided.

Nacirema culture is characterized by a highly developed market economy which has evolved in a rich natural habitat. While much of the people's time is devoted to economic pursuits, a large part of the fruits of these labors and a considerable portion of the day are spent in ritual activity. The focus of this activity is the human body, the appearance and health of which loom as a dominant concern in the ethos of the people. While such a concern is certainly not unusual, its ceremonial aspects and associated philosophy are unique.

The fundamental belief underlying the whole system appears to be that the human body is ugly and that its natural tendency is to debility and disease. Incarcerated in such a body, man's only hope is to avert these characteristics through the use of the powerful influences of ritual and ceremony. Every household has one or more shrines devoted to this purpose. The more powerful individuals in the society have several shrines in their houses and, in fact, the opulence of a house is often referred to in terms of the number of such ritual centers it possesses. Most houses are of wattle and daub construction, but the shrine rooms of the more wealthy are walled with stone. Poorer families imitate the rich by applying pottery plaques to their shrine walls.

While each family has at least one such shrine, the rituals associated with it are not family ceremonies but are private and secret. The rites are normally only discussed with children, and then only during the period when they are being initiated into these mysteries. I was able, however, to establish sufficient rapport with the natives to examine these shrines and to have the rituals described to me.

The focal point of the shrine is a box or chest which is built into the wall. In this chest are kept the many charms and magical potions without which no native believes he could live. These preparations are secured from a variety of specialized practitioners. The most powerful of these are the medicine men, whose assistance must be rewarded with substantial gifts. However, the medicine men do not provide the curative potions for their clients, but decide what the ingredients should be and then write them down in an ancient and secret language. This writing is understood only by the medicine men and by the herbalists who, for another gift, provide the required charm.

The charm is not disposed of after it has served its purpose, but is placed in the charm-box of the household shrine. As these magical materials are specific for certain ills, and the real or imagined maladies of the people are many, the charm-box is usually full to overflowing. The magical packets are so numerous that people forget what their purposes were and fear to use them again. While the natives are very vague on this point, we can only assume that the idea in retaining all the old magical materials is that their presence in the charm-box, before which the body rituals are conducted, will in some way protect the worshipper.

Beneath the charm-box is a small font. Each day every member of the family, in succession, enters the shrine room, bows his head before the charm–box, mingles different sorts of holy water in the font, and proceeds with a brief rite of ablution. The holy waters are secured from the Water Temple of the community, where the priests conduct elaborate ceremonies to make the liquid ritually pure.

In the hierarchy of magical practitioners, and below the medicine men in prestige, are specialists whose designation is best translated "holy-mouth-men." The Nacirema have an almost pathological horror of and fascination with the mouth, the condition of which is believed to have a supernatural influence on all social relationships. Were it not for the rituals of the mouth, they believe that their teeth would fall out, their gums bleed, their jaws shrink, their friends desert them, and their lovers reject them. They also believe that a strong relationship exists between oral and moral characteristics. For example, there is a ritual ablution of the mouth for children which is supposed to improve their moral fiber.

The daily body ritual performed by everyone includes a mouth-rite. Despite the fact that these people are so punctilious about care of the mouth, this rite involves a practice which strikes the uninitiated stranger as revolting. It was reported to me that the ritual consists of inserting a small bundle of hog hairs into the mouth, along with certain magical powders and then moving the bundle in a highly formalized series of gestures.

In addition to the private mouth-rite, the people seek out a holy-mouth-man once or twice a year. These practitioners have an impressive set of paraphernalia, consisting of a variety of augers, awls, probes, and prods. The use of these objects in the exorcism of the evils of the mouth involves almost unbelievable ritual torture of the client. The holy-mouth-man opens the client's mouth and, using the above-mentioned tools, enlarges any holes which decay may have created in the teeth. Magical materials are put into these holes. If there are no naturally occurring holes in the teeth, large sections of one or more teeth are gouged out so that the supernatural substance can be applied. In the client's view, the purpose of these ministrations is to arrest decay and to draw friends. The extremely sacred and traditional character of the rite is evident in the fact that the natives return to the holy-mouth-men year after year, despite the fact that their teeth continue to decay.

It is to be hoped that, when a thorough study of the Nacirema is made, there will be careful inquiry into the personality structure of these people. One has but to watch the gleam in the eye of a holy-mouth-man, as he jabs an awl into an exposed nerve, to suspect that a certain amount of sadism is involved. If this can be established, a very interesting pattern emerges, for most of the population shows definite masochistic tendencies. It was to these that Professor Linton referred in discussing a distinctive part of the daily body ritual which is performed only by men. This part of the rite involves scraping and lacerating the surface of the face with a sharp instrument. Special women's rites are performed only four times during each lunar month, but what they lack in frequency is made up in barbarity. As part of this ceremony, women bake their heads in small ovens for about an hour. The theoretically interesting point is that what seems to be a preponderantly masochistic people have developed sadistic specialists.

The medicine men have an imposing temple, or *latipso,* in every community of any size. The more elaborate ceremonies required to treat very sick patients can only be performed at this temple. These ceremonies involve not only the thaumaturge but a permanent group of vestal maidens who move sedately about the temple chambers in distinctive costume and headdress.

The *latipso* ceremonies are so harsh that it is phenomenal that a fair proportion of the really sick natives who enter the temple ever recover. Small children whose indoctrination is still incomplete have been known to resist attempts to take them to the temple because "that is where you go to die." Despite this fact, sick adults are not only willing but eager to undergo the protracted ritual purification, if they can afford to do so. No matter how ill the supplicant or how grave the emergency, the guardians of many temples will not admit a client if he cannot give a rich gift to the custodian. Even after one has gained admission and survived the ceremonies, the guardians will not permit the neophyte to leave until he makes still another gift.

The supplicant entering the temple is first stripped of all his or her clothes. In everyday life the Nacirema avoids exposure of his body and its natural functions. Bathing and excretory acts are performed only in the secrecy of the household shrine, where they are ritualized as part of the body-rites. Psychological shock results from the fact that body secrecy is suddenly lost upon entry into the *latipso.* A man, whose own wife has never seen him in an excretory act, suddenly finds himself naked and assisted by a vestal maiden while he performs his natural functions into a sacred vessel. This sort of ceremonial treatment is necessitated by the fact that the excreta are used by a diviner to ascertain the course and nature of the client's sickness. Female clients, on the other hand, find their naked bodies are subjected to the scrutiny, manipulation and prodding of the medicine men.

Few supplicants in the temple are well enough to do anything but lie on their hard beds. The daily ceremonies, like the rites of the holy-mouth-men, involve discomfort and torture. With ritual precision, the vestals awaken their miserable charges each dawn and roll them about on their beds of pain while performing ablutions, in the formal movements of which the maidens are highly trained. At other times they insert magic wands in the supplicant's mouth or force him to eat substances which are supposed to be healing. From time to time the medicine men come to their clients and jab magically treated needles into their flesh. The fact that these temple ceremonies may not cure, and may even kill the neophyte, in no way decreases the people's faith in the medicine men.

There remains one other kind of practitioner, known as a "listener." This witch-doctor has the power to exorcise the devils that lodge in the heads of people who have been bewitched. The Nacirema believe that parents bewitch their own children. Mothers are particularly suspected of putting a curse on children while teaching them the secret body rituals. The counter-magic of the witch-doctor is unusual in its lack of ritual. The patient simply tells the "listener" all his troubles and fears, beginning with the earliest difficulties he can remember. The memory displayed by the Nacirema in these exorcism sessions is truly remarkable. It is not uncommon for the patient to bemoan the rejection he felt upon being weaned as a babe, and a few individuals even see their troubles going back to the traumatic effects of their own birth.

In conclusion, mention must be made of certain practices which have their base in native esthetics but which depend upon the pervasive aversion to the natural body and its functions. There are ritual fasts to make fat people thin and ceremonial feasts to make thin people fat. Still other rites are used to make women's breasts larger if they are small, and smaller if they are large. General dissatisfaction with breast shape is symbolized in the fact that the ideal form is virtually outside the range of human variation. A few women afflicted with almost inhuman hypermammary development are so idolized that they make a handsome living by simply going from village to village and permitting the natives to stare at them for a fee.

Reference has already been made to the fact that excretory functions are ritualized, routinized, and relegated to secrecy. Natural reproductive functions are similarly distorted. Intercourse is taboo as a topic and scheduled as an act. Efforts are made to avoid pregnancy by the use of magical materials or by limiting intercourse to certain phases of the moon. Conception is actually very infrequent. When pregnant, women dress so as to hide their condition. Parturition takes place in secret, without friends or relatives to assist, and the majority of women do not nurse their infants.

Our review of the ritual life of the Nacirema has certainly shown them to be a magic-ridden people. It is hard to understand how they have managed to exist so long under the burdens which they have imposed upon themselves. But even such exotic customs as these take on real meaning when they are viewed with the insight provided by Malinowski when he wrote (1948:70):

> Looking from far and above, from our high places of safety in the developed civilization, it is easy to see all the crudity and irrelevance of magic. But without its power and guidance early man could not have mastered his practical difficulties as he has done, nor could man have advanced to the higher stages of civilization.

References

Linton, R. (1936). *The study of man.* New York: D. Appleton-Century Co.

Malinowski, B. (1948). *Magic, science, and religion.* Glencoe, IL: The Free Press.

Murdock, G. P. (1949). *Social structure.* New York: The Macmillan Co.

❂ ❂ ❂

Questions

1. We might find many things strange about the Nacirema. What might the Nacirema find strange about us? List three possibilities and explain your choices.

2. Use the reading to explain and cite examples of the following concepts: value, norm, and sanction.

3. What benefit might we derive from studying the Nacirema way of life?

4. Miner studied the Nacirema from an anthropological perspective; as a sociologist who wants to understand the Nacirema, what would you do differently in studying them?

5. What role does the listener play in Nacirema culture?

6. Explain the role of magic in the daily lives of the Nacirema.

7. Many readers finish this article without realizing that "Nacirema" is "American" spelled backwards. Why did Miner write about Americans as if we were a strange tribe? What insights do we gain about ourselves by taking this perspective?

Manifesto of the Communist Party

KARL MARX AND FRIEDRICH ENGELS

Karl Marx's and Friedrich Engels' Communist Manifesto laid the theoretical foundation for what sociologists have since labeled the "conflict" perspective. This work details the nature of social relations between the bourgeoisie (the middle and upper classes) and the proletariat (the working class), paying particular attention to the role that the means of production play. The work clearly outlines the nature of the political economy and the process by which class inequality emerges and is maintained.

☺ Bourgeois and Proletarians[1]

The history of all hitherto existing society is the history of class struggles.

Freeman and slave, patrician and plebeian, lord and serf, guild-master and journeyman, in a word, oppressor and oppressed, stood in constant opposition to one another, carried on an uninterrupted, now hidden, now open fight, a fight that each time ended, either in a revolutionary reconstitution of society at large, or in the common ruin of the contending classes.

In the earlier epochs of history, we find almost everywhere a complicated arrangement of society into various orders, a manifold gradation of social rank. In ancient Rome we have patricians, knights, plebeians, slaves; in the Middle Ages, feudal lords, vassals, guild-mas-

Manifesto of the Communist Party, Part I, by Karl Marx and Friedrich Engels, 1848.

ters, journeymen, apprentices, serfs; in almost all of these classes, again, subordinate gradations.

The modern bourgeois society that has sprouted from the ruins of feudal society, has not done away with class antagonisms. It has but established new classes, new conditions of oppression, new forms of struggle in place of the old ones.

Our epoch, the epoch of the bourgeoisie, possesses, however, this distinctive feature; it has simplified the class antagonisms. Society as a whole is more and more splitting up into two great hostile camps, into two great classes directly facing each other: Bourgeoisie and Proletariat.

From the serfs of the Middle Ages sprang the chartered burghers of the earliest towns. From these burgesses the first elements of the bourgeoisie were developed.

The discovery of America, the rounding of the Cape, opened up fresh ground for the rising bourgeoisie. The East Indian and Chinese markets, the [colonization] of America, trade with the colonies, the increase in the means of exchange and in commodities generally, gave to commerce, to navigation, to industry, an impulse never before known, and thereby, to the revolutionary element in the tottering feudal society, a rapid development.

The feudal system of industry, under which industrial production was monopolized by close guilds, now no longer sufficed for the growing wants of the new markets. The manufacturing system took its place. The guild-masters were pushed on one side by the manufacturing middle class; division of labor between the different corporate guilds vanished in the face of division of labor in each single workshop.

Meantime the markets kept ever growing, the demand, ever rising. Even manufacture no longer sufficed. Thereupon, steam and machinery revolutionized industrial production. The place of manufacture was taken by the giant, Modern Industry, the place of the industrial middle class, by industrial millionaires, the leaders of whole industrial armies, the modern bourgeois.

Modern industry has established the worldmarket, for which the discovery of America paved the way. This market has given an immense development to commerce, to navigation, to communication by land. This development has, in its turn, reacted on the extension of industry; and in proportion as industry, commerce, navigation, railways extended, in the same proportion the bourgeoisie developed, increased its capital, and pushed into the background every class handed down from the Middle Ages.

We see, therefore, how the modern bourgeoisie is itself the product of a long course of development, of a series of revolutions in the modes of production and of exchange.

Each step in the development of the bourgeoisie was accompanied by a corresponding political advance of that class. An oppressed class under the sway of the feudal nobility, an armed and self-governing association in the mediaeval commune,[2] here independent urban republic (as in Italy and Germany), there taxable "third estate" of the monarchy (as in France), afterwards, in the period of manufacture proper, serving either the semi-feudal or the absolute monarchy as a counterpoise against the nobility, and, in fact, cornerstone of the great monarchies in general, the bourgeoisie has at last, since the establishment of Modern Industry and of the world-market, conquered for itself, in the modern representative State, exclusive political sway. The executive of the modern State is but a committee for managing the common affairs of the whole bourgeoisie.

The bourgeoisie, historically, has played a most revolutionary part.

The bourgeoisie, wherever it has got the upper hand, has put an end to all feudal, patriarchal, idyllic relations. It has pitilessly torn asunder the motley feudal ties that bound man to his "natural superiors," and has left remaining no other nexus between man and man than naked self-interest, than callous "cash payment." It has drowned the most heavenly ecstasies of religious fervour, of chivalrous enthusiasm, of philistine sentimentalism, in the icy water of egotistical calculation. It has resolved personal worth into exchange value, and in place of the numberless indefeasible chartered freedoms, has set up that single, unconscionable freedom—Free Trade. In one word, for exploitation, veiled by religious and political illusions, it has substituted naked, shameless, direct, brutal exploitation.

The bourgeoisie has stripped of its halo every occupation hitherto honoured and looked up to with reverent awe. It has converted the physician, the lawyer, the priest, the poet, the man of science, into its paid [wage-laborers].

The bourgeoisie has torn away from the family its sentimental veil, and has reduced the family relation to a mere money relation.

The bourgeoisie has disclosed how it came to pass that the brutal display of vigour in the Middle Ages, which Reactionists so much admire, found its fitting complement in the most slothful indolence. It has been the first to show what man's activity can bring about. It has accomplished wonders far surpassing Egyptian pyramids, Roman aqueducts, and Gothic cathedrals; it has conducted expeditions that put in the shade all former Exoduses of nations and crusades.

The bourgeoisie cannot exist without constantly revolutionizing the instruments of production, and thereby the relations of production, and with them the whole relations of society. Conservation of the old modes of production in unaltered form, was, on the contrary, the first condition of existence for all earlier industrial classes. Constant revolutionizing of production, uninterrupted disturbance of all social conditions, everlasting uncertainty and agitation distinguish the bourgeois epoch from all earlier ones. All fixed, fast-frozen relations, with their train of ancient and venerable prejudices and opinions, are swept away, all new-formed ones become antiquated before they can ossify. All that is solid melts into air, all that is holy is profaned, and man is at last compelled to face with sober senses, his real conditions of life, and his relations with his kind.

The need of a constantly expanding market for its products chases the bourgeoisie over the whole surface of the globe. It must nestle everywhere, settle everywhere, establish [connections] everywhere.

The bourgeoisie has through its exploitation of the world-market given a cosmopolitan character to production and consumption in every country. To the great chagrin of Reactionists, it has drawn from under the feet of industry the national ground on which it stood. All old-established national industries have been destroyed or are daily being destroyed. They are dislodged by new industries, whose introduction becomes a life and death question for all civilised nations, by industries that no longer work up indigenous raw material, but raw material drawn from the remotest zones; industries whose products are consumed, not only at home, but in every quarter of the globe. In place of the old wants, satisfied by the productions of the country, we find new wants, requiring for their satisfaction the products of distant lands and climes. In place of the old local and national seclusion and self-sufficiency, we have intercourse in every direction, universal interdependence of nations. And as in material, so also in intellectual production. The intellectual creations of individual nations become common property. National one-sidedness and narrow-mindedness become more and more impossible, and from the numerous national and local literatures there arises a world-literature.

The bourgeoisie, by the rapid improvement of all instruments of production, by the immensely facilitated means of communication, draws all, even the most barbarian, nations into civilization. The cheap prices of its commodities are the heavy artillery with which it batters down all Chinese walls, with which it forces the barbarians' intensely obstinate hatred of foreigners to capitulate. It compels all nations, on pain of extinction, to adopt the bourgeois mode of production; it compels them to introduce what it calls civilization into their midst, i.e., to become bourgeois themselves. In a word, it creates a world after its own image.

The bourgeoisie has subjected the country to the rule of the towns. It has created enormous cities, has greatly increased the urban population as compared with the rural, and has thus rescued a considerable part of the population from the idiocy of rural life. Just as it has made the country dependent on the towns, so it has made barbarian and semi-barbarian countries dependent on the civilised ones, nations of peasants on nations of bourgeois, the East on the West.

The bourgeoisie keeps more and more doing away with the scattered state of the population, of the means of production, and of property. It has agglomerated population, centralized means of production, and has concentrated property in a few hands. The necessary consequence of this was political centralization. Independent, or but loosely connected provinces, with separate interests, laws, governments and systems of taxation, became lumped together in one nation, with one government, one code of laws, one national class interest, one frontier and one customs-tariff.

The bourgeoisie, during its rule of scarce one hundred years, has created more massive and more colossal productive forces than have all preceding generations together. Subjection of Nature's forces to man, machinery, application of chemistry to industry and agriculture, steam-navigation, railways, electric telegraphs, clearing of whole continents for cultivation, canalization of rivers, whole populations conjured out of the ground—what earlier century had even a presentiment that such productive forces slumbered in the lap of social labor?

We see then: The means of production and of exchange on whose foundation the bourgeoisie built itself up, were generated in feudal society. At a certain stage in the development of these means of production and of exchange, the conditions under which feudal society produced and exchanged, the feudal organization of agriculture and manufacturing industry, in one word, the feudal relations of property became no longer compatible with the already developed productive forces; they became so many fetters. They had to burst asunder; they were burst asunder.

Into their places stepped free competition, accompanied by a social and political constitution adapted to it, and by the economical and political sway of the bourgeois class.

A similar movement is going on before our own eyes. Modern bourgeois society with its relations of production, of exchange and of property, a society that has conjured up such gigantic means of production and of exchange, is like the sorcerer, who is no longer able to control the powers of the nether world whom he has called up by his spells. For many a decade past the history of industry and commerce is but the history of the revolt of modern productive forces against modern conditions of production, against the property relations that are the conditions for the existence of the bourgeoisie and of its rule. It is enough to mention the commercial crises that by their periodical return put on its trial, each time more threateningly, the existence of the entire bourgeois society. In these crises a great part not only of the existing products, but also of the previously created productive forces, are periodically destroyed. In these crises there breaks out an epidemic that, in all earlier epochs, would have seemed an absurdity—the epidemic of overproduction. Society suddenly finds itself put back into a state of momentary barbarism; it appears as if a famine, a universal war of devastation had cut off the supply of every means of subsistence; industry and commerce seem to be destroyed; and why? Because there is too much civilization, too much means of subsistence, too much industry, too much commerce. The productive forces at the disposal of society no longer tend to further the development of the conditions of bourgeois property; on the contrary, they have become too powerful for these conditions, by which they are fettered, and so soon as they overcome these fetters, they bring disorder into the whole of bourgeois society, endanger the existence of bourgeois property. The conditions of bourgeois society are too narrow to comprise the wealth created by them. And how does the bourgeoisie get over these crises? On the one hand by enforced destruction of a mass of productive forces; on the other, by the conquest of new markets, and by the more thorough exploitation of the old ones. That is to say, by paving the way for more extensive and more destructive crises, and by diminishing the means whereby crises are prevented.

The weapons with which the bourgeoisie felled feudalism to the ground are now turned against the bourgeoisie itself.

But not only has the bourgeoisie forged the weapons that bring death to itself; it has also called into existence the men who are to wield those weapons—the modern working class—the proletarians.

In proportion as the bourgeoisie, i.e., capital, is developed, in the same proportion is the proletariat, the modern working class, developed, a class of laborers, who live only so long as they find work, and who find work only so long as their labor increases capital. These laborers, who must sell themselves piecemeal, are a commodity, like every other article of commerce, and are consequently exposed to all the vicissitudes of competition, to all the fluctuations of the market.

Owing to the extensive use of machinery and to division of labor, the work of the proletarians has lost all individual character, and, consequently, all charm for the workman. He becomes an appendage of the machine, and it is only the most simple, most monotonous and most easily acquired knack that is required of him. Hence, the cost of production of a workman is restricted, almost entirely, to the means of subsistence that he requires for his maintenance, and for the propagation of his race. But the price of a commodity, and also of labor, is equal to its cost of production. In proportion, therefore, as the repulsiveness of the work increases, the wage decreases. Nay more, in proportion as the use of machinery and division of labor increases, in the same proportion the burden of toil also increases, whether by prolongation of the working hours, by increase of the work enacted in a given time, or by increased speed of the machinery, etc.

Modern industry has converted the little workshop of the patriarchal master into the great factory of the industrial capitalist. Masses of laborers, crowded into the factory, are organized like soldiers. As privates of the industrial army they are placed under the command of a perfect hierarchy of officers and sergeants. Not only are they the slaves of the bourgeois class, and of the bourgeois State, they are daily and hourly enslaved by the machine, by the over-looker, and, above all, by the individual bourgeois manufacturer himself. The more openly this despotism proclaims gain to be its end and aim, the more petty, more hateful and the more embittering it is.

The less the skill and exertion or strength implied in manual labor, in other words the more modern industry becomes developed, the more is the labor of men superseded by that of women. Differences of age and sex have no longer any distinctive social validity for the working class. All are instruments of labor, more or less expensive to use, according to their age and sex.

No sooner is the exploitation of the laborer by the manufacturer, so far, at an end, that he receives his wages in cash, than he is set upon by the other portions of the bourgeoisie, the landlord, the shop-keeper, the pawnbroker, etc.

The lower strata of the middle class—the small tradespeople, shopkeepers, and retired tradesmen generally, the handicraftsmen and peasants—all these sink gradually into the proletariat, partly because their diminutive capital does not suffice for the scale on which Modern Industry is carried on, and is swamped in the competition with the large capitalists, partly because their specialised skill is rendered worthless by new methods of production. Thus the proletariat is recruited from all classes of the population.

The proletariat goes through various stages of development. With its birth begins its struggle with the bourgeoisie. At first the contest is carried on by individual laborers, then by the workpeople of a factory, then by the operatives of one trade, in one locality, against the individual bourgeois who directly exploits them. They direct their attacks not against the bourgeois conditions of production, but against the instruments of production themselves; they destroy imported wares that compete with their labor, they smash to pieces machinery, they set factories ablaze, they seek to restore by force the vanished status of the workman of the Middle Ages.

At this stage the laborers still form an incoherent mass scattered over the whole country, and broken up by their mutual competition. If anywhere they unite to form more compact bodies, this is not yet the consequence of their own active union, but of the union of the bourgeoisie, which class, in order to attain its own political ends, is compelled to set the whole proletariat in motion, and is moreover yet, for a time, able to do so. At this stage, therefore, the proletarians do not fight their enemies, but the enemies of their enemies, the remnants of absolute monarchy, the landowners, the non-industrial bourgeois, the petty bourgeoisie. Thus the whole historical movement is concentrated in the hands of the bourgeoisie; every victory so obtained is a victory for the bourgeoisie.

But with the development of industry the proletariat not only increases in number, it becomes concentrated in greater masses, its strength grows, and it feels that strength more. The various interests and conditions of life within the ranks of the proletariat are more and more equalized, in proportion as machinery obliterates all distinctions of labor, and nearly everywhere reduces wages to the same low level. The growing competition among the bourgeois, and the resulting commercial crises, make the wages of the workers ever more fluctuating. The unceasing improvement of machinery, ever more rapidly developing, makes their livelihood more and more precarious; the collisions between individual workmen and individual bourgeois take more and more the character of collisions between two classes. Thereupon the workers begin to form combinations (Trades' Unions) against the bourgeois; they club together in order to keep up the rate of wages; they found permanent associations in order to make provision beforehand for these occasional revolts. Here and there the contest breaks out into riots.

Now and then the workers are victorious, but only for a time. The real fruit of their battles lies, not in the immediate result, but in the ever expanding union of the workers. This union is helped on by the improved means of communication that are created by modern industry, and that place the workers of different localities in contact with one another. It was just this contact that was needed to centralize the numerous local struggles, all of the same character, into one national struggle between classes. But every class struggle is a political struggle. And that union, to attain which the burghers of the Middle Ages, with their miserable highways, required centuries, the modern proletarians, thanks to railways, achieve in a few years.

This organization of the proletarians into a class, and consequently into a political party, is continually being upset again by the competition between the workers themselves. But it ever rises up again, stronger, firmer, mightier. It compels legislative recognition of particular interests of the workers, by taking advantage of the divisions among the bourgeoisie itself. Thus the Ten-Hours-Bill in England was carried.

Altogether collisions between the classes of the old society further, in many ways, the course of development of the proletariat. The bourgeoisie finds itself involved in a constant battle. At first with the aristocracy; later on, with those portions of the bourgeoisie itself, whose interests have become antagonistic to the progress of industry; at all times, with the bourgeoisie of foreign countries. In all these battles it sees itself compelled to appeal to the proletariat, to ask for its help, and thus, to drag it into the political arena. The bourgeoisie itself, therefore, supplies the proletariat with its own elements of political and general education, in other words, it furnishes the proletariat with weapons for fighting the bourgeoisie.

Further, as we have already seen, entire sections of the ruling classes are, by the advance of industry, precipitated into the proletariat, or are at least threatened in their conditions of existence. These also supply the proletariat with fresh elements of enlightenment and progress.

Finally, in times when the class-struggle nears the decisive hour, the process of dissolution going on within the ruling class, in fact within the whole range of old society, assumes such a violent, glaring character, that a small section of the ruling class cuts itself adrift, and joins the revolutionary class, the class that holds the future in its hands. Just as, therefore, at an earlier period, a section of the nobility went over to the bourgeoisie, so now a portion of the bourgeoisie goes over to the proletariat, and in particular, a portion of the bourgeois ideologists, who have raised themselves to the level of comprehending theoretically the historical movements as a whole.

Of all the classes that stand face to face with the bourgeoisie today, the proletariat alone is a really revolutionary class. The other classes decay and finally disappear in the face of modern industry; the proletariat is its special and essential product.

The lower-middle class, the small manufacturer, the shopkeeper, the artisan, the peasant, all these fight against the bourgeoisie, to save from extinction their existence as fractions of the middle class. They are therefore not revolutionary, but conservative. Nay more, they are reactionary, for they try to roll back the wheel of history. If by chance they are revolutionary, they are so, only in view of their impending transfer into the proletariat, they thus defend not their present, but their future interests, they desert their own standpoint to place them-selves at that of the proletariat.

The "dangerous class," the social scum, that passively rotting mass thrown off by the lowest layers of old society, may, here and there, be swept into the movement by a proletarian revolution; its conditions of life, however, prepare it far more for the part of a bribed tool of reactionary intrigue.

• • •

Hitherto, every form of society has been based, as we have already seen, on the antagonism of oppressing and oppressed classes. But in order to oppress a class, certain conditions must be assured to it under which it can, at least, continue its slavish existence. The serf, in the period of serfdom, raised himself to membership in the com-mune, just as the petty bourgeois, under the yoke of feudal abso-lutism, managed to develop into a bourgeois. The modern laborer, on the contrary, instead of rising with the progress of industry, sinks deeper and deeper below the conditions of existence of his own class. He becomes a pauper, and pauperism develops more rapidly than population and wealth. And here it becomes evident, that the bour-geoisie is unfit any longer to be the ruling class in society, and to impose its conditions of existence upon society as an overriding law. It is unfit to rule, because it is incompetent to assure an existence to its slave within his slavery, because it cannot help letting him sink into such a state, that it has to feed him, instead of being fed by him. Society can no longer live under this bourgeoisie, in other words, its existence is no longer compatible with society.

The essential condition for the existence, and for the sway of the bourgeois class, is the formation and augmentation of capital; the condition for capital is wage-labor. Wage-labor rests exclusively on competition between the laborers. The advance of industry, whose involuntary promoter is the bourgeoisie, replaces the isolation of the laborers, due to competition, by their involuntary combination, due to association. The development of Modern Industry, therefore, cuts from under its feet the very foundation on which the bourgeoisie pro-duces and appropriates products. What the bourgeoisie therefore produces, above all, are its own grave-diggers. Its fall and the victory of the proletariat are equally inevitable.

Endnotes

[1]By *bourgeoisie* is meant the class of modern capitalists, owners of the means of social production and employers of wage-labor. By *proletariat*, the class of modern wage-laborers who, having no means of production of their own, are reduced to selling their labor-power in order to live.

[2]"Commune" was the name taken, in France, by the nascent towns even before they had conquered from their feudal lords and masters, local self-government and political rights as "the Third Estate." Generally speaking, for the economical development of the bourgeoisie, England is here taken as the typical country, for its political development, France.

❧ ❧ ❧

Questions

1. How do Marx and Engels define class conflict? What is the basis of this conflict?

2. According to Marx and Engels, which class can be considered the "most revolutionary"? Which class most supports the status quo?

3. How do the bourgeoisie help undermine their own status as the ruling class?

4. According to Marx and Engels, how does capitalism benefit the proletariat? How does capitalism benefit the bourgeoisie?

The Amish: A Small Society

JOHN A. HOSTETLER

This classic article presents the Amish community as a place where practical knowledge, custom, and personal associations take precedence over science, critical knowledge, abstract associations, and modern conveniences. While contemporary Amish society is different from the way John Hostetler portrays it here, this article does shed light on the workings of a folk society.

*S*mall communities, with their distinctive character—where life is stable and intensely human—are disappearing. Some have vanished from the face of the earth, others are dying slowly, but all have undergone changes as they have come into contact with an expanding machine civilization. The merging of diverse peoples into a common mass has produced tension among members of the minorities and the majority alike.

The Old Order Amish, who arrived on American shores in colonial times, have survived in the modern world in distinctive, viable, small communities. They have resisted the homogenization process more successfully than others. In planting and harvest time one can see their bearded men working the fields with horses and their women hanging out the laundry in neat rows to dry. Many American people have seen Amish families, with the men wearing broad-brimmed black hats and the women in bonnets and long dresses, in railway depots or bus terminals. Although the Amish have

"The Amish: A Small Society," by John A. Hostetler, reprinted from *Amish Society*, 1980, pp. 3–12.

lived with industrialized America for over two and a half centuries, they have moderated its influence on their personal lives, their families, communities, and their values.

The Amish are often perceived by other Americans to be relics of the past who live an austere, inflexible life dedicated to inconvenient and archaic customs. They are seen as renouncing both modern conveniences and the American dream of success and progress. But most people have no quarrel with the Amish for doing things the old-fashioned way. Their conscientious objection was tolerated in wartime, for after all, they are meticulous farmers who practice the virtues of work and thrift.

. . . The Amish are a church, a community, a spiritual union, a conservative branch of Christianity, a religion, a community whose members practice simple and austere living, a familistic entrepreneuring system, and an adaptive human community. . . .

The Amish are in some ways a little commonwealth, for their members claim to be ruled by the law of love and redemption. The bonds that unite them are many. Their beliefs, however, do not permit them solely to occupy and defend a particular territory. They are highly sensitive in caring for their own. They will move to other lands when circumstances force them to do so.

Commonwealth implies a place, a province, which means any part of a national domain that geographically and socially is sufficiently unified to have a true consciousness of its unity. Its inhabitants feel comfortable with their own ideas and customs, and the "place" possesses a sense of distinction from other parts of the country. Members of a commonwealth are not foot-loose. They have a sense of productivity and accountability in a province where "the general welfare" is accepted as a day-to-day reality. Commonwealth has come to have an archaic meaning in today's world, because when groups and institutions become too large, the sense of commonwealth or the common good is lost. Thus it is little wonder that the most recent dictionaries of the American English language render the meaning of commonwealth as "obsolescent." In reality, the Amish are in part a commonwealth. There is, however, no provision for outcasts.

It may be argued that the Amish have retained elements of wholesome provincialism, a saving power to which the world in the future will need more and more to appeal. Provincialism need not turn to ancient narrowness and ignorance, confines from which many have sought to escape. A sense of province or commonwealth, with its cherished love of people and self-conscious dignity, is a necessary basis for relating to the wider world community. Respect for locality, place, custom, and local idealism can go a long way toward checking the monstrous growth of consolidation in the nation and thus help to save human freedom and individual dignity.

. . . Anthropologists, who have compared societies all over the world, have tended to call semi-isolated peoples "folk societies," "primitives," or merely "simple societies." These societies constitute an altogether different type in contrast to the industrialized, or so-called civilized, societies.

The "folk society," as conceptualized by Robert Redfield,[1] is a small, isolated, traditional, simple, homogeneous society in which oral communication and conventionalized ways are important factors in integrating the whole life. In such an ideal-type society, shared practical knowledge is more important than science, custom is valued more than critical knowledge, and associations are personal and emotional rather than abstract and categoric.

Folk societies are uncomfortable with the idea of change. Young people do what the old people did when they were young. Members communicate intimately with one another, not only by word of mouth but also through custom and symbols that reflect a strong sense of belonging to one another. A folk society is *Gemeinschaft-like;* there is a strong sense of "we-ness." Leadership is personal rather than institutionalized. There are no gross economic inequalities. Mutual aid is characteristic of the society's members. The goals of life are never stated as matters of doctrine, but neither are they questioned. They are implied by the acts that constitute living in a small society. Custom tends to become sacred. Behavior is strongly patterned, and acts as well as cultural objects are given symbolic meaning that is often pervasively religious. Religion is diffuse and all-pervasive. In the typical folk society, planting and harvesting are as sacred in their own ways as singing and praying.

The folk model lends itself well to understanding the tradition-directed character of Amish society. The heavy weight of tradition can scarcely be explained in any other way. The Amish, for example, have retained many of the customs and small-scale technologies that were common in rural society in the nineteenth century. Through a process of syncretism, Amish religious values have been fused with an earlier period of simple country living when everyone farmed with horses and on a scale where family members could work together. The Amish exist as a folk or "little" community in a rural subculture within the modern state. . . . The outsider who drives through an Amish settlement cannot help but recognize them by their clothing, farm homes, furnishings, fields, and other material traits of culture. Although they speak perfect English with outsiders, they speak a dialect of German among themselves.

Amish life is distinctive in that religion and custom blend into a way of life. The two are inseparable. The core values of the community are religious beliefs. Not only do the members worship a deity they understand through the revelation of Jesus Christ and the Bible, but their patterned behavior has a religious dimension. A distinctive way of life permeates daily life, agriculture, and the application of energy to economic ends. Their beliefs determine their conceptions of the self, the universe, and man's place in it. The Amish world view recognizes a certain spiritual worth and dignity in the universe in its natural form. Religious considerations determine hours of work and the daily, weekly, seasonal, and yearly rituals associated with life experience. Occupation, the means and destinations of travel, and choice of friends and mate are determined bv religious considerations. Religious and work attitudes are not far distant from each other. The universe includes the divine, and Amish society itself is considered divine insofar as the Amish recognize themselves as "a chosen people of God." The Amish do not seek to master nature or to work against the elements, but try to work with them. The affinity between

Amish society and nature in the form of land, terrain, and vegetation is expressed in various degrees of intensity.

Religion is highly patterned, so one may properly speak of the Amish as a tradition-directed group. Though allusions to the Bible play an important role in determining their outlook on the world, and on life after death, these beliefs have been fused with several centuries of struggling to survive in community. Out of intense religious experience, societal conflict, and intimate agrarian experience, a mentality has developed that prefers the old rather than the new. While the principle seems to apply especially to religion, it has also become a charter for social behavior. "The old is the best, and the new is of the devil" has become a prevalent mode of thought. By living in closed communities where custom and a strong sense of togetherness prevail, the Amish have formed an integrated way of life and a folk-like culture. Continuity of conformity and custom is assured and the needs of the individual from birth to death are met within an integrated and shared system of meanings. Oral tradition, custom, and conventionality play an important part in maintaining the group as a functioning whole. To the participant, religion and custom are inseparable. Commitment and culture are combined to produce a stable human existence.

. . . A century ago, hardly anyone knew the Amish existed. A half-century ago they were viewed as an obscure sect living by ridiculous customs, as stubborn people who resisted education and exploited the labor of their children. Today the Amish are the unwilling objects of a thriving tourist industry on the eastern seaboard. They are revered as hard-working, thrifty people with enormous agrarian stamina, and by some, as islands of sanity in a culture gripped by commercialism and technology run wild.

Endnote

[1]Redfield, R. (1947). The folk society. *American Journal of Sociology, 52,* 293–308. See also his book *The little community* (1955). Chicago: University of Chicago Press.

◉ ◉ ◉

Questions

1. Why do some people see the Amish as "relics of the past"? Do you agree with this assessment? Why or why not?

2. What is a folk society? How does this folk model help explain traditional Amish society?

3. What is the role of religion in Amish society? How does this compare with the role of religion in mainstream American society?

4. Suppose you lived in the Amish community described in this article. What would you say to a tourist who asked you why you avoided technology that would make your life easier?

Parents' Socialization of Children

D. TERRI HEATH

The family unit is the primary agent of socialization in most societies. However, the majority of studies focus on the socializing effect of parents within a single culture. Furthermore, many of us are familiar mostly with our own family experiences (either as a child or parent) and those of our peers. Unfortunately, this means that our knowledge is limited by culture and class. In this selection, D. Terri Heath compares parenting styles and socializing effects by summarizing studies from a range of countries, including India, Japan, Israel, Thailand, Malawi, South Africa, and the United States. As you read, think about the ways in which your own experiences differ from those of adolescents in other countries and social classes.

*S*tudents interested in cross-cultural research learn quickly that there are more similarities than differences in the experience of parenthood for people of different countries. Worldwide, parents have for centuries been responsible for the socialization of their children. Although it is true that parents receive assistance from others (e.g., extended family, neighbors, and professional caregivers) in fulfilling these obligations, societies throughout the world charge parents with the primary protection, socialization, and nurturance of the children they bear or adopt. Communities mandate these obligations out of a belief that parents are the most suitable adults to rear the children they bear. Parents are assigned legal responsibility to raise their children to be productive, responsible adults in accordance with the expectations of each particular community.

. . .

❧ A Typology of Parenting Styles

The particular balance of these three components (control, power, and support) reflects the childrearing style of the parent. This area of research was energized by Baumrind's (1966) categorization of childrearing into authoritative, permissive, and authoritarian parenting styles and their associated influences on children. *Authoritative* parents are firm in their limits but warm and nurturing in their approach. They explain their reasons for their actions, encourage parent-child discussions about problems, and are responsive to their children's needs. They recognize their own power as parents and use this power to gain compliance in their children if reasoning is ineffective. The children of authoritative parents are usually self-reliant, self-controlled, cheerful, cooperative with adults, achievement oriented, and friendly with peers.

Permissive parents avoid supervision and control of their children either by not establishing standards of acceptable behavior for their children or by setting standards that are lower than their children's capabilities. They are accepting of their children and consult with them on family matters. They encourage autonomy, use reasoning, and are rarely punitive. Permissive parents may either indulge or ignore their children's needs. The children of permissive parents are usually aggressive, aimless, domineering, lacking in self-control and self-reliance, and noncompliant with adults.

Authoritarian parents demand obedience from their children, impose and enforce many rules and restrictions, and favor punitive methods to gain compliance. They value and encourage order and tradition, do not permit parent-child negotiations, and are uncompromising in their standards and rules. The children of authoritarian parents are usually fearful, moody, aimless, unhappy, easily annoyed, and less able to cope effectively with stressful circumstances (Jaffe, 1991).

Baumrind concludes that it is authoritative parenting that fosters those qualities associated with Western notions of social competence in youths: social responsibility, vitality, independence, achievement, friendliness, and cooperativeness (Baumrind, 1975, 1978). Few researchers have tested Baumrind's typology and theories on parenting practices in either developing countries or Eastern developed countries (e.g., Japan). This type of cross-cultural research is critically important in furthering our understanding of cultural differences of Baumrind's typology and resultant child outcomes.

❃ Cross-Cultural Research Examples: Parenting Styles

Because space limitations here preclude a comprehensive presentation of this literature, . . . selected studies illustrate the variety of cross-cultural work in this area. The examples come from China, . . . the United States, and Israel. The first illustrative example, from China, was included here because it describes the influence of parental control, support, and power even when parents are only able to interact with their children a few hours each week. . . . [Second] is an illustrative example from the Mexican American subculture in the United States. Researchers here examined one of the subdimensions of control, coercion via corporal punishment, in a comparative study between native-born and foreign-born mothers. The last illustrative example is indirectly related to parental support. Mothers in two different cultures, Japanese and Israeli, support identical behaviors in their children but label these behaviors as either obedient (Japan) or autonomous (Israel), depending on which is more valued in their respective culture.

China

A team of six researchers recently completed "the first large-scale psychological study of socialization in China" (Zhengyuan, Wen, Mussen, Jian-Xian, Chang-Min, & Zi-Fang, 1991, p. 241). Using research on U.S. samples as models, this team documented the complex relationship between childrearing and child behaviors that exists in contemporary Chinese culture.

China has a long, rich history of collectivism and places a priority on community over individual needs. Although there have been recent internal challenges to this established ideology, China remains a model for parenting practices within a collective society. For example, even when their children are very young, many Chinese parents bring them to child centers before breakfast and retrieve them after supper, for an average of 10 to 11 hours in care each day, six days a week. With children in group care for such a significant portion of their childhood days, can parents influence the development of their children during the few hours each week available to them? A team of researchers surveyed 2,254 Chinese children, ages three to six, and their parents to assess the influence of various subdimensions of parental support and control on children's personality development (Zhengyuan et al., 1991). The results suggest that parents have a significant influence on the development of their child's personality even though the amount of parent-child interaction time is limited in many Chinese families. Chinese parents who exert strong control over children foster the development of good character, positive attitudes toward others, self-confidence, self- control, a high frustration tolerance, and positive attitudes toward work. Chinese parents who use inductive discipline (e.g., reasoning and persuasion methods even if the child does something to make them very angry) contribute to the development of self-control, self-confidence, independence, and positive attitudes toward work in their children. When parents encourage independence in their children, they help children develop positive attitudes toward others, self-confidence, independence, self-control, high tolerance for frustration, and positive attitudes toward work. Parents who demonstrate a respect for individuality have children who are curious, show positive attitudes toward others and work, are self-confident, independent, demonstrate high levels of self-control, and show good character. Finally, intellectual stimulation by parents is associated with children who are independent and self-confident and show a high frustration tolerance and good character. In sum, Chinese parents appear to be powerful socialization agents for their children even though their children spend few hours each week in the presence of parents. Differences in parenting styles contribute to significant differences in child behavior and personality development for Chinese families.

. . .

Foreign-Born and Native-Born Mexican American Subculture in the United States

There has been much speculation about the influence of culture on parental control and its subdimensions, especially among subcultures in the United States. High rates of reported child maltreatment have been linked to the perceived tendency among minority populations in the United States to use corporal punishment as a disciplinary strategy. But in a recent study of foreign-born and native-born Mexican American mothers in the United States, mothers in both groups chose corporal punishment as their last choice of control method when their children misbehaved. Therefore, no cultural differences were apparent. For both groups, mothers were most likely to use "no television/no play with a friend" and least likely to use "spanking" as their most common method of control. "Scolding" and "verbal reasoning" ranked second and third, respectively. However, there were subtle yet significant differences in how these mothers carried out this control. Foreign-born mothers were more likely to use "physical discipline" and "verbal reasoning" than were native-born mothers because they often used a combination of these two methods. They would first spank their child and then explain the reasons for the spanking. Native-born mothers more often used scolding than the combination of spanking and verbal reasoning (Buriel, Mercado, Rodriguez, & Chavez, 1991). The researchers concluded that Mexican American mothers did not choose corporal punishment as their preferred style of control. Although there were subtle differences between foreign-born and native-born Mexican American mothers on how control was administered, the preferred method for both groups was withdrawal of privileges rather than physical punishment. This challenges the notion that the high rates of reported child maltreatment among minority populations are a result of a culturally based reliance on methods of corporal punishment for parental control.

*J*apan and *J*srael

The last illustrative study in this section compares an Asian culture and a Middle Eastern one on the value of autonomy (independence) and obedience. The results suggest that parents use supportive techniques to encourage identical behaviors in each culture but label these behaviors as either autonomous or obedient according to whichever trait is more valued in their respective cultures.

Israeli and Japanese cultures are based on family cohesiveness, educational achievement, and collectivism. However, unlike Japanese culture, Israel also values a Western-based emphasis on individualism. This individualism promotes a parental emphasis upon developing independence and self-sufficiency in children. Japanese parents expect obedience to parents who teach early mastery of skills that demonstrate emotional maturity, self-control, self-reliance, and compliance with adult authority (Osterweil & Nagano, 1991). When Japanese mothers of preschoolers are compared with Israeli mothers of preschoolers on their views of independence and obedience in their children, the cultural differences become apparent. Although obedience is defined by both groups as compliance with parental demands, Japanese mothers are more likely to describe their child as obedient when they perform personal care functions (e.g., brushing teeth and dressing self) than do Israeli mothers who report similar functions as examples of autonomy. In other words, on these indicators of instrumental independence (e.g., child gets dressed, washes, and goes to school by him/herself) Israeli mothers more often express these as examples of independence, whereas Japanese mothers more often use these same examples to reflect obedience. In examining emotional independence, some interesting differences emerge between these two cultures. Israeli mothers emphasize a child's ability to be alone as an example of emotional independence; they appreciate it because they tend to value initiative in self-expression and the capacity for self-occupation. However, Japanese mothers value the development of the capacity for establishing social relationships and view it as the measure of emotional independence. Osterweil and Nagano (1991) conclude that "instrumental independence is viewed as a manifestation of separateness in Israel, but in Japan it indicates a close relationship with mother and compliance with her wishes" (p. 373). Therefore, it appears that both Israeli and Japanese mothers value independence but for different reasons. Israeli mothers value it as an indication of separation between mother and child, whereas Japanese mothers value independence as an indication of a child's closeness, as manifested in obedience to teachings about social competence.

Summary

From the cross-cultural research presented in this section, it is apparent that there are more similarities than differences in parents' socialization of children across cultures. This discussion of parental socialization techniques describes and illustrates how the balance and interaction of parental control, power, and support result in particular child behaviors.

Although Chinese parents spend little time each week with their young children, they serve as powerful socialization agents in the development of their children's personalities. . . . Although much speculation exists about why minority populations are overrepresented in reports of child maltreatment in the United States, it is apparently not because corporal punishment is a preferred method of parental control for either native-born or foreign-born Mexican Americans. Finally, parental support of particular child behaviors encourages the development of what Israeli mothers describe as autonomy and Japanese mothers describe as obedience.

◉ Parental Class Influences

In nearly every culture, parental differences in class result in different expectations of and outcomes for children. In industrialized societies, class is most commonly measured by socioeconomic status, education, accumulated wealth, and occupation. However, these measures have sometimes failed to discriminate class statuses in developing countries so contemporary researchers have begun to identify measures such as housing conditions, proficiency in the dominant language, and the demands placed on the children's labor as more relevant measures of class in some cultures (Lockheed, Fuller, & Nyirongo 1989). In general, higher class, however measured, is associated with: 1) parents who encourage their children, invest more time helping them in academic activities, and hold greater academic aspirations for them; and 2) children who exhibit higher reading scores, greater academic motivation, and greater self-esteem (Amato & Ochiltree, 1986; Gecas, 1979; Kohn, 1977; Maccoby, 1980; Lockheed et al., 1989). These qualities often result in higher academic performance.

Family background variables appear to influence status attainment in children via three interconnected clusters of influences, commonly referred to as the Wisconsin Model (Falk & Cosby, 1975; Hanson, 1983; Otto & Haller, 1979). Family-of-origin variables (e.g., mother's and father's educational attainments) specify the family's socioeconomic status and social circumstances. The family-of-origin variables join with personal characteristic variables (e.g., child's IQ) to influence sons and daughters to achieve levels of academic achievement compatible with their family's social position, expectations, and personal ability. These influences are further modified by social psychological variables (e.g., academic performance, significant others, and aspirations). Thus, family-of-origin variables create a class position for the family, which limits the number and range of significant others in the child's environment who communicate role expectations and support specific aptitudes in the child (Otto, 1986; Sewell, Haller, & Ohlendorf, 1970). This milieu is further shaped by the personal characteristics of the child that influence their occupational aspirations. Furthermore, the occupational experiences of parents are often linked to their socialization practices in childrearing, which give children the tools to succeed in specific occupations (Farmer, 1985; Peterson, Rollins, Thomas, & Heaps, 1982). Consequently, educational attainment is closely associated with occupational status because occupations require specific academic prerequisites (Wilson, Peterson, & Wilson, 1993).

In examining successful children, family processes are also important. Those children who are academic achievers have parents who set standards that are both challenging and attainable, and these parents encourage and support their children in their attempts to meet these challenges. Such parents are knowledgeable about what their child is capable of achieving. Children who are encouraged to meet a challenge that is too difficult are vulnerable to failure. Children who consistently fail are unwilling to try new experiences. On the other hand, parents who fail to challenge their children often raise children who are bored and lack high self-esteem. Balancing challenge with opportunities to succeed results in children who take appropriate risks and demonstrate high self-esteem.

Differences in home environments have an additional, significant impact on which children will excel academically. In industrialized countries, children who live in homes in which reading material for children and adults is present, television is deemphasized, and children are encouraged to explore and solve problems are more likely to succeed in their academic careers. Although fewer researchers have investigated parallel contributions to success for children living in developing countries, it is intuitive to expect that when demands for children's labor are less and housing and sanitary conditions are better, children probably achieve greater literacy and academic success. Five components of family life are associated with school achievement: 1) high levels of verbal interaction between parent and child (e.g., asking children questions and permitting children to participate in meal conversations), 2) high expectations by parents for the child's achievement, 3) a warm and nurturing parent-child relationship, 4) an authoritative style of parental discipline (Baumrind, 1968) (e.g., demands for maturity, inductive control techniques, and high levels of parental support), and 5) parental belief that the child is capable of success (Hess & Holloway, 1984).

Occupations of parents also play a significant role in the childrearing and therefore success outcomes of children. Parents' attitudes toward childrearing have been found to correlate with their occupations, partially explaining the differences between parents who foster academically successful children and those who do not. Working-class parents participate in the labor force in positions that demand reliability, respect, and adherence to rules. In turn, they value and teach such qualities as conformity, orderliness, and obedience to their children. Because middle-class parents work in jobs that demand creativity, ambition, independence, and self-control, these parents emphasize autonomy and internalized control. Like working-class parents, those qualities that enable middle-class parents to succeed at work become the foundation for what they teach their children (Kohn, 1977; Peterson & Rollins, 1987). Both sets of values can aid children in their academic success, but especially so if parents value education and support academic achievement in their children.

However, social forces outside the family may have a competing influence. For example, Peters (1981) reports that black U.S. families place a greater emphasis on qualities that conflict with the behavior encouraged for U.S. school children in the classroom. Because educational institutions are operated predominantly by white, educated, middle-class teachers and administrators, the school environment may be more supportive of children who exhibit parallel middle-class behaviors (e.g., self-assertion and independence) than of children who exhibit behaviors learned in black, working-class families (respect for elders and authority figures).

Let us turn now to research from around the globe on the role of parents, their socioeconomic status, and education levels in the fostering of academically successful children. Some studies found parents' class status to be the primary influence in academic achievement and others found that parents' educational attainment exerted the strongest influence. Both factors appear to be important to children's academic success. Five examples from vastly different cultures illustrate this nearly worldwide relationship.

The Mizos of India

Mizoram is a state in northeastern India inhabited almost entirely by a tribal people known as Mizos. Agriculture is the primary occupation of the Mizos people, with all able-bodied adults participating in the work. Men clear the jungle for new fields, and women sow the seeds, weed, and harvest the crops. Arranged marriages, once the standard, are now gradually diminishing within the Mizos culture, and free selection of marital partners is more common today. However, a brideprice is still paid to the bride's relatives by the groom. When the couple bears children, responsibility for childrearing rests with them. All Mizos parents, irrespective of their status and wealth, consider the education of their children a privilege, yet it is the higher-status families that report greater parent-child interaction, which, in turn, leads to significantly greater academic achievement for boys (Sudhir & Sailo, 1989). Boys who experienced greater parent-child interaction demonstrated significantly higher achievement scores in general science and social science. However, girls who experienced greater parent-child interaction showed no significant differences in academic achievement from girls who experienced lower parent-child interaction. One cultural explanation for this gender difference is that given the male-dominated patrilineal culture of the Mizos, boys are more encouraged to compete and achieve than are girls (who may even be discouraged from academic achievement) even though both girls and boys have legal access to formal educational opportunities (Sudhir & Sailo, 1989). In this situation, greater parent-child interaction has no effect on girls' achievement because the cultural behavior of the society neutralizes any academic achievement differences between daughters of higher-socioeconomic-status parents and those of lesser-status parents.

Thailand and Malawi

In the developing countries of Asia's Thailand and Africa's Malawi, family background appears to influence the school performance of youth in a variety of ways. In Thailand, the influence of family background on the mathematics scores of 8th-grade students paralleled findings in many industrialized countries; higher mathematics scores were associated with higher paternal occupational status, higher maternal education, higher per capita income for the district, and use of the language of instruction in the home (Lockheed et al., 1989). In Malawi, however, these conventional measures of family background were not associated with differences in mathematics scores of similar-age children in 4th and 7th grades. When measures of class more relevant for a developing country were used, students who did well in mathematics were associated with: 1) a greater number of modern attributes of their home (e.g., modern house without a thatched roof, ownership of a radio, and electricity), 2) congruence between the language of home and instruction, and 3) less demand for child labor by the parents. Consequently, family background and class status demonstrate a fairly consistent association with academic success when they are measured in a culturally relevant manner.

Urban Blacks and Whites in Great Britain

An example from Great Britain further illustrates that time spent with children is associated with improved academic achievement, and that time invested is often a function of parental education (Hamner &

Turner, 1985). When two cultural subgroups of inner-city London six-year-olds were compared, researchers found that race and educational attainment of the mother both influenced the amount of time mothers spent with their children reading, doing mathematics, and writing. Black (Afro Caribbean) mothers read aloud to their children more often than did white mothers. Children of more highly educated mothers spent more time on all learning activities than did children of mothers with less education (Plewis, Mooney & Creeser, 1990).

The Xhosa of South Africa

The black Xhosa-speaking people of Transkei, South Africa, offer yet another example of the relationship between parent education and children's academic achievement. The socioeconomic status (SES) of Xhosa-speaking students, ages 13 to 17, and of average ability (as measured on a standardized aptitude test) was categorized as either low, middle, or high SES. When these three groups of students were compared on academic ability, the academic performance of each youth was associated with his/her parents' SES. Students in the higher SES category scored better on academic achievement tests than did students in either the middle or low SES categories. Furthermore, taken separately, maternal and paternal aspirations for academic achievement increased the child's academic performance. In other words, the aspirations of each parent appeared to have separate, yet powerful, influences on the academic performance of both daughters and sons in this South African subculture (Cherian, 1991).

Thailand and the United States

In addition to the important influence of parents' education and SES on academic achievement in children, parental encouragement also appears to exert a clear influence on children's academic success as described earlier. When comparing the perceptions of their parents' encouragement of the mathematics skills of Thai and U.S. adolescents (age 13), some clear trends emerge. Strong parental encouragement of success in mathematics is associated with adolescents who are less anxious when doing mathematics, and who do not view mathematics as more appropriate for males than females. Both Thai and U.S. adolescents hold more positive views of the usefulness and importance of mathematics to society, as well as more positive views of themselves as learners of mathematics, when they believe their parents encourage them to succeed in mathematics. Furthermore, there are no differences between Thai and U.S. students in these relationships, which lends support for the universality of this relationship between parental encouragement for success and children's academic achievement (Tocci & Engelhard, 1991).

Summary

Socioeconomic status, amount of parent–child interaction, parental education, and parental encouragement of success in a specific academic subject all demonstrate positive significant effects on children's academic performance. Using examples from vastly different cultures, economies, and political states, it appears that parental time invested in children, with its resultant payoff in greater academic achievement, is more common among higher SES families. This may be partly the result of possessing greater resources, enabling these parents to spend more time in such pursuits with their children.

However, we must use caution in interpreting these seemingly consistent results. Another plausible explanation for these findings is that the measures researchers used to test academic achievement in these studies may measure the skills taught to middle- and higher-class children more than the skills taught to lower-class children by less educated parents. For example, a child who lives in a remote, agricultural village in a developing country may be exceptionally gifted in the tasks required of the local industry but may not be able to demonstrate these on a standardized academic instrument. More studies are needed from developing countries, to understand cross-cultural similarities and differences in academic achievement. A separate but related problem in this area is the lack of attention to the issue of literacy. By necessity, this section has been limited to discussion on the more narrow topic of academic achievement because of the dearth of cross-cultural studies of parental influences on literacy. When sociologists and psychologists invest more research resources into the examination of cultures in developing countries, future literature in this area may focus on the broader concept of literacy, a more elementary skill but of great global value.

. . .

❂ Conclusion

In reviewing the literature on cross-cultural research on parent-child relations . . . , a clear trend became increasingly apparent. When parents are more involved and/or have greater expectations of their children's behavior, children demonstrate better outcomes. As is apparent from the illustrative examples, greater parental involvement is an active involvement, not a passive one. It is acquired not simply by the amount of time parents and children spend together but rather by how that time is spent. An involved parent is not one who spends the majority of the day near his/her child but rarely interacting with the child. It is, instead, the parent who uses opportunities to share activities such as teaching the child a local trade, reading together, or fostering a close, supportive relationship through companionship. This active, involved parent appears much more likely to rear a successful child. Illustrative cross-cultural examples presented here of high-quality interaction between parents and children, such as spending time reading together in Great Britain, establishing firm limits and offering support in China, and engaging adolescents in activities with parents and tribal elders in the United States has been associated with better child outcomes. These patterns emerged even when examining parent-son versus parent-daughter relations, relationships among family members in developing versus developed countries, or parent-child relationships in families that resided in Western cultures versus Eastern ones.

. . . Using currently available cross-cultural literature, there appears to be little cross-cultural difference in this association, further supporting the argument that there are more similarities than differences in parental influences on children across cultures. However, this conclusion is based on currently available literature. Parental involvement and parental expectations are broad, general concepts. It is likely that when future cross-cultural research designs include subdimensions of these two broad concepts, results may offer descriptions of cultural differences in parental involvement and expectations for children around the world.

References

Amato, P. R., & Ochiltree, G. (1986). Family resources and the development of child competence. *Journal of Marriage and the Family, 48*, 47–56.

Baumrind, D. (1968). Authoritarian vs. authoritative parental control. *Adolescence, 3*, 255–272.

Cherian, V. I. (1991). Parental aspiration and academic achievement of Xhosa children. *Psychological Reports, 68*(2), 547–553.

Falk, W. W., & Cosby, A. G. (1975). Women and the status attainment process. *Social Science Quarterly, 56*, 307–314.

Farmer, H. S. (1985). Model of career and achievement motivation for women and men. *Journal of Counseling Psychology, 32*, 363–390.

Gecas, V. (1979). The influence of social class on socialization. In W. R. Burr, R. Hill, F. I. Nye, & I. L. Reiss (Eds.), *Contemporary theories about the family* (Vol. 1, pp. 365–404). New York: Free Press.

Hamner, T. J., & Turner, P. H. (1985). *Parenting in contemporary society*. Englewood Cliffs, NJ: Prentice Hall.

Hanson, S. L. (1983). A family life-cycle approach to socioeconomic attainment of working women. *Journal of Marriage and the Family, 45*, 323–338.

Hess, R. D., & Holloway, S. D. (1984). Family and school as educational institutions. In R. D. Parke (Ed.), *Review of child development research* (Vol. 7, pp. 179–222). Chicago: University of Chicago Press.

Kohn, M. L. (1977). *Class and conformity: A study in values* (2nd ed.). Chicago: University of Chicago Press.

Lockheed, M. E., Fuller, B., & Nyirongo, R. (1989). Family effects on students' achievement in Thailand and Malawi. *Sociology of Education, 62*, 239–256.

Maccoby, E. E. (1980). *Social development: Psychological growth and the parent-child relationship*. New York: Harcourt Brace Jovanovich.

Otto, L. B. (1986). Family influences on youth's occupational aspirations and achievements. In G. K. Leigh & G. W. Peterson (Eds.), *Adolescents in families* (pp. 226–255). Cincinnati: South-Western.

Otto, L. B., & Haller, A. O. (1979). Evidence for a social-psychological view of the status attainment process: Four studies compared. *Social Forces, 57*, 887–914.

Peters, M. F. (1981). "Making it" black family style: Building on the strengths of black families. In N. Stinnett (Ed.), *Family strengths: Roots of well-being*. Lincoln: University of Nebraska Press.

Peterson, G. W., & Rollins, B. C. (1987). Parent-child socialization. In M. B. Sussman & S. K. Steinmetz (Eds.), *Handbook of marriage and the family* (pp. 471–507). New York: Plenum Press.

Peterson, G. W., Rollins, B. C., Thomas, D. L., & Heaps, L. K. (1982). Social placement of adolescents: Sex-role influences on family decisions regarding the careers of youth. *Journal of Marriage and the Family, 44*, 647–661.

Plewis, I., Mooney, A., & Creeser, R. (1990). Time on educational activities at home and educational progress in infant school. *British Journal of Educational Psychology, 60*(3), 330–337.

Sewell, W. H., Haller, A. O., & Ohlendorf, G. W. (1970). The educational and early occupational status attainment process: Replication and revision. *American Sociological Review, 35*, 1014–1027.

Sudhir, M. A., & Sailo, L. (1989). Parent-child interaction and academic achievement among secondary school students in Aizawi. *Indian Journal of Psychometry and Education, 20*(1), 19–28.

Tocci, C. M., & Engelhard, G. (1991). Achievement, parental support, and gender differences in attitudes toward mathematics. *Journal of Educational Research, 84*(5), 280–286.

Wilson, S. M., Peterson, G. W., & Wilson, P. (1993). The process of educational and occupational attainment of adolescent females from low-income, rural families. *Journal of Marriage and the Family, 55*, 158–175.

☻ ☻ ☻

Questions

1. Define authoritative, permissive, and authoritarian parenting. How are authoritative and authoritarian parenting styles alike? How are they different?

2. How much variation is there in parenting styles across countries and cultures?

3. How do Chinese parents manage to be strong agents of socialization despite spending so little time with their children?

4. How does nativity (i.e., place of birth) affect parenting style for Mexican Americans? How does "culture" help explain these differences?

5. In the United States, how is class associated with parental involvement and influence?

6. How consistent are the influences of class on adolescent behavior across countries and cultures? What limitations does the author place on these similarities?

7. To what degree did your own relations with your parents reflect the patterns discussed by Heath? Could your parents be classified as permissive, authoritative, or authoritarian in their parenting styles? Which tactics and strategies from the other two styles did your parents also employ?

Dyads, Triads, and Larger Groups

GEORG SIMMEL

The most fundamental building block for any group or organization is the dyad, a pair of individuals who interact with one another. In this classic work, Georg Simmel introduces the concept of the dyad and discusses its fundamental characteristics. He then expands his discussion to include triads and larger groups, and theorizes about the changing nature of social relations.

. . .

☻ The Dyad

. . .

Everyday experiences show the specific character that a relationship attains by the fact that only two elements participate in it. A common fate or enterprise, an agreement or secret between two persons, ties each of them in a very different manner than if even only three have a part in it. This is perhaps most characteristic of the secret. General experience seems to indicate that this minimum of two, with which the secret ceases to be the property of the one individual, is at the same time the maximum at which its preservation is relatively secure. A secret religious-political society . . . formed in the beginning of the nineteenth century in France and Italy, had different degrees among its members. The real secrets of the society were known only to the higher degrees; but a discussion of these secrets could take place only between any two members of the high degrees.

"Dyads, Triads, and Larger Groups," by Georg Simmel, reprinted from *The Sociology of Georg Simmel,* translated by Kurt H. Wolff, 1950. Copyright © by The Free Press. pp. 118–144.

The limit of two was felt to be so decisive that, where it could not be preserved in regard to knowledge, it was kept. . . . More generally speaking, the difference between the dyad and larger groups consists in the fact that the dyad has a different relation to each of its two elements than have larger groups to *their* members. Although, for the outsider, the group consisting of two may function as an autonomous, super-individual unit, it usually does not do so for its participants. Rather, each of the two feels himself confronted only by the other, not by a collectivity above him. The social structure here rests immediately on the one and on the other of the two, and the secession of either would destroy the whole. The dyad, therefore, does not attain that super-personal life which the individual feels to be independent of himself. As soon, however, as there is a sociation of three, a group continues to exist even in case one of the members drops out.

• • •

In the dyad, the sociological process remains, in principle, within personal interdependence and does not result in a structure that grows beyond its elements. This also is the basis of "intimacy." The "intimate" character of certain relations seems to me to derive from the individual's inclination to consider that which distinguishes him from others, that which is individual in a qualitative sense, as the core, value, and chief matter of his existence. The inclination is by no means always justifiable; in many people, the very opposite—that which is typical, which they share with many—is the essence and the substantial value of their personality. The same phenomenon can be noted in regard to groups. They, too, easily make their specific content, that is shared only by the members, not by outsiders, their center and real fulfillment. Here we have the form of intimacy.

• • •

It is obvious that the intimacy of the dyad is closely tied up with its sociological specialty, not to form a unit transcending the two members. For, in spite of the fact that the two individuals would be its only participants, this unit would nevertheless constitute a third element which might interpose itself between them. The larger the group is, the more easily does it form an objective unit up and above its members, and the less intimate does it become: the two characteristics are intrinsically connected. The condition of intimacy consists in the fact that the participants in a given relationship see only one another, and do not see, at the same time, an objective, super-individual structure which they feel exists and operates on its own. Yet in all its purity, this condition is met only rarely even in groups of as few as three. Likewise, the third element in a relation between two individuals—the unit which has grown out of the interaction among the two—interferes with the most intimate nature of the dyad; and this is highly characteristic of its subtler structure. Indeed, it is so fundamental that even marriages occasionally succumb to it, namely, when the first child is born.

· · ·

Neither of the two members can hide what he has done behind the group, nor hold the group responsible for what he has failed to do. Here the forces with which the group surpasses the individual—indefinitely and partially, to be sure, but yet quite perceptibly—cannot compensate for individual inadequacies, as they can in larger groups. There are many respects in which two united individuals accomplish more than two isolated individuals. Nevertheless, the decisive characteristic of the dyad is that each of the two must actually accomplish something, and that in case of failure only the other remains—not a super-individual force, as prevails in a group even of three. The significance of this characteristic, however, is by no means only negative (referring, that is, to what it excludes). On the contrary, it also makes for a close and highly specific coloration of the dyadic relationship. Precisely the fact that each of the two knows that he can depend only upon the other and on nobody else, gives the dyad a special consecration—as is seen in marriage and friendship, but also in more external associations, including political ones, that consist of two groups. In respect to its sociological destiny and in regard to any other destiny that depends on it, the dyadic element is much more frequently confronted with All or Nothing than is the member of the larger group.

❧ The Triad vs. the Dyad

This peculiar closeness between two is most clearly revealed if the dyad is contrasted with the triad. For among three elements, each one operates as an intermediary between the other two, exhibiting the twofold function of such an organ, which is to unite and to separate. Where three elements, A, B, C, constitute a group, there is, in addition to the direct relationship between A and B, for instance, their indirect one, which is derived from their common relation to C. The fact that two elements are each connected not only by a straight line—the shortest—but also by a broken line, as it were, is an enrichment from a formal-sociological standpoint. Points that cannot be contacted by the straight line are connected by the third element, which offers a different side to each of the other two, and yet fuses these different sides in the unity of its own personality. Discords between two parties which they themselves cannot remedy, are accommodated by the third or by absorption in a comprehensive whole.

Yet the indirect relation does not only strengthen the direct one. It may also disturb it. No matter how close a triad may be, there is always the occasion on which two of the three members regard the third as an intruder. The reason may be the mere fact that he shares in certain moods which can unfold in all their intensity and tenderness only when two can meet without distraction: the sensitive union of two is always irritated by the spectator. It may also be noted how extraordinarily difficult and rare it is for three people to attain a really uniform mood—when visiting a museum, for instance, or looking at a landscape—and how much more easily such a mood emerges between two. A and B may stress and harmoniously feel their m, because the n which A does not share with B, and the x which B does not share with A, are at once spontaneously conceded to be individual prerogatives located, as it were, on another plane. If, however, C joins the company, who shares n with A and x with B, the result is that (even under this scheme, which is the one most favorable to the unity of the whole) harmony of feeling is made completely impossible. Two may actually be *one* party, or may stand entirely beyond any question of party. But it is usual for just such finely tuned combinations of three at once to result in three parties of two persons each, and thus to destroy the unequivocal character of the relations between each two of them.

The sociological structure of the dyad is characterized by two phenomena that are absent from it. One is the intensification of relation by a third element, or by a social framework that transcends both members of the dyad. The other is any disturbance and distraction of pure and immediate reciprocity. In some cases it is precisely this absence which makes the dyadic relationship more intensive and strong. For, many otherwise underdeveloped, unifying forces that derive from more remote psychical reservoirs come to life in the feeling of exclusive dependence upon one another and of hopelessness that cohesion might come from anywhere but immediate interaction. Likewise, they carefully avoid many disturbances and dangers into which confidence in a third party and in the triad itself might lead the two. This intimacy, which is the tendency of relations between two persons, is the reason why the dyad constitutes the chief seat of jealousy.

· · ·

❧ Dyads, Triads, and Larger Groups

Dyads thus have very specific features. This is shown not only by the fact that the addition of a third person completely changes them, but also, and even more so, by the common observation that the further expansion to four or more by no means correspondingly modifies the group any further. For instance, a marriage with one child has a character which is completely different from that of a childless marriage, but it is not significantly different from a marriage with two or more children. To be sure, the difference resulting from the advent of the second child is again much more considerable than is that which results from the third. But this really follows from the norm mentioned: in many respects, the marriage with one child is a relation consisting of two elements—on the one hand, the parental unit, and on the other, the child. The second child is not only a fourth member of a relation but, sociologically speaking, also a third, with the peculiar effects of the third member.

• • •

In short, the sociological situation between the superordinate and the subordinate is completely changed as soon as a third element is added. Party formation is suggested instead of solidarity. . . . It is seen in all these cases that the triad is a structure completely different from the dyad but not, on the other hand, specifically distinguished from four or more members.

☙ ☙ ☙

Questions

1. How is intimacy related to the dyad?

2. What does Simmel mean that dyads are "frequently confronted with All or Nothing"?

3. How does the fundamental nature of the dyad change when a third element is added?

4. How do the dyad and triad differ in terms of social relations and power?

5. Think about your closest personal friend; you were likely a dyad at some point in time. How did your relationship change when a third person was added? What effect did the third person have on the cohesiveness of the group and the intimacy between you and your original friend?

The Presentation of Self in Everyday Life

ERVING GOFFMAN

Erving Goffman's most lasting contributions to sociology are likely his writings on "impression management." This concept is crucial for understanding what's known as the symbolic interactionist perspective—the belief that interactions are constructed based on the use of mutually understood symbols, objects and language. In the introduction to his classic text, The Presentation of Self in Everyday Life, *Goffman presents several key concepts including impression management, the "situation," and sign-vehicles. While reading this selection, think about how these concepts lay the groundwork for the eventual introduction of "front-stage" and "back-stage" and how these concepts are critical for understanding human interaction.*

*W*hen an individual enters the presence of others, they commonly seek to acquire information about him or to bring into play information about him already possessed. They will be interested in his general socio-economic status, his conception of self, his attitude toward them, his competence, his trustworthiness, etc. Although some of this information seems to be sought almost as an end in itself, there are usually quite practical reasons for acquiring it. Information about the individual helps to define the situation, enabling others to know in advance what he will expect of them and what they may expect of him. Informed in these ways, the others will know how best to act in order to call forth a desired response from him.

For those present, many sources of information become accessible and many carriers (or "sign-vehicles") become available for conveying this information. If unacquainted with the individual, observers can glean clues from his conduct and appearance which allow them to apply their previous experience with individuals roughly similar to the one before them or, more important, to apply untested stereotypes to him. They can also assume from past experience that only individuals of a particular kind are likely to be found in a given social setting. They can rely on what the individual says about himself or on documentary evidence he provides as to who and what he is. If they know, or know of, the individual by virtue of experience prior to the interaction, they can rely on assumptions as to the persistence and generality of psychological traits as a means of predicting his present and future behavior.

However, during the period in which the individual is in the immediate presence of the others, few events may occur which directly provide the others with the conclusive information they will need if they are to direct wisely their own activity. Many crucial facts lie beyond the time and place of interaction or lie concealed within it. For example, the "true" or "real" attitudes, beliefs, and emotions of the individual can be ascertained only indirectly, through his avowals or through what appears to be involuntary expressive behavior. Similarly, if the individual offers the others a product or service, they will often find that during the interaction there will be no time and place immediately available for eating the pudding that the proof can be found in. They will be forced to accept some events as conventional or natural signs of something not directly available to the senses. In Ichheiser's terms,[1] the individual will have to act so that he intentionally or unintentionally *expresses* himself, and the others will in turn have to be *impressed* in some way by him. . . .

Taking communication in both its narrow and broad sense, one finds that when the individual is in the immediate presence of others, his activity will have a promissory character. The others are likely to find that they must accept the individual on faith, offering him a just return while he is present before them in exchange for something whose true value will not be established until after he has left their presence. (Of course, the others also live by inference in their dealings with the physical world, but it is only in the world of social interaction that the objects about which they make inferences will purposely facilitate and hinder this inferential process.) The security that they justifiably feel in making inferences about the individual will vary, of course, depending on such factors as the amount of information they already possess about him, but no amount of such past evidence can entirely obviate the necessity of acting on the basis of inferences. As William I. Thomas suggested:

> It is also highly important for us to realize that we do not as a matter of fact lead our lives, make our decisions, and reach our goals in everyday life either statistically or scientifically. We live by inference. I am, let us say, your guest. You do not know, you cannot determine scientifically, that I will not steal your money or your spoons. But inferentially I will not, and inferentially you have me as a guest.[2]

Let us now turn from the others to the point of view of the individual who presents himself before them. He may wish them to think highly of him, or to think that he thinks highly of them, or to perceive how in fact he feels toward them, or to obtain no clear-cut impression; he may wish to ensure sufficient harmony so that the interaction can be sustained, or to defraud, get rid of, confuse, mislead, antagonize, or insult them. Regardless of the particular objective which the individual has in mind and of his motive for having this objective, it will be in his interests to control the conduct of the others, especially their responsive treatment of him. This control is achieved largely by influencing the definition of the situation which the others come to formulate, and he can influence this definition by expressing himself in such a way as to give them the kind of impression that will lead them to act voluntarily in accordance with his own plan. Thus, when an individual appears in the presence of others, there will usually be some reason for him to mobilize his activity so that it will convey an impression to others which it is in his interests to convey. Since a girl's dormitory mates will glean evidence of her popularity from the calls she receives on the phone, we can suspect that some girls will arrange for calls to be made, and Willard Waller's finding can be anticipated:

> It has been reported by many observers that a girl who is called to the telephone in the dormitories will often allow herself to be called several times, in order to give all the other girls ample opportunity to hear her paged.[3]

Of the two kinds of communication—expressions given and expressions given off—this report will be primarily concerned with the latter, with the more theatrical and contextual kind, the non-verbal, presumably unintentional kind, whether this communication be purposely engineered or not. As an example of what we must try to examine, I would like to cite at length a novelistic incident in which Preedy, a vacationing Englishman, makes his first appearance on the beach of his summer hotel in Spain:

> But in any case he took care to avoid catching anyone's eye. First of all, he had to make it clear to those potential companions of his holiday that they were of no concern to him whatsoever. He stared through them, round them, over them—eyes lost in space. The beach might have been empty. If by chance a ball was thrown his way, he looked surprised; then let a smile of amusement lighten his face (Kindly Preedy), looked round dazed to see that there were people on the beach, tossed it back with a smile to himself and not a smile at the people, and then resumed carelessly his nonchalant survey of space.
>
> But it was time to institute a little parade, the parade of the Ideal Preedy. By devious handlings he gave any who wanted to look a chance to see the title of his book—a Spanish translation of Homer, classic thus, but not daring, cosmopolitan too—and then gathered together his

beach-wrap and bag into a neat sand-resistant pile (Methodical and Sensible Preedy), roll slowly to stretch at ease his huge frame (Big-Cat Preedy), and tossed aside his sandals (Carefree Preedy, after all).

The marriage of Preedy and the sea! There were alternative rituals. The first involved the stroll that turns into a run and a dive straight into the water, thereafter smoothing into a strong splashless crawl towards the horizon. But of course not really to the horizon. Quite suddenly he would turn on to his back and thrash great white splashes with his legs, somehow thus showing that he could have swum further had he wanted to, and then would stand up a quarter out of water for all to see who it was.

The alternative course was simpler, it avoided the cold-water shock and it avoided the risk of appearing too high-spirited. The point was to appear to be so used to the sea, the Mediterranean, and this particular beach, that one might as well be in the sea as out of it. It involved a slow stroll down and into the edge of the water—not even noticing his toes were wet, land and water all the same to him!—with his eyes up at the sky gravely surveying portents, invisible to others, of the weather (Local Fisherman Preedy).[4]

The novelist means us to see that Preedy is improperly concerned with the extensive impressions he feels his sheer bodily action is giving off to those around him. We can malign Preedy further by assuming that he has acted merely in order to give a particular impression, that this is a false impression, and that the others present receive either no impression at all, or, worse still, the impression that Preedy is affectedly trying to cause them to receive this particular impression. But the important point for us here is that the kind of impression Preedy thinks he is making is in fact the kind of impression that others correctly and incorrectly glean from someone in their midst.

I have said that when an individual appears before others his actions will influence the definition of the situation which they come to have. Sometimes the individual will act in a thoroughly calculating manner, expressing himself in a given way solely in order to give the kind of impression to others that is likely to evoke from them a specific response he is concerned to obtain. Sometimes the individual will be calculating in his activity but be relatively unaware that this is the case. Sometimes he will intentionally and consciously express himself in a particular way, but chiefly because the tradition of his group or social status require this kind of expression and not because of any particular response (other than vague acceptance or approval) that is likely to be evoked from those impressed by the expression. Sometimes the traditions of an individual's role will lead him to give a well-designed impression of a particular kind and yet he may be neither consciously nor unconsciously disposed to create such an impression. The others, in their turn, may be suitably impressed by the individual's efforts to convey something, or may misunderstand the situation and come to conclusions that are warranted neither by the individual's intent nor by the facts. In any case, in so far as the others act *as if* the individual had conveyed a particular impression, we may take a functional or pragmatic view and say that the individual has "effectively" projected a given definition of the situation and "effectively" fostered the understanding that a given state of affairs obtains.

There is one aspect of the others' response that bears special comment here. Knowing that the individual is likely to present himself in a light that is favorable to him, the others may divide what they witness into two parts; a part that is relatively easy for the individual to manipulate at will, being chiefly his verbal assertions, and a part in regard to which he seems to have little concern or control, being chiefly derived from the expressions he gives off. The others may then use what are considered to be the ungovernable aspects of his expressive behavior as a check upon the validity of what is conveyed by the governable aspects. In this a fundamental asymmetry is demonstrated in the communication process, the individual presumably being aware of only one stream of his communication, the witnesses of this stream and one other. For example, in Shetland Isle one crofter's wife, in serving native dishes to a visitor from the mainland of Britain, would listen with a polite smile to his polite claims of liking what he was eating; at the same time she would take note of the rapidity with which the visitor lifted his fork or spoon to his mouth, the eagerness with which he passed food into his mouth, and the gusto expressed in chewing the food, using these signs as a check on the stated feelings of the eater. The same woman, in order to discover what one acquaintance (A) "actually" thought of another acquaintance (B), would wait until B was in the presence of A but engaged in conversation with still another person (C). She would then covertly examine the facial expressions of A as he regarded B in conversation with C. Not being in conversation with B, and not being directly observed by him, A would sometimes relax usual constraints and tactful deceptions, and freely express what he was "actually" feeling about B. This Shetlander, in short, would observe the unobserved observer.

Now given the fact that others are likely to check up on the more controllable aspects of behavior by means of the less controllable, one can expect that sometimes the individual will try to exploit this very possibility, guiding the impression he makes through behavior felt to be reliably informing.[5] For example, in gaining admission to a tight social circle, the participant observer may not only wear an accepting look while listening to an informant, but may also be careful to wear the same look when observing the informant talking to others; observers of the observer will then not as easily discover where he actually stands. A specific illustration may be cited from Shetland Isle. When a neighbor dropped in to have a cup of tea, he would ordinarily wear at least a hint of an expectant warm smile as he passed through the door into the cottage. Since lack of physical obstructions outside the cottage and lack of light within it usually made it possible to observe the visitor unobserved as he approached the house, islanders sometimes took pleasure in watching the visitor drop whatever expression he was manifesting and replace it with a sociable one just before reaching the door. However, some visitors, in appreciating that this examination was occurring, would blindly adopt a social face a long distance from the house, thus ensuring the projection of a constant image.

This kind of control upon the part of the individual reinstates the symmetry of the communication process, and sets the stage for a kind of information game—a potentially infinite cycle of concealment, discovery, false revelation, and rediscovery. It should be added that since the others are likely to be relatively unsuspicious of the presumably unguided aspect of the individual's conduct, he can gain much by controlling it. The others of course may sense that the individual is manipulating the presumably spontaneous aspects of his behavior, and seek in this very act of manipulation some shading of conduct that the individual has not managed to control. This again provides a check upon the individuals behavior, this time his presumably uncalculated behavior, thus re-establishing the asymmetry of the communication process. Here I would like only to add the suggestion that the arts of piercing an individual's effort at calculated unintentionality seem better developed than our capacity to manipulate our own behavior, so that regardless of how many steps have occurred in the information game, the witness is likely to have the advantage over the actor, and the initial asymmetry of the communication process is likely to be retained.

When we allow that the individual projects a definition of the situation when he appears before others, we must also see that the others, however passive their role may seem to be, will themselves effectively project a definition of the situation by virtue of their response to the individual and by virtue of any lines of action they initiate to him. Ordinarily the definitions of the situation projected by the several different participants are sufficiently attuned to one another so that open contradiction will not occur. I do not mean that there will be the kind of consensus that arises when each individual present candidly expresses what he really feels and honestly agrees with the expressed feelings of the others present. This kind of harmony is an optimistic ideal and in any case not necessary for the smooth working of society. Rather, each participant is expected to suppress his immediate heartfelt feelings, conveying a view of the situation which he feels the others will be able to find at least temporarily acceptable. The maintenance of this surface of agreement, this veneer of consensus, is facilitated by each participant concealing his own wants behind statements which assert values to which everyone present feels obliged to give up service.

• • •

Given the fact that the individual effectively projects a definition of the situation when he enters the presence of others, we can assume that events may occur within the interaction which contradict, discredit, or otherwise throw doubt upon this projection. When these disruptive events occur, the interaction itself may come to a confused and embarrassed halt. Some of the assumptions upon which the responses of the participants had been predicated become untenable, and the participants find themselves lodged in an interaction for which the situation has been wrongly defined and is now no longer defined. At such moments the individual whose presentation has been discredited may feel ashamed while the others present may feel hostile, and all the participants may come to feel ill at ease, nonplussed, out of countenance, embarrassed, experiencing the kind of anomy that is generated when the minute social system of face-to-face interaction breaks down.

In stressing the fact that the initial definition of the situation projected by an individual tends to provide a plan for the co-operative activity that follows—in stressing this action point of view—we must not overlook the crucial fact that any projected definition of the situation also has a distinctive moral character. It is this moral character of projections that will chiefly concern us in this report. Society is organized on the principle that any individual who possesses certain social characteristics has a moral right to expect that others will value and treat him in a correspondingly appropriate way. Connected with this principle is a second, namely that an individual who implicitly or explicitly signifies that he has certain social characteristics ought to have this claim honored by others and ought in fact to be what he claims he is. In consequence, when an individual projects a definition of the situation and thereby makes an implicit or explicit claim to be a person of a particular kind, he automatically exerts a moral demand upon the others, obliging them to value and treat him in the manner that persons of his kind have a right to expect. He also implicitly forgoes all claims to be things he does not appear to be[6] and hence forgoes the treatment that would be appropriate for such individuals. The others find, then, that the individual has informed them as to what is and as to what they ought to see as the "is."

* * *

To summarize, then, I assume that when an individual appears before others he will have many motives for trying to control the impression they receive of the situation. . . . The issues dealt with by stagecraft and stage management are sometimes trivial but they are quite general; they seem to occur everywhere in social life, providing a clear-cut dimension for formal sociological analysis.

Endnotes

[1]Ichheiser, G. (1949). Misunderstandings in human relations. Supplement to *The American Journal of Sociology, 55*, 6–7.

[2]Quoted in Volkart, E. H. (Ed.) (1951). *Social behavior and personality.* Contributions of W. I. Thomas to Theory and Social Research. New York: Social Science Research Council, 5.

[3]Waller, W. The rating and dating complex. *American Sociological Review. 2*, 730.

[4]Sansom, W. (1956). *A contest of ladies.* London: Hogarth, 230–232.

[5]The widely read and rather sound writings of Stephen Potter are concerned in part with signs that can be engineered to give a shrewd observer the apparently incidental cues he needs to discover concealed virtues the gamesman does not in fact possess.

[6]This role of the witness in limiting what it is the individual can be has been stressed by Existentialists, who see it as a basic threat to individual freedom. See Sartre, J.-P. (1956). *Being and nothingness.* (H. E. Barnes, Trans.). New York: Philosophical Library, 365 ff.

Questions

1. Define "sign-vehicles." What is the significance of sign-vehicles?

2. How does the "definition of the situation" affect the presentation of the self?

3. According to Goffman, there are two components of any projected behavior: the governable and the ungovernable. What is the value of the ungovernable aspect of behavior?

4. The concept that Goffman is most known for is "impression management," which includes a front-stage and back-stage component. Explain how the concepts introduced in this selection lead to the development of the front-stage, back-stage distinction.

The McDonaldization of Society

GEORGE RITZER

According to George Ritzer, our society has become increasingly McDonaldized. That is, we constantly search for ways to maximize efficiency in diverse social settings. In this article, Ritzer explains how organizations like McDonald's have influenced other aspects of our social structure through their emphasis on rationality, efficiency, control, and predictability. As you read this article, think about the ways in which your own life has become McDonaldized.

*M*cDonaldization implies a search for maximum efficiency in increasingly numerous and diverse social settings. *Efficiency* means choosing the optimum means to a given end. Let me clarify this definition. First, the truly optimum means to an end is rarely found. Rather, optimum in this definition implies the attempt to find and use the *best possible* means. . . .

In a McDonaldized society, people rarely search for the best means to an end on their own. Rather, they rely on the optimum means that have been previously discovered and institutionalized in a variety of social settings. Thus, the best means may be part of a technology, written into an organization's rules and regulations, or taught to employees during the process of occupational socialization. It would be inefficient if people always had to discover for themselves the optimum means to ends. . . .

◉ The Fast-Food Industry: We Do It All for Them

Although the fast-food restaurant did not create the yearning for efficiency, it has helped turn it into a nearly universal desire. Many sectors of society have had to change in order to operate in the efficient manner demanded by those accustomed to life in the fast lane of the fast-food restaurant. . . .

In the early 1950s, the dawn of the era of the fast-food restaurant, the major alternative to fast food was the home-cooked meal made mostly from ingredients previously purchased at various markets. . . .

But the home-cooked meal was, and still is, a relatively inefficient way to eat. It requires going to the market, preparing the ingredients, cooking the food, eating it, and cleaning up afterward. The restaurant has long been a more efficient alternative in terms of effort.

But restaurants can also be inefficient—it may take several hours to go to a restaurant, consume a meal, and then return home. The desire for more efficient restaurants led to the rise of some of the ancestors of the fast-food restaurants—diners, cafeterias, and early drive-through or drive-in restaurants. . . .

Above all else, Ray Kroc was impressed by the efficiency of the McDonald brothers' operation, as well as the enormous profit potential of such a system applied at a large number of sites. Here is how Kroc described his initial reactions to the McDonald's system:

> I was fascinated by the simplicity and effectiveness of the system.
>
> . . . each step in producing the limited menu was stripped down to its essence and accomplished with a minimum of effort. They sold hamburgers and cheeseburgers only. The burgers were . . . all fried the same way.[1]

• • •

Kroc and his associates experimented with each component of the hamburger to increase the efficiency of producing and serving it.

For example, they started with only partially sliced buns that arrived in cardboard boxes. The griddle workers had to spend time opening the boxes, separating the buns, slicing them in half, and discarding the leftover paper and cardboard. Eventually, they found that buns sliced completely in half could be used more efficiently. In addition, buns were made efficient by having them separated and shipped in reusable boxes. The meat patty received similar attention. For example, the paper between the patties had to have just the right amount of wax so that the patties would readily slide off the paper and onto the grill. Kroc made it clear that he aimed at greater efficiency:

> The purpose of all these refinements, and we never lost sight of it, was to make our griddle man's job easier to do quickly and well. And the other considerations of cost cutting, inventory control, and so forth were important to be sure, but they were secondary to the critical detail of what happened there at the smoking griddle. This was the vital passage of our *assembly-line,* and the product had to flow through it smoothly or the whole plant would falter.[2] (Italics added.)

• • •

Getting diners into and out of the fast-food restaurant has also been streamlined. As three observers put it, McDonald's has done "everything to speed the way from secretion to excretion."[3] Parking lots adjacent to the restaurant offer readily available parking spots. It's a short walk to the counter, and although there is sometimes a line, food is usually quickly ordered, obtained, and paid for. The highly limited menu makes the diner's choice easy in contrast to the many choices available in other restaurants. With the food obtained, it is but a few steps to a table and the beginning of the "dining experience." Because there is little inducement to linger, the diners generally gather the leftover paper, styrofoam, and plastic, discard them in a nearby trash receptacle, and get back in their cars to drive to the next (often McDonaldized) activity.

Not too many years ago, those in charge of fast-food restaurants discovered that the drive-through window made this whole process far more efficient. McDonald's opened its first drive-through in 1975 in Oklahoma City; within four years, almost half its restaurants had one. Instead of the "laborious" and "inefficient" process of parking the car, walking to the counter, waiting in line, ordering, paying, carrying the food to the table, eating, and disposing of the remnants, the drive-through window offered diners the option of driving to the window (perhaps waiting in a line of cars), ordering, paying, and driving off with the meal. You could eat while driving if you wanted to be even more efficient. The drive-through window is also efficient for the fast-food restaurant. As more and more people use the drive-through window, fewer parking spaces, tables, and employees are needed. Further, consumers take their debris with them as they drive away, thereby eliminating the need for additional trash receptacles and employees to empty those receptacles periodically.

• • •

☺ Higher Education: *Just Fill* in the *Box*

In the educational system, specifically the university (now being dubbed "McUniversity"[4]), you can find many examples of the pressure for greater efficiency. One is the machine-graded, multiple-choice examination. In a much earlier era, students were examined individually by their professors. This may have been a good way to find out what students knew, but it was highly labor-intensive and inefficient. Later, the essay examination became very popular. While grading a set of essays was more efficient than giving individual oral examinations, it was still relatively inefficient and time-consuming. Enter the multiple-choice examination, the grading of which was a snap. In fact, graduate assistants could grade it, making it even more efficient for the professor. Now there are computer-graded examinations that maximize efficiency for both professors and graduate assistants. They even offer advantages to students, such as making it easier to study and limiting the effect of the subjective views of the grader on the grading process.

The multiple-choice examination still left the professor saddled with the inefficient task of composing the necessary sets of questions.

Furthermore, at least some of the questions had to be changed each semester because new students were likely to gain possession of old exams. The solution: Textbook companies provided professors with books (free of charge) full of multiple-choice questions to accompany textbooks required for use in large classes. However, the professor still had to retype the questions or have them retyped. Recently, publishers have begun to provide these sets of questions on computer disks. Now all the professor needs to do is select the desired questions and let the printer do the rest. With these great advances in efficiency, professors now can choose to have very little to do with the entire examination process, from question composition to grading.

Publishers have provided other services to make teaching more efficient for those professors who adopt their textbooks. With the adoption of a textbook, a professor may receive many materials with which to fill class hours—lecture outlines, computer simulations, discussion questions, videotapes, movies, even ideas for guest lecturers and student projects. Professors who choose to use all these devices need do little or nothing on their own for their classes. A highly efficient means of teaching, this approach frees up time for other much more valued activities (by professors, but not students) such as writing and research.

Finally, worth noting is the development of a relatively new type of "service" on college campuses. For a nominal fee, students are provided with lecture notes, from instructors, teaching assistants, and top-notch students, for their courses. No more inefficient note-taking, in fact, no more inefficient class attendance. Students are free to pursue more valuable activities such as poring over arcane journals in the graduate library or watching the "soaps."

· · ·

Home Cooking (and Related Phenomena)

Given the efficiency of the fast-food restaurant, the home kitchen has had to grow more efficient or face total extinction. Had the kitchen not grown more efficient, a comedian could have envisioned a time when the kitchen would have been replaced by a large, comfortable telephone lounge used for calling Domino's for pizza delivery.

One key to the salvation of the kitchen is the microwave oven.[5] Far more efficient than conventional ovens for preparing a meal, the microwave has streamlined the process of cooking. Microwaves are usually faster than other ovens, and people can also prepare a wider array of foods in them. Perhaps most important, they spawned a number of microwavable foods (including soup, pizza, hamburgers, fried chicken, french fries, and popcorn) that permit the efficient preparation of the fare people usually find in fast-food restaurants. For example, one of the first microwavable foods produced by Hormel was an array of biscuit-based breakfast sandwiches "popularized in recent years by many of the fast-food chains," most notably McDonald's and its Egg McMuffin.[6] . . . In fact, many food companies now employ people who continually scout fast-food restaurants for new ideas. As one executive put it, "Instead of having a breakfast sandwich at McDonald's, you can pick one up from the freezer of your grocery store."[7] . . . Instead of getting into the car, driving to the restaurant, and returning home, people need only pop the desired foods in the microwave. . . .

Another reason efficiency in the kitchen has not damaged the fast-food business is that fast food offers many advantages over the "home-cooked" microwaved dinner. For one, people can have dinner out rather than just another meal at home. For another, as Stan Luxenberg has pointed out in *Roadside Empires,* McDonald's offers more than an efficient meal; it offers fun—brightly lit, colorful, and attractive settings, garish packaging, special inducements to children, giveaways, contests—in short, it offers a carnival-like atmosphere in which to buy and consume fast food.[8] Thus, faced with the choice of an efficient meal at home or one in a fast-food restaurant, many people will choose the latter.

• • •

The McDonaldization of food preparation and consumption has also reached the booming diet industry. Diet books promising all sorts of shortcuts to weight loss are often at the top of the best-seller lists. Losing weight is normally difficult and time-consuming, hence the lure of diet books that promise to make weight loss easier and quicker, that is, more efficient.

For those on a diet, and many people are on more or less perpetual diets, the preparation of low-calorie food has been streamlined. Instead of cooking diet foods from scratch, they may now purchase an array of prepared diet foods in frozen and/or microwavable form. For those who do not wish to go through the inefficient process of eating these diet meals, there are products even more streamlined such as diet shakes (Slim-Fast, for example) that can be "prepared" and consumed in a matter of seconds.

The issue of dieting points outside the home to the growth of diet centers such as Jenny Craig and Nutri/System. Nutri/System sells dieters, at substantial cost, prepackaged freeze-dried food. In what is close to the ultimate in streamlined cooking, all the dieter need do is add water. Freeze-dried foods are also efficient for Nutri/System, because they can be efficiently packaged, transported, and stored. Furthermore, the dieter's periodic visits to a Nutri/System center are efficiently organized. A counselor is allotted ten minutes with each client. During that brief time, the counselor takes the client's weight, blood pressure, and measurements, asks routine questions, fills out a chart, and devotes whatever time is left to "problem solving." If the session extends beyond the allotted ten minutes and other clients are waiting, the receptionist will buzz the counselor's room. Counselors learn their techniques at Nutri/System University where, after a week of training (no inefficient years of matriculation here), they earn certification and an NSU diploma.

Shopping

Shopping has also grown more efficient. The department store obviously is a more efficient place in which to shop than a series of specialty shops dispersed throughout the city or suburbs. The shopping mall increases efficiency by bringing a wide range of department stores and specialty shops under one roof. Kowinski describes the mall as "an extremely efficient and effective selling machine."[9] It is cost-efficient for retailers because it is the collection of shops and department stores ("mail synergy") that brings in throngs of people. And it is efficient for consumers because in one stop they can visit numerous shops, have lunch at a "food court" (likely populated by many fast-food chains), see a movie, have a drink, and go to an exercise or diet center.

The drive for shopping efficiency did not end with the malls. Seven-Eleven and its clones have become drive-up, if not drive-through, minimarkets. For those who need only a few items, it is far more efficient (albeit more costly) to pull up to a highly streamlined Seven-Eleven than to run to a supermarket. . . .

In recent years, catalogues (e.g., L.L. Bean, Lands' End) have become more popular. They enable people to shop from the comfort of their homes. Still more efficient, though it may lead to many hours in front of the TV, is home-television shopping. A range of products are paraded before viewers, who can purchase them simply by phoning in and conveniently charging their purchases. The latest advance in home shopping is the "scanfone," an at-home phone machine that includes "a pen-sized bar-code scanner, a credit card magnetic-strip reader, and a key pad." The customer merely "scans items from a bar-coded catalogue and also scans delivery dates and payment methods. The orders are then electronically relayed to the various stores, businesses, and banks involved."[10] Some mall operators fear that they will ultimately be put out of business because of the greater efficiency of shopping at home.

. . .

Entertainment

With the advent of videotapes and video-rental stores, many people no longer deem it efficient to drive to their local theater to see a movie. Movies can now be viewed, often more than one at a sitting, in people's own dens. Those who wish even greater efficiency can buy one of the new television sets that enables viewers to see a movie while also watching a favorite TV show on an inset on the screen.

The largest video rental franchise in the United States, Blockbuster, predictably "considers itself the McDonald's of the video business."[11] . . . However, Blockbuster may already be in danger of replacement by even more efficient alternatives such as the pay-per-view movies offered by many cable companies. Instead of trekking to the video store, people just turn to the proper channel and phone the cable company. New small dishes allow people access to a wider range of video offerings. Now in the experimental stage, video-on-demand systems may some day allow people to order the movies available in video stores from the comfort of their homes. . . . Just as the video store replaced many movie theaters, video stores themselves may soon make way for even more efficient alternatives.

. . . Travel to exotic foreign locales has also grown more streamlined. The best example of this is the package tour. Take, for example, a thirty-day tour of Europe. To make it efficient, tourists visit only the major locales in Europe. Buses hurtle through cities, allowing tourists to glimpse the maximum number of sites in the time allowed. At particularly interesting or important sights, the bus may slow down or even stop to permit some picture taking. At the most important locales, a brief stopover is planned; there, a visitor can hurry through the site, take a few pictures, buy a souvenir, then hop back on the bus to head to the next attraction. The package tour can be seen as a mechanism that permits the efficient transport of people from one locale to another.

. . .

Dehumanization of Customers and Employees

. . . The fast-food restaurant offers its employees a dehumanizing work setting. Said Burger King workers, "A moron could learn this job, it's so easy" and "Any trained monkey could do this job."[12] Workers can use only a small portion of their skills and abilities. This is irrational from the organization's viewpoint, because it could obtain much more from its employees for the money (however negligible) it pays them. . . .

The minimal skill demands of the fast-food restaurant are also irrational from the employee's perspective. Besides not using all their skills, employees are not allowed to think and be creative on the job. This leads to a high level of resentment, job dissatisfaction, alienation, absenteeism, and turnover among those who work in fast-food restaurants.[13] In fact, the fast-food industry has the highest turnover rate—approximately 300% a year—of any industry in the United States. That means that the average fast-food worker lasts only about four months; the entire work force of the fast-food industry turns over approximately three times a year. . . .

The fast-food restaurant also dehumanizes the customer. By eating on a sort of assembly line, the diner is reduced to an automaton made to rush through a meal with little gratification derived from the dining experience or from the food itself. The best that can usually be said is that it is efficient and it is over quickly.

Some customers might even feel as if they are being fed like livestock in a highly rationalized manner. This point was made on TV a number of years ago in a *Saturday Night Live* skit, "Trough and Brew," a parody of a small fast-food chain called "Burger and Brew." In the skit, some young executives learn that a new fast-food restaurant called Trough and Brew has opened, and they decide to try it for lunch. When they enter the restaurant, bibs are tied around their necks. Then, they discover what resembles a pig trough filled with chili and periodically refilled by a waitress scooping new supplies from a bucket. The customers bend over, stick their heads into the trough, and lap up the chili as they move along the trough making high-level business decisions. Every so often they come up for air and lap some beer from the communal "brew basin." After they have finished their "meal," they pay their bills "by the head." Since their faces are smeared with chili, they are literally "hosed off" before they leave the restaurant. The young executives are last seen being herded out of the restaurant, which is being closed for a half-hour so that it can be "hosed down." *Saturday Night Live* was clearly ridiculing the fact that fast-food restaurants tend to treat their customers like lower animals.

Customers are also dehumanized by scripted interactions, and other efforts to make interactions uniform. "Uniformity is incompatible when human interactions are involved. Human interactions that are mass-produced may strike consumers as dehumanizing if the routinization is obvious or manipulative if it is not."[14] Dehumanization occurs when prefabricated interactions take the place of authentic human relationships.

. . .

Another dehumanizing aspect of fast-food restaurants is that they minimize contact among human beings. For example, the nature of the fast-food restaurant makes the relationships between employees and customers fleeting at best. Because the average employee works part-time and stays only a few months, even the regular customer can rarely develop a personal relationship with him or her. All but gone are the days when one got to know well a waitress at a diner or the short order cook at a local greasy spoon. Few are the places where an employee knows who you are and knows what you are likely to order.

Contact between workers and customers is very short. It takes little time at the counter to order, receive the food, and pay for it. Both employees and customers are likely to feel rushed and to want to move on, customers to their dinner and employees to the next order. There is virtually no time for customer and counterperson to interact in such a context. This is even truer of the drive-through window, where thanks to the speedy service and the physical barriers, the server is even more distant.

These highly impersonal and anonymous relationships are heightened by the training of employees to interact in a staged, scripted, and limited manner with customers. Thus, the customers may feel that they are dealing with automatons rather than with fellow human beings. For their part, the customers are supposed to be, and often are, in a hurry, so they also have little to say to the McDonald's employee. Indeed, it could be argued that one of the reasons the fast-food restaurants succeed is that they are in time with our fast-paced and impersonal society. . . . People in the modern world

want to get on with their business without unnecessary personal relationships. The fast-food restaurant gives them precisely what they
want.

Not only the relationships between employee and customer, but
other potential relationships are limited greatly. Because employees
remain on the job for only a few months, satisfying personal relationships among employees are unlikely to develop. . . .

Relationships among customers are largely curtailed as well.
Although some McDonald's ads would have people believe otherwise,
gone for the most part are the days when people met in the diner or
cafeteria for coffee or a meal and lingered to socialize. Fast-food
restaurants clearly do not encourage such socializing. If nothing else,
the chairs by design make people uncomfortable, so that they move
on quickly. The drive-through windows completely eliminate the
possibility of interaction with other customers.

· · ·

Fast-food restaurants also tend to have negative effects on other
human relationships. There is, for example, the effect on the family,
especially the so-called "family meal." The fast-food restaurant is not
conducive to a long, leisurely, conversation-filled dinnertime.
Furthermore, as the children grow into their teens, the fast-food
restaurant can lead to separate meals as the teens go at one time with
their friends, and the parents go at another time. Of course, the
drive-through window only serves to reduce further the possibility of
a family meal. The family that gobbles its food while driving on to its
next stop can hardly enjoy "quality time." Here is the way one journalist describes what is happening to the family meal:

> Do families who eat their suppers at the Colonel's, swinging
> on plastic seats, or however the restaurant is arranged, say
> grace before picking up a crispy brown chicken leg? Does
> dad ask junior what he did today as he remembers he forgot
> the piccalilli and trots through the crowds over to the count-
> er to get some? Does mom find the atmosphere conducive to
> asking little Mildred about the problems she was having with

third conjugation French verbs, or would it matter since otherwise the family might have been at home chomping down precooked frozen food, warmed in the microwave oven and watching "Hollywood Squares"?[15]

There is much talk these days about the disintegration of the family, and the fast-food restaurant may well be a crucial contributor to that disintegration. In fact, as implied above, dinners at home may now not be much different from meals at the fast-food restaurant. Families tended to stop having lunch together by the 1940s and breakfast together by the 1950s. Today, the family dinner is following the same route. Even at home, the meal will probably not be what it once was. Following the fast-food model, people have ever more options to "graze," "refuel" nibble on this, or snack on that, rather than sit down at a formal meal. Also, because it may seem inefficient to do nothing but just eat, families are likely to watch television while they are eating. Furthermore, the din, to say nothing of the lure, of dinnertime TV programs such as *Wheel of Fortune* is likely to make it difficult for family members to interact with one another.

A key technology in the destruction of the family meal is the microwave oven and the vast array of microwavable foods it helped generate.[16] More than 70% of American households have a microwave oven. A *Wall Street Journal* poll indicated that Americans consider the microwave their favorite household product. In fact, the microwave in a McDonaldizing society is seen as an advance over the fast-food restaurant. Said one consumer researcher, "It has made even fast-food restaurants not seem fast because at home you don't have to wait in line." As a general rule, consumers demand meals that take no more thin ten minutes to microwave, whereas in the past people were more often willing to spend a half hour or even an hour cooking dinner. This emphasis on speed has, of course, brought with it lower quality, but people do not seem to mind this loss: "We're just not as critical of food as we used to be."[17]

• • •

ℋomogenization

Another dehumanizing effect of the fast-food restaurant is that it has increased homogenization in the United States and, increasingly, throughout the world. This decline in diversity is manifest in the extension of the fast-food model to all sorts of ethnic foods. People are hard-pressed to find an authentically different meal in an ethnic fast-food chain. The food has been rationalized and compromised so that it is acceptable to the tastes of virtually all diners. Paradoxically, while fast-food restaurants have permitted far more people to experience ethnic food, the food that they eat has lost many of its distinguishing characteristics. The settings are also all modeled after McDonald's in one way or another.

The expansion of these franchises across the United States means that people find little difference between regions and between cities. Tourists find more familiarity and less diversity as they travel around the nation, and this is increasingly true on a global scale. Exotic settings are increasingly likely sites for American fast-food chains. The McDonald's and Kentucky Fried Chicken in Beijing are but two examples of this. . . . The spread of American and indigenous fast food throughout much of the world causes less and less diversity from one setting to another. The human craving for new and diverse experiences is being limited, if not progressively destroyed, by the spread of fast-food restaurants. The craving for diversity is being supplanted by the desire for uniformity and predictability.

• • •

☻ Conclusion

• • •

Although I have emphasized the irresistibility of McDonaldization, . . . my fondest hope is that I am wrong. . . . I hope that people can resist McDonaldization and create instead a more reasonable, more human world.

A few years ago, McDonald's was sued by the famous French chef, Paul Bocuse, for using his picture on a poster without his permission. Enraged, Bocuse said, "How can I be seen promoting this tasteless, boneless food in which everything is soft." Nevertheless, Bocuse seemed to acknowledge the inevitability of McDonaldization: "There's a need for this kind of thing . . . and trying to get rid of it seems to me to be as futile as trying to get rid of the prostitutes in the Bois de Bologne."[18] Lo and behold, two weeks later, it was announced that the Paris police had cracked down on prostitution in the Bois de Bologne. Said a police spokesperson, "There are none left." Thus, just as chef Bocuse was wrong about the prostitutes, perhaps I am wrong about the irresistibility of McDonaldization. Yet, before I grow overly optimistic, it should be noted that "everyone knows that the prostitutes will be back as soon as the operation is over. In the spring, police predict, there will be even more than before."[19] Similarly, it remains likely that no matter how intense the opposition, the future will bring with it more rather than less McDonaldization. Even if this proves to be the case, it is my hope that you will follow some of the advice outlined in this chapter for protesting and mitigating the worst effects of McDonaldization. Faced with Max Weber's iron cage and image of a future dominated by the polar night of icy darkness and hardness, I hope that if nothing else, you will consider the words of the poet Dylan Thomas: "Do not go gentle into that good night. . . . Rage, rage against the dying of the light."[20]

Endnotes

[1]Kroc, R. (1977). *Grinding it out.* New York: Berkeley Medallion Books, p. 8.

[2]Kroc, R. (1977). *Grinding it out.* New York: Berkeley Medallion Books, pp. 96–97.

[3]Kroker, A., Kroker, M., & Cook, D. (1989). *Panic encyclopedia: The definitive guide to the postmodern scene.* New York: St. Martin's Press, p. 119.

[4]Parker, M., & Jary, D. (1995). The McUniversity: Organization, management and academic subjectivity. *Organization, 2,* 1–19.

[5]"The microwave cooks up a new way of life. (1989, September 19). *Wall Street Journal,* p. B1; Microwavable foods—Industry's response to consumer demands for convenience. (1987). *Food Technology, 41,* 52–63.

[6]"Microwavable foods—Industry's response to consumer demands for convenience. *Food Technology, 41,* 54.

[7]Shapiro, E. (1991, October 14). A page from fast food's menu. *New York Times,* pp. D1, D3.

[8]Luxenberg, S. (1985). *Roadside empires: How the chains franchised America.* New York: Viking.

[9]Kowinski, W. S. (1985). *The malling of America: An inside look at the great consumer paradise.* New York: Morrow, p. 61.

[10]Swisher, K. (1992, April 16) Companies unveil "scanfone" shopping service. *Washington Post,* pp. B1, B15.

[11]Potts, M. (1991, December 9). Blockbuster struggle with merger script. *Washington Post/Washington Business,* p. 24; Shapiro, E. (1992, February 21). Market place: A mixed outlook for Blockbuster. *New York Times,* p. D6.

[12]Reiter, E. (1991). *Making fast food.* Montreal and Kingston: McGill-Queen's University Press, pp. 150, 167.

[13]Leidner disagrees with this, arguing that McDonald's "workers expressed relatively little dissatisfaction with the extreme routinization." See Leidner, R. (1993). *Fast food, fast talk: Service work and the routinization of everyday life.* Berkeley: University of California Press, p. 134. One could ask, however, whether this indicates a McDonaldizing society in which people, accustomed to the process, simply accept it as an inevitable part of their work.

[14]Leidner, R. (1993). *Fast food, fast talk: Service work and the routinization of everyday life.* Berkeley-University of California Press, p. 30.

[15]von Hoffman, N. (1978, November 23). The fast-disappearing family meal. *Washington Post,* p. C4.

[16]Visser, M. (1989, December). A meditation on the microwave. *Psychology Today,* pp. 38ff.

[17]"The microwave cooks up a new way of life. (1989, September 19). *Wall Street Journal,* p. B1.

[18]Cohen, R. (1992, February 18). Faux pas by McDonald's in Europe. *New York Times,* p. D1.

[19]Two quotes from Waxman, S. (1992, March 2). Paris's sex change operation. *Washington Post,* p. B1.

[20]Thomas, D. (1952). *The collected poems of Dylan Thomas.* "Do Not Go Gentle into That Good Night." New York: New Directions, p. 128.

❧ ❧ ❧

Questions

1. What is McDonaldization?

2. What are some negative outcomes of McDonaldization? What are some of the positive outcomes?

3. How has McDonaldization resulted in social change? What effect has this change had on our culture? On the world?

4. Describe some ways in which your life has become McDonaldized. What can you do to fight McDonaldization in your life?

5. Have you ever worked for McDonald's or another McDonaldized business? If so, does the behind-the-scenes reality compare with what the customer sees? How do your experiences compare with those described in the article?

The Normality of Crime

EMILE DURKHEIM

What is normal for a society? What is pathological? While most of us might think of crime as abnormal and therefore something that should be eliminated, Emile Durkheim disagrees. In this classic essay, Durkheim addresses the conditions under which a behavior emerges, and uses crime to illustrate the necessary role of pathological behavior in society.

• • •

*I*f there is a fact whose pathological nature appears indisputable, it is crime. All criminologists agree on this score. Although they explain this pathology differently, they nonetheless unanimously acknowledge it. However, the problem needs to be treated less summarily.

. . . Crime is not only observed in most societies of a particular species, but in all societies of all types. There is not one in which criminality does not exist, although it changes in form and the actions which are termed criminal are not everywhere the same. Yet everywhere and always there have been men who have conducted themselves in such a way as to bring down punishment upon their heads. If at least, as societies pass from lower to higher types, the crime rate (the relationship between the annual crime figures and population figures) tended to fall, we might believe that, although still remaining a normal phenomenon, crime tended to lose that character of normality. Yet there is no single ground for believing such a regression to be real. Many facts would rather seem to point to the existence of a movement in the opposite direction. From the beginning of the century statistics provide us with a means of following the progression of criminality. It has everywhere increased, and in France the increase is of the order of 300 per cent. Thus there is no phenomenon which represents more incontrovertibly all the symptoms of normality, since it appears to be closely bound up with the conditions of all collective life. To make crime a social illness would be to concede that sickness is not something accidental, but on the contrary derives in certain cases from the fundamental constitution of the living creature. This would be to erase any distinction between the physiological and the pathological. It can certainly happen that crime itself has normal forms; this is what happens, for instance, when it reaches an excessively high level. There is no doubt that this excessiveness is pathological in nature. What is normal is simply that criminality exists, provided that for each social type it does not reach or go beyond a certain level which it is perhaps not impossible to fix in conformity with the previous rules.[1]

We are faced with a conclusion which is apparently somewhat paradoxical. Let us make no mistake: to classify crime among the phenomena of normal sociology is not merely to declare that it is an inevitable though regrettable phenomenon arising from the incorrigible wickedness of men; it is to assert that it is a factor in public health, an integrative element in any healthy society. At first sight this result is so surprising that it disconcerted even ourselves for a long time. However, once that first impression of surprise has been overcome it is not difficult to discover reasons to explain this normality and at the same time to confirm it.

In the first place, crime is normal because it is completely impossible for any society entirely free of it to exist.

Crime, as we have shown elsewhere, consists of an action which offends certain collective feelings which are especially strong and clear-cut. In any society, for actions regarded as criminal to cease, the feelings that they offend would need to be found in each individual consciousness without exception and in the degree of strength requisite to counteract the opposing feelings. Even supposing that this condition could effectively be fulfilled, crime would not thereby disappear; it would merely change in form, for the very cause which made the well-springs of criminality to dry up would immediately open up new ones.

Indeed, for the collective feelings, which the penal law of a people at a particular moment in its history protects, to penetrate individual consciousnesses that had hitherto remained closed to them, or to assume greater authority—whereas previously they had not possessed enough—they would have to acquire an intensity greater than they had had up to then. The community as a whole must feel them more keenly, for they cannot draw from any other source the additional force which enables them to bear down upon individuals who formerly were the most refractory. For murderers to disappear, the horror of bloodshed must increase in those strata of society from which murderers are recruited; but for this to happen the abhorrence must increase throughout society. Moreover, the very absence of crime would contribute directly to bringing about that result, for a sentiment appears much more respectable when it is always and uniformly respected. But we overlook the fact that these strong states of the common consciousness cannot be reinforced in this way without the weaker states, the violation of which previously gave rise to mere breaches of convention, being reinforced at the same time, for the weaker states are no more than the extension and attenuated form of the stronger ones. Thus, for example, theft and mere misappropriation of property offend the same altruistic sentiment, the respect for other people's possessions. However, this sentiment is offended less strongly by the latter action than the former. Moreover, since the average consciousness does not have sufficient intensity of feeling to feel strongly about the lesser of these two offences, the latter is the object of greater tolerance. This is why the misapppropriator is merely censured, while the thief is punished. But if this sentiment grows stronger, to such a degree that it extinguishes in the consciousness the tendency to theft that men possess, they will become more sensitive to these minor offences, which up to then had had only a marginal effect upon them. They will react with greater intensity against these lesser faults, which will become the object of severer condemnation, so that, from the mere moral errors that they were, some will pass into the category of crimes. For example, dishonest contracts or those fulfilled dishonestly, which only incur public censure or civil redress, will become crimes. Imagine a community of saints in an exemplary and perfect monastery. In it crime as such will be unknown but faults that appear venial to the ordinary person will arouse the same scandal as does normal crime in ordinary consciences. If therefore that community has the power to judge and punish, it will term such acts criminal and deal with them as such. It is for the same reason that the completely honourable man judges his slightest moral failings with a severity that the mass of people reserves for acts that are truly criminal. In former times acts of violence against the person were more frequent than they are today because respect for individual dignity was weaker. As it has increased, such crimes have become less frequent, but many acts which offended against that sentiment have been incorporated into the penal code, which did not previously include them.[2]

In order to exhaust all the logically possible hypotheses, it will perhaps be asked why this unanimity should not cover all collective sentiments without exception, and why even the weakest sentiments should not evoke sufficient power to forestall any dissentient voice. The moral conscience of society would be found in its entirety in every individual, endowed with sufficient force to prevent the commission of any act offending against it, whether purely conventional failings or crimes. But such universal and absolute uniformity is utterly impossible, for the immediate physical environment in which each one of us is placed, our hereditary antecedents, the social influences upon which we depend, vary from one individual to another and consequently cause a diversity of consciences. It is impossible for everyone to be alike in this matter, by virtue of the fact that we each have our own organic constitution and occupy different areas in space. This is why, even among lower peoples where individual originality is very little developed, such originality does however exist. Thus, since there cannot be a society in which individuals do not diverge to some extent from the collective types, it is also inevitable that among these deviations some assume a criminal character. What confers upon them this character is not the intrinsic importance of the acts but the importance which the common consciousness ascribes to them. Thus if the latter is stronger and possesses sufficient authority to make these divergences very weak in absolute terms, it will also be more sensitive and exacting. By reacting against the slightest deviations with an energy which it elsewhere employs against those that are more weighty, it endues them with the same gravity and will brand them as criminal.

Thus crime is necessary. It is linked to the basic conditions of social life, but on this very account is useful, for the conditions to which it is bound are themselves indispensable to the normal evolution of morality and law.

Indeed today we can no longer dispute the fact that not only do law and morality vary from one social type to another, but they even change within the same type if the conditions of collective existence are modified. Yet for these transformations to be made possible, the collective sentiments at the basis of morality should not prove unyielding to change, and consequently should be only moderately intense. If they were too strong, they would no longer be malleable. Any arrangement is indeed an obstacle to a new arrangement; this is even more the case the more deep-seated the original arrangement. The more strongly a structure is articulated, the more it resists modification: this is as true for functional as for anatomical patterns. If there were no crimes, this condition would not be fulfilled, for such a hypothesis presumes that collective sentiment would have attained a degree of intensity unparalleled in history. Nothing is good indefinitely and without limits. The authority which the moral consciousness enjoys must not be excessive, for otherwise no one would dare to attack it and it would petrify too easily into an immutable form. For it to evolve, individual originality must be allowed to manifest itself. But so that the originality of the idealist who dreams of transcending his era may display itself, that of the criminal, which falls short of the age, must also be possible. One does not go without the other.

Nor is this all. Beyond this indirect utility, crime itself may play a useful part in this evolution. Not only does it imply that the way to necessary changes remains open, but in certain cases it also directly prepares for these changes. Where crime exists, collective sentiments are not only in the state of plasticity necessary to assume a new form, but sometimes it even contributes to determining beforehand the shape they will take on. Indeed, how often is it only an anticipation of the morality to come, a progression towards what will be! According to Athenian law, Socrates was a criminal and his condemnation was entirely just. However, his crime—his independence of thought—was useful not only for humanity but for his country. It served to prepare a way for a new morality and a new faith, which the Athenians then needed because the traditions by which they had hitherto lived no longer corresponded to the conditions of their existence. Socrates's case is not an isolated one, for it recurs periodically in history. The freedom of thought that we at present enjoy could never have been asserted if the rules that forbade it had not been violated before they were solemnly abrogated. However, at the time the violation was a crime, since it was an offence against sentiments still keenly felt in the average consciousness. Yet this crime was useful since it was the prelude to changes which were daily becoming more necessary. Liberal philosophy has had as its precursors heretics of all kinds whom the secular arm rightly punished through the Middle Ages and has continued to do so almost up to the present day.

From this viewpoint the fundamental facts of criminology appear to us in an entirely new light. Contrary to current ideas, the criminal no longer appears as an utterly unsociable creature, a sort of parasitic element, a foreign, unassimilable body introduced into the bosom of society. He plays a normal role in social life. For its part, crime must no longer be conceived of as an evil which cannot be circumscribed closely enough. Far from there being cause for congratulation when it drops too noticeably below the normal level, this apparent progress assuredly coincides with and is linked to some social disturbance. Thus the number of crimes of assault never falls so low as it does in times of scarcity.[3] Consequently, at the same time, and as a reaction, the theory of punishment is revised, or rather should be revised. If in fact crime is a sickness, punishment is the cure for it and cannot be conceived of otherwise; thus all the discussion aroused revolves round knowing what punishment should be to fulfil its role as a remedy. But if crime is in no way pathological, the object of punishment cannot be to cure it and its true function must be sought elsewhere.

• • •

Endnotes

[1]From the fact that crime is a phenomenon of normal sociology it does not follow that the criminal is a person normally constituted from the biological and psychological viewpoints. The two questions are independent of each other. This independence will be better understood when we have shown later the difference which exists between psychical and sociological facts.

[2]Calumny, insults, slander, deception, etc.

[3]But, although crime is a fact of normal sociology, it does not follow that we should not abhor it. Pain has likewise nothing desirable about it: the individual detests is just as society detests crime, and yet it is a normal physiological function. Not only does it necessarily derive from the very constitution of every living creature, but it plays a useful and irreplaceable role in life. Thus it would be a peculiar distortion to represent our thinking as an apologia for crime. We would not even have envisaged protesting against such an interpretation were we not aware of the strange accusations and misunderstandings to which one is exposed in undertaking to study moral facts objectively and to speak of them in language that is not commonly used.

Questions

1. Why does Durkheim contend that crime is not only normal, but necessary?

2. How does crime contribute to the development of (or important changes in) a society?

3. Given Durkheim's view of crime, how effective can we expect social sanctions and reform efforts to be in deterring crime?

4. Think of specific crimes that are committed on your campus. How would Durkheim explain the existence or prevalence of these crimes?

On Being Sane in Insane Places

D. L. ROSENHAN
Stanford University

D. L. Rosenhan wondered, "If sanity and insanity exist, how shall we know them?" By having pseudopatients check themselves into psychiatric hospitals and record their experiences as mental patients, Rosenhan learned that staff members did not realize that these individuals were actually mentally healthy. Moreover, the experiences recorded by the pseudopatients provide a rich account of the role of powerlessness, depersonalization, and labeling that occur in mental institutions. It also explains how the institutional structure and environment contribute to the problem of these processes.

If sanity and insanity exist, how shall we know them?

The question is neither capricious nor itself insane. However much we may be personally convinced that we can tell the normal from the abnormal, the evidence is simply not compelling. It is commonplace, for example, to read about murder trials wherein eminent psychiatrists for the defense are contradicted by equally eminent psychiatrists for the prosecution on the matter of the defendant's sanity. More generally, there are a great deal of conflicting data on the reliability, utility, and meaning of such terms as "sanity," "insanity," "mental illness," and "schizophrenia." Finally, as early as 1934, Benedict suggested that normality and abnormality are not universal.[1] What is viewed as normal in one culture may be seen as quite aberrant in another. Thus, notions of normality and abnormality may not be quite as accurate as people believe they are.

To raise questions regarding normality and abnormality is in no way to question the fact that some behaviors are deviant or odd. Murder is deviant. So, too, are hallucinations. Nor does raising such questions deny the existence of the personal anguish that is often associated with "mental illness."

Anxiety and depression exist. Psychological suffering exists. But normality and abnormality, sanity and insanity, and the diagnoses that flow from them may be less substantive than many believe them to be.

At its heart, the question of whether the sane can be distinguished from the insane (and whether degrees of insanity can be distinguished from each other) is a simple matter: do the salient characteristics that lead to diagnoses reside in the patients themselves or in the environments and contexts in which observers find them? . . . The belief has been strong and patients present symptoms, that those symptoms can be categorized and, implicitly, that the sane are distinguishable from the insane. More recently, however, this belief has been questioned. . . . The view has grown that psychological categorization of mental illness is useless at best and downright harmful, misleading, and pejorative at worst. Psychiatric diagnoses, in this view, are in the minds of the observers and are not valid summaries of characteristics displayed by the observed.[2-3]

Gains can be made in deciding which of these is more nearly accurate by getting normal people (that is, people who do not have, and have never suffered, symptoms of serious psychiatric disorders) admitted to psychiatric hospitals and then determining whether they were discovered to be sane and, if so, how. If the sanity of such pseudopatients were always detected, there would be a prima facie evidence that a sane individual can be distinguished from the insane context in which he is found. Normality (and presumably abnormality) is distinct enough that it can be recognized wherever it occurs, for it is carried within the person. If, on the other hand, the sanity of the pseudopatients were never discovered, serious difficulties would arise for those who support traditional modes of psychiatric diagnosis. Given that the hospital staff was not incompetent, that the pseudopatient had been behaving as sanely as he had been outside of the hospital, and that it had never been previously suggested that he belonged in a psychiatric hospital, such an unlikely outcome would support the view that psychiatric diagnosis betrays little about the patient but much about the environment in which an observer finds him.

This article describes such an experiment. Eight sane people gained secret admission to 12 different hospitals. Their diagnostic experiences constitute the data of the first part of this article; the remainder is devoted to a description of their experiences in psychiatric institutions. . . .

❂ Pseudopatients and Their Settings

The eight pseudopatients were a varied group. One was a psychology graduate student in his 20's. The remaining seven were older and "established." Among them were three psychologists, a pediatrician, a psychiatrist, a painter, and a housewife. Three pseudopatients were women, five were men. All of them employed pseudonyms, lest their alleged diagnoses embarrass them later. Those who were in mental health professions alleged another occupation in order to avoid the special attentions that might be accorded by staff, as a matter of courtesy or caution, to ailing colleagues. With the exception of myself (I was the first pseudopatient and my presence was known to the hospital administrator and chief psychologist and, so far as I can tell, to them alone), and the presence of pseudopatients and the nature of the research program was not known to the hospital staffs.

The settings were similarly varied. In order to generalize the findings, admission into a variety of hospitals was sought. The 12 hospitals in the sample were located in five different states on the East and West coasts. Some were old and shabby, some were quite new. Some were research-oriented, others not. Some had good staff-patient ratios, others were quite understaffed. Only one was a strictly private hospital. All of the others were supported by state or federal funds or, in one instance, by university funds.

After calling the hospital for an appointment, the pseudopatient arrived at the admissions office complaining that he had been hearing voices. Asked what the voices said, he replied that they were often unclear, but as far as he could tell they said "empty," "hollow," and "thud." The voices were unfamiliar and were the same sex as the pseudopatient. The choice of these symptoms was occasioned by their apparent similarity to existential symptoms. Such symptoms are alleged to arise from painful concerns about the perceived meaninglessness of one's life. It is as if the hallucinating person were saying, "My life is empty and hollow." . . .

Beyond alleging the symptoms and falsifying name, vocation, and employment, no further alterations of person, history, or circumstances were made.

The significant events of the pseudopatient's life history were presented as they had actually occurred. Relationships with parents and siblings, with spouse and children, with people at work and in school, consistent with the aforementioned exceptions, were described as they were or had been. Frustrations and upsets were described along with joys and satisfactions. These facts are important to remember. If anything, they strongly biased the subsequent results in favor of detecting sanity, since none of their histories or current behaviors were seriously pathological in any way.

Immediately upon admission to the psychiatric ward, the pseudopatient ceased simulating *any* symptoms of abnormality. In some cases, there was a brief period of mild nervousness and anxiety, since none of the pseudopatient really believed that they would be admitted so easily. Indeed, their shared fear was that they would be immediately exposed as frauds and greatly embarrassed. Moreover, many of them had never visited a psychiatric ward; even those who had, nevertheless had some genuine fears about what might happen to them. Their nervousness, then, was quite appropriate to the novelty of the hospital setting, and it abated rapidly.

Apart from that short-lived nervousness, the pseudopatient behaved on the ward as he "normally" behaved. The pseudopatient spoke to patients and staff as he might ordinarily. Because there is uncommonly little to do on a psychiatric ward, he attempted to engage others in conversation. When asked by staff how he was feeling, he indicated that he was fine, that he no longer experienced symptoms. He responded to instructions from attendants, to calls for medication (which was not swallowed), and to dining-hall instructions. Beyond such activities as were available to him on the admissions ward, he spent his time writing down his observations about the ward, its patients, and the staff. Initially these notes were written "secretly," but as it soon became clear that no one much cared, they were subsequently written on standard tablets of paper in such public places as the dayroom. No secret was made of these activities. . . .

❂ The Normal Are Not Detectably Sane

Despite their public "show" of sanity, the pseudopatients were never detected. Admitted, except in one case, with a diagnosis of schizophrenia, each was discharged with a diagnosis of schizophrenia "in remission." The label "in remission" should in no way be dismissed as a formality, for at no time during any hospitalization had any question been raised about any pseudopatient's simulation. Nor are there any indications in the hospital records that the pseudopatient's status was suspect. Rather, the evidence is strong that, once labeled schizophrenic, the pseudopatient was stuck with that label. If the pseudopatient was to be discharged, he must naturally be "in remission"; but he was not sane, nor, in the institution's view, had he ever been sane.

The uniform failure to recognize sanity cannot be attributed to the quality of the hospitals, for, although there were considerable variations among them, several are considered excellent. Nor can it be alleged that there was simply not enough time to observe the pseudopatients. Length of hospitalization ranged from 7 to 52 days, with an average of 19 days. The pseudopatients were not, in fact, carefully observed, but this failure clearly speaks more to traditions within psychiatric hospitals than to lack of opportunity.

Finally, it cannot be said that the failure to recognize the pseudopatients' sanity was due to the fact that they were not behaving sanely. While there was clearly some tension present in all of them, their daily visitors could detect no serious behavioral consequences—nor, indeed, could other patients. It was quite common for the patients to "detect" the pseudopatients' sanity. During the first three hospitalizations, when accurate counts were kept, 35 of a total of 118 patients on the admissions ward voiced their suspicions, some vigorously. "You're not crazy. You're a journalist, or a professor [referring to the continual note-taking]. You're checking up on the hospital." While most of the patients were reassured by the pseudopatient's insistence that he had been sick before he came in but was fine now, some continued to believe that the pseudopatient was sane throughout his hospitalization. The fact that the patients often recognized normality when staff did not raises important questions.

Failure to detect sanity during the course of hospitalization may be due to the fact that physicians operate with a strong bias toward what the statisticians call the type 2 error. This is to say that physicians are more inclined to call a healthy person sick (a false positive, type 2) than a sick person healthy (a false negative, type 1). The reasons for this are not hard to find: it is clearly more dangerous to misdiagnose illness than health. Better to err on the side of caution, to suspect illness even among the healthy.

But what holds for medicine does not hold equally well for psychiatry. Medical illnesses, while unfortunate, are not commonly pejorative. Psychiatric diagnoses, on the contrary, carry with them personal, legal, and social stigmas. It was therefore important to see whether the tendency toward diagnosing the sane insane could be reversed. The following experiment was arranged at a research and teaching hospital whose staff had heard these findings but doubted that such an error could occur in their hospitals. The staff was informed that at some time during the following 3 months, one or more pseudopatients would attempt to be admitted into the psychiatric hospital. Each staff member was asked to rate each patient who presented himself at admissions or on the ward according to the likelihood that the patient was a pseudopatient. A 10-point scale was used, with a 1 and 2 reflecting high confidence that the patient was a pseudopatient.

Judgments were obtained on 193 patients who were admitted for psychiatric treatment. All staff who had had sustained contact with or primary responsibility for the patient—attendants, nurses, psychiatrists, physicians, and psychologists—were asked to make judgments. Forty-one patients were alleged, with high confidence, to be pseudopatients by at least one member of the staff. Twenty-three were considered suspect by at least one psychiatrist. Nineteen were suspected by one psychiatrist, *and* one other staff member. Actually, no genuine pseudopatient (at least from my group) presented himself during this period.

The experiment is instructive. It indicates that the tendency to designate sane people as insane can be reversed when the stakes (in this case, prestige and diagnostic acumen) are high. But what can be said of the 19 people who were suspected of being "sane" by one psychiatrist and another staff member? Were these people truly "sane," or was it rather the case that in the course of avoiding the type 2 error the staff tended to make more errors of the first sort—calling the crazy "sane"? There is no way of knowing. But one thing is certain: any diagnostic process that lends itself so readily to massive errors of this sort cannot be a very reliable one.

◉ The Stickiness of Psychodiagnostic Labels

Beyond the tendency to call the healthy sick—a tendency that accounts better for diagnostic behavior on admission than it does for such behavior after a lengthy period of exposure—the data speaks to the massive role of labeling in psychiatric assessment. Having once been labeled schizophrenic, there is nothing the pseudopatient can do to overcome the tag. The tag profoundly colors others' perceptions of him and his behavior.

From one viewpoint, these data are hardly surprising, for it has long been known that elements are given meaning by the context in which they occur. Gestalt psychology made this point vigorously, and Asch demonstrated that there are "central" personality traits (such as "warm" versus "cold") which are so powerful that they markedly color the meaning of other information in forming an impression of a given personality. "Insane," "schizophrenic," "manic-depressive," and "crazy" are probably among the most powerful of such central traits. Once a person is designated abnormal, all of his other behaviors and characteristics are colored by that label. Indeed, that label is so powerful that many of the pseudopatients' normal behaviors were overlooked entirely or profoundly misinterpreted. Some examples may clarify this issue.

. . .

All pseudopatients took extensive notes publicly. Under ordinary circumstances, such behavior would have raised questions in the minds of observer, as, in fact, it did among patients. Indeed, it seemed so certain that the notes would elicit suspicion that elaborate precautions were taken to remove them from the ward each day. But the precautions proved needless. The closest any staff member came to questioning these notes occurred when one pseudopatient asked his physician what kind of medication he was receiving and began to write down the response. "You needn't write it," he was told gently. "If you have trouble remembering, just ask me again."

If no questions were asked of the pseudopatients, how was their writing interpreted? Nursing records for three patients indicate that the writing was seen as an aspect of their pathological behavior. "Patient engages in writing behavior" was the daily nursing comment on one of the pseudopatients who was never questioned about his writing. Given that the patient is in the hospital, he must be psychologically disturbed. And given that he is disturbed, continuous writing must be a behavioral manifestation of that disturbance, perhaps a subset of the compulsive behaviors that are sometimes correlated with schizophrenia.

One tacit characteristic of psychiatric diagnosis is that it locates the sources of aberration within the individual and only rarely within the complex of stimuli that surrounds him. Consequently, behaviors that are stimulated by the environment are commonly misattributed to the patient's disorder. For example, one kindly nurse found a pseudopatient pacing the long hospital corridors. "Nervous, Mr. X?" she asked. "No, bored," he said.

The notes kept by pseudopatients are full of patient behaviors that were misinterpreted by well-intentioned staff. Often enough, a patient would go "berserk" because he had, wittingly or unwittingly, been mistreated by, say, an attendant. A nurse coming upon the scene would rarely inquire even cursorily into the environmental stimuli of the patient's behavior. Rather, she assumed that his upset derived from his pathology, not from his present interactions with other staff members. Occasionally, the staff might assume that the patient's family (especially when they had recently visited) or other patients had stimulated the outburst. But never were the staff found to assume that one of themselves or the structure of the hospital had anything to do with a patient's behavior. One psychiatrist pointed to a group of patients who were sitting outside the cafeteria entrance half an hour before lunchtime. To a group of young residents he indicated that such behavior was characteristic of the oral-acquisitive nature of the syndrome. It seemed not to occur to him that there were very few things to anticipate in a psychiatric hospital besides eating.

A psychiatric label has a life and an influence of its own. Once the impression has been formed that the patient is schizophrenic, the expectation is that he will continue to be schizophrenic. When a sufficient amount of time has passed, during which the patient has done nothing bizarre, he is considered to be in remission and available for discharge. But, the label endures beyond discharge, with the unconfirmed expectation that he will behave as a schizophrenic again. Such labels, conferred by mental health professionals, are as influential on the patient as they are on his relatives and friends, and it should not surprise anyone that the diagnosis acts on all of them as self-fulfilling prophecy. Eventually, the patient himself accepts the diagnosis, with all of its surplus meanings and expectations, and behaves accordingly.

The inferences to be made from these matters are quite simple. Much as Zigler and Phillips have demonstrated that there is enormous overlap in the symptoms presented by patients who have been variously diagnosed,[4] so there is enormous overlap in the behaviors of the sane and the insane. The sane are not "sane" all of the time. We lose our tempers "for no good reason." We are occasionally depressed or anxious, again for no good reason. And we may find it difficult to get along with one or another person—again for no reason that we can specify. Similarly, the insane are not always insane. Indeed, it was the impression of the pseudopatient while living with them that they were sane for long periods of time—that the bizarre behaviors upon which their diagnoses were allegedly predicated constituted only a small fraction of their total behavior. If it makes no sense to label ourselves permanently depressed on the basis of an occasional depression, then it takes better evidence than is presently available to label all patients insane or schizophrenic on the basis of bizarre behaviors or cognitions. It seems more useful, as Mischel[5] has pointed out, to limit our discussions to *behaviors,* the stimuli that provoke them, and their correlates. . . .

☻ The Experience of Psychiatric Hospitalization

The term "mental illness" is of recent origin. It was coined by people who were humane in their inclinations and who wanted very much to raise the station of (and the public's sympathies toward) the psychologically disturbed from that of witches and "crazies" to one that was akin to the physically ill. And they were at least partially successful, for the treatment of the mentally ill *has* improved considerably over the years. But while treatment has improved, it is doubtful that people really regard the mentally ill in the same way that they view the physically ill. A broken leg is something one recovers from, but mental illness allegedly endures forever. A broken leg does not threaten the observer, but a crazy schizophrenic? There is by now a host of evidence that attitudes toward the mentally ill are characterized by fear, hostility, aloofness, suspicion, and dread.[6] The mentally ill are society's lepers. . . .

Consider the structure of the typical psychiatric hospital. Staff and patients are strictly segregated. Staff have their own living space, including their dining facilities, bathrooms, and assembly places. The glassed quarters that contain the professional staff, which the pseudopatients came to call "the cage," sit out on every dayroom. The staff emerge primarily for caretaking purposes—to give medication, to conduct a therapy or group meeting, to instruct or reprimand a patient. Otherwise, staff keep to themselves, almost as if the disorder that afflicts their changes is somehow catching.

So much is patient-staff segregation the rule that, for four public hospitals in which an attempt was made to measure the degree to which staff and patients mingle, it was necessary to use "time out of the staff cage" as the operational measure. While it was not the case that all time spent out of the cage was spent mingling with patients (attendants, for example, would occasionally emerge to watch television in the dayroom), it was the only way in which one could gather reliable data on time for measuring.

The average amount of time spent by attendants outside of the cage was 11.3 percent (range, 3 to 52 percent). This figure does not represent only time spent mingling with patients, but also includes time spent on such chores as folding laundry, supervising patients while they shave, directing ward clean-up, and sending patients to off-ward activities. It was the relatively rare attendant who spent time talking with patients or playing games with them. It proved impossible to obtain a "percent mingling time" for nurses, since the amount of time they spent out of the cage was too brief. Rather, we counted instances of emergence from the cage. On the average, daytime nurses emerged from the cage 11.5 times per shift, including instances when they left the ward entirely (range, 4 to 39 times). Late afternoon and night nurses were even less available, emerging on the average 9.4 times per shift (range, 4 to 41 times). Data on early morning nurses, who arrived usually after midnight and departed at 8 a.m., are not available because patients were asleep during most of this period.

Physicians, especially psychiatrists, were even less available. They were rarely seen on the wards. Quite commonly, they would be seen only when they arrived and departed, with the remaining time being spent in their offices or in the cage. On the average, physicians emerged on the ward 6.7 times per day (range, 1 to 17 times). It proved difficult to make an accurate estimate in this regard, since physicians often maintained hours that allowed them to come and go at different times.

The hierarchical organization of the psychiatric hospital has been commented on before,[7] but the latent meaning of that kind of organization is worth noting again. Those with the most power have least to do with patients, and those with the least power are most involved with them. Recall, however, that the acquisition of role-appropriate behaviors occurs mainly through the observation of others, with the most powerful having the most influence. Consequently, it is understandable that attendants not only spend more time with patients than do any other members of the staff—that is required by their station in the hierarchy—but also, insofar as they learn from their superiors' behavior, spend as little time with patients as they can. Attendants are seen mainly in the cage, which is where the models, the action, and the power are.

I turn now to a different set of studies, those dealing with staff response to patient-initiated contact. It has long been known that the amount of time a person spends with you can be an index of your significance to him. If he initiates and maintains eye contact, there is reason to believe that he is considering your requests and needs. If he pauses to chat or actually stops and talks, there is added reason to infer that he is individuating you. In four hospitals, the pseudopatient approached the staff member with a request which took the following form: "Pardon me, Mr. [or Dr. or Mrs.] X, could you tell me when I will be eligible for grounds privileges?" (or ". . . when I will be presented at the staff meeting?" or ". . . when I am likely to be discharged?"). While the content of the question varied according to the appropriateness of the target and the pseudopatient's (apparent) current needs the form was always a courteous and relevant request for information. Care was taken never to approach a particular member of the staff more than once a day, lest the staff member become suspicious or irritated. In examining these data, remember that the behavior of the pseudopatients was neither bizarre nor disruptive. One could indeed engage in good conversation with them.

The data for these experiments are shown in Table 1, separately for physicians (column 1) and for nurses and attendants (column 2). Minor differences between these four institutions were overwhelmed by the degree to

TABLE 1 *Self-initiated contact by pseudopatients with psychiatrists and nurses and attendants, compared to contact with other groups*

| | Psychiatric Physicians | | University campus (nonmedical) | | University medical center hospitals | |
	(1) Psychiatrists	(2) Nurses and attendants	(3) Faculty	(4) "Looking for a psychiatrist"	(5) "Looking for an internist"	(6) No additional comment
Responses						
Moves on, head averted (%)	71	88	0	0	0	0
Makes eye contact (%)	23	10	0	11	0	0
Pauses and chats (%)	2	2	0	11	0	10
Stops and talks (%)	4	0.5	100	78	100	90
Mean number of questions answered (out of 6)	*	*	6	3.8	4.8	4.5
Respondents (No.)	13	47	14	18	15	10
Attempts (No.)	185	1283	14	18	15	10

which staff avoided continuing contacts that patients had initiated. By far, their most common response consisted of either a brief response to the question, offered while they were "on the move" and with head averted, or no response at all.

The encounter frequently took the following bizarre form: (pseudopatient) "Pardon me, Dr. X. Could you tell me when I am eligible for grounds privileges?" (physician) "Good morning, Dave. How are you today?" (Moves off without waiting for a response.)

It is instructive to compare these data with data recently obtained at Stanford University. It has been alleged that large and eminent universities are characterized by faculty who are so busy that they have no time for students. For this comparison, a young lady approached individual faculty members who seemed to be walking purposefully to some meeting or teaching engagement and asked them the following six questions:

1. "Pardon me, could you direct me to Encina Hall?" (at the medical school: ". . . to the Clinical Research Center?").
2. "Do you know where Fish Annex is?" (there is no Fish Annex at Stanford).
3. "Do you teach here?"
4. "How does one apply for admission to the college?" (at the medical school: ". . . to the medical school?").
5. "Is it difficult to get in?"
6. "Is there financial aid?"

Without exception, as can be seen in Table 1 (column 3), all of the questions were answered. No matter how rushed they were, all respondents not only maintained eye contact, but stopped to talk. Indeed, many of the respondents went out of their way to direct or take the questioner to the office she was seeking, to try to locate "Fish Annex," or to discuss with her the possibilities of being admitted to the university.

Similar data, also shown in Table 1 (columns 4, 5, and 6), were obtained in the hospital. Here too, the young lady came prepared with six questions. After the first questions, however, she remarked to 18 of her respondents (column 4) "I'm looking for a psychiatrist," and to 15 others (column 5), "I'm looking for an internist." Ten other respondents received no inserted comment (column 6). The general degree of cooperative responses is considerably higher for these university groups than it was for pseudopatients in psychiatric hospitals. Even so, differences are apparent within the medical school setting. Once having indicated that she was looking for a psychiatrist, the degree of cooperation elicited was less than when she sought an internist.

• • •

◉ The Sources of Depersonalization

What are the origins of depersonalization? I have already mentioned two. First are attitudes held by all of us toward the mentally ill—including those who treat them—attitudes characterized by fear, distrust, and horrible expectations on the one hand, and benevolent intentions on the other. Our ambivalence leads in this instance as in others, to avoidance.

Second, and not entirely separate, the hierarchical structure of the psychiatric hospital facilitates depersonalization. Those who are at the top have least to do with patients, and their behavior inspires the rest of the staff. Average daily contact with psychiatrists, psychologists, residents, and physicians combined ranged from 3.9 to 25.1 minutes, with an overall mean of 6.8 (six pseudopatients over a total of 129 days of hospitalization). Included in this average are time spent in the admissions interview, ward meetings in the presence of a senior staff member, group and individual psychotherapy contacts, case presentation conferences, and discharge meetings. Clearly, patients do not spend much time in interpersonal contact with doctoral staff. And doctoral staff serve as models for nurses and attendants.

There are probably other sources. Psychiatric installations are presently in serious financial straits. Staff shortages are pervasive, staff time at a premium. Something has to give, and that something is patient contact. Yet, while financial stresses are realities, too much can be made of them. I have the impression that the psychological forces that result in depersonalization are much stronger than the fiscal ones and that the addition of more staff would not correspondingly improve patient care in this regard. The incidence of staff meetings and the enormous amount of record-keeping on patients, for example, have not been as substantially reduced as has patient contact. Priorities exist, even during hard times. Patient contact is not a significant priority in the traditional psychiatric hospital, and fiscal pressures do not account for this. Avoidance and depersonalization may.

Heavy reliance upon psychotropic medication tacitly contributes to depersonalization by convincing staff that treatment is indeed being conducted and that further patient contact may not be necessary. Even here, however, caution needs to be exercised in understanding the role of psychotropic drugs. If patients were powerful rather than powerless, if they were viewed as interesting individuals rather than diagnostic entities, if they were socially sig-nificant rather than social lepers, if their anguish truly and wholly compelled our sympathies and concerns, would we not *seek* contact with them, despite the availability of medications? Perhaps for the pleasure of it all?

☙ The Consequences of Labeling and Depersonalization

Whenever the ratio of what is known to what needs to be known approaches zero, we tend to invent "knowledge" and assume that we understand more than we actually do. We seem unable to acknowledge that we simply don't know. The needs for diagnosis and remediation of behavioral and emotional problems are enormous. But rather than acknowledge that we are just embarking on understanding, we continue to label patients "schizophrenic," "manic-depressive," and "insane," as if in those words we had captured the essence of understanding. The facts of the matter are that we have known for a long time that diagnoses are often not useful or reliable, but we have nev-ertheless continued to use them. We now know that we cannot distinguish insanity from sanity. It is depressing to consider how that information will be used.

Not merely depressing, but frightening. How many people, one won-ders, are sane but not recognized as such in our psychiatric institutions? How many have been needlessly stripped of their privileges of citizenship, from the right to vote and drive to that of handling their own accounts? How many have feigned insanity in order to avoid the criminal consequences of their behavior, and conversely, how many would rather stand trial than live inter-minably in a psychiatric hospital—but are wrongly thought to be mentally ill? How many have been stigmatized by well-intentioned, but nevertheless, erroneous, diagnoses? On the last point, recall again that a "type 2 error" in psychiatric diagnosis does not have the same consequences it does in med-ical diagnosis. A diagnosis of cancer that has been found to be in error is cause for celebration. But psychiatric diagnoses are rarely found to be in error. The label sticks, a mark of inadequacy forever.

Finally, how many patients might be "sane" outside the psychiatric hos-pital but seem insane in it—not because craziness resides in them, as it were, but because they are responding to a bizarre setting, one that may be unique to institutions which harbor nether people? Goffman[3] calls the process of socialization to such institutions "mortification"—an apt metaphor that includes the processes of depersonalization that have been described here. And while it is impossible to know whether the pseudopatients' responses to these processes are characteristic of all inmates—they were, after all, not real patients—it is difficult to believe that these processes of socialization to a psychiatric hospital provide useful attitudes or habits of response for living in the "real world."

◉ Summary and Conclusion

It is clear that we cannot distinguish the sane from the insane in psychiatric hospitals. The hospital itself imposes a special environment in which the meanings of behavior can easily be misunderstood. The consequences to patients hospitalized in such an environment—the powerlessness, depersonalization, segregation, mortification, and self-labeling—seem undoubtedly counter-therapeutic.

I do not, even now, understand this problem well enough to perceive solutions. But two matters seem to have some promise. The first concerns the proliferation of community mental health facilities, of crisis intervention centers, of the human potential movement, and of behavior therapies that, for all of their own problems, tend to avoid psychiatric labels, to focus on specific problems and behaviors, and to retain the individual in a relatively non-pejorative environment. Clearly, to the extent that we refrain from sending the distressed to insane places, our impressions of them are less likely to be distorted. . . .

The second matter that might prove promising speaks to the need to increase the sensitivity of mental health workers and researchers to the *Catch 22* position of psychiatric patients. Simply reading materials in this area will be of help to some such workers and researchers. For others, directly experiencing the impact of psychiatric hospitalization will be of enormous use. Clearly, further research into the social psychology of such total institutions will both facilitate treatment and deepen understanding.

I and the other pseudopatients in the psychiatric setting had distinctly negative reactions. We do not pretend to describe the subjective experiences of true patients. Theirs may be different from ours, particularly with the passage of time and the necessary process of adaptation to one's environment. But we can and do speak to the relatively more objective indices of treatment within the hospital. It could be a mistake, and a very unfortunate one, to consider that what happened to us derived from malice or stupidity on the part of the staff. Quite the contrary, our overwhelming impression of them was of people who really cared, who were committed and who were uncommonly intelligent. Where they failed, as they sometimes did painfully, it would be more accurate to attribute those failures to the environment in which they, too, found themselves than to personal callousness. Their perceptions and behavior were controlled by the situation, rather than being motivated by a malicious disposition. In a more benign environment, one that was less attached to global diagnosis, their behaviors and judgment might have been more benign and effective.

Endnotes

[1]Benedict, R. (1954). *J. Gen Psychol.*, *10*, 59.

[2]See in this regard H. Becker. (1963). *Outsiders: Studies in the sociology of deviance.* New York: Free Press.

[3]Goffman, E. (1961). *Asylums.* Garden City, NY: Doubleday.

[4]Zigler, E., & Phillips, L. (1961). *J. Abnorm. Soc. Psychol.*, *63*, 69. New York: Wiley.

[5]Mischel, W. (1968). *Personality and assessment.* New York: Wiley.

[6]Sarbin, T. R., & Mancuso, J. C. (1967). *J. Clin. Consult. Psychol.*, *35*, 159; Sarbin, T. R. *ibid.* 31, 447 (1967); Nunnally, J. C. Jr., (1961). *Popular conceptions of mental health.* Holt, Rinehart & Winston.

[7]Stanton, H. H., & Schwartz, M. S. (1954). *The mental hospital: A study of institutionalized participation in psychiatric illness and treatment.* New York: Basic Books.

❂ ❂ ❂

Questions

1. How successful were the "normal" individuals at being checked into psychiatric hospitals?

2. Once they were in the hospital and began to behave normally, how many of these "patients" were revealed as *not* being "crazy"? What does this phenomenon imply about the power of the label that the hospital staff applied to the individuals?

3. How much contact did the professional staff have with the patients in this study? How would you characterize the interactions that did occur between patients and staff?

4. How did the structure and organization of the hospital contribute to the depersonalization of the patients?

5. What are some consequences of labeling a person as mentally ill?

6. This study was conducted in the late sixties/early seventies. How might the behaviors and experiences of the mentally ill be similar today? Different? In answering, focus on the interactions between the mentally ill and those around them (i.e., "normals"). Do the stigma and label of mental illness have the same effect on individuals today that Rosenhan observed several decades ago?

The Power Elite

C. WRIGHT MILLS

"The power elite" is an expression clearly associated with the work of C. Wright Mills. Today, the term is widely used in organizational sociology, political sociology, and other areas. It also has connotations of social conflict, which is not necessarily what Mills had in mind. As you read this piece, think about which sociological perspective the power elite would most closely align with theoretically and whether Mills's original conceptualization is accurately portrayed in more contemporary works.

Except for the unsuccessful Civil War, changes in the power system of the United States have not involved important challenges to its basic legitimations. Even when they have been decisive enough to be called "revolutions," they have not involved the "resort to the guns of a cruiser, the dispersal of an elected assembly by bayonets, or the mechanisms of a police state."[1] Nor have they involved, in any decisive way, any ideological struggle to control masses. Changes in the American structure of power have generally come about by institutional shifts in the relative positions of the political, the economic, and the military orders.

. . .

The Nature of the Power Elite

We study history, it has been said, to rid ourselves of it, and the history of the power elite is a clear case for which this maxim is correct. Like the tempo of American life in general, the long-term trends of

"The Power Elite," by C. Wright Mills, reprinted from *The Power Elite,* 1956. Copyright © by Oxford University Press. pp. 269–297.

the power structure have been greatly speeded up since World War II, and certain newer trends within and between the dominant institutions have also set the shape of the power elite. . . .

I. In so far as the structural clue to the power elite today lies in the political order, that clue is the decline of politics as genuine and public debate of alternative decisions—with nationally responsible and policy-coherent parties and with autonomous organizations connecting the lower and middle levels of power with the top levels of decision. America is now in considerable part more a formal political democracy than a democratic social structure, and even the formal political mechanics are weak.

The long-time tendency of business and government to become more intricately and deeply involved with each other has, in the fifth epoch, reached a new point of explicitness. The two cannot now be seen clearly as two distinct worlds. It is in terms of the executive agencies of the state that the rapprochement has proceeded most decisively. The growth of the executive branch of the government, with its agencies that patrol the complex economy, does not mean merely the "enlargement of government" as some sort of autonomous bureaucracy: it has meant the ascendancy of the corporation's man as a political eminence. . . .

II. In so far as the structural clue to the power elite today lies in the enlarged and military state, that clue becomes evident in the military ascendancy. The warlords have gained decisive political relevance, and the military structure of America is now in considerable part a political structure. The seemingly permanent military threat places a premium on the military and upon their control of men, material, money, and power; virtually all political and economic actions are now judged in terms of military definitions of reality: the higher warlords have ascended to a firm position within the power elite of the fifth epoch. . . .

III. In so far as the structural clue to the power elite today lies in the economic order, that clue is the fact that the economy is at once a permanent-war economy and a private-corporation economy. American capitalism is now in considerable part a military capitalism, and the most important relation of the big corporation to the state rests on the coincidence of interests between military and corporate needs, as defined by warlords and corporate rich. Within the elite as a whole, this coincidence of interest between the high military and the corporate chieftains strengthens both of them and further subordinates the role of the merely political men. Not politicians, but corporate executives, sit with the military and plan the organization of war effort. . . .

The power elite is composed of political, economic, and military men, but this instituted elite is frequently in some tension: it comes together only on certain coinciding points and only on certain occasions of "crisis." In the long peace of the nineteenth century, the military were not in the high councils of state, not of the political directorate, and neither were the economic men—they made raids upon the state but they did not join its directorate. During the thirties, the political man was ascendant. Now the military and the corporate men are in top positions.

Of the three types of circle that compose the power elite today, it is the military that has benefited the most in its enhanced power, although the corporate circles have also become more explicitly entrenched in the more public decision-making circles. It is the professional politician that has lost the most, so much that in examining the events and decisions, one is tempted to speak of a political vacuum in which the corporate rich and the high warlord, in their coinciding interest, rule.

It should not be said that the three "take turns" in carrying the initiative, for the mechanics of the power elite are not often as deliberate as that would imply. At times, of course, it is—as when political men, thinking they can borrow the prestige of generals, find that they must pay for it, or, as when during big slumps, economic men feel the need of a politician at once safe and possessing vote appeal. Today all three are involved in virtually all widely ramifying decisions. Which of the three types seems to lead depends upon "the tasks of the period" as they, the elite, define them. Just now, these tasks center upon "defense" and international affairs. Accordingly, as we have seen, the military are ascendant in two senses: as personnel and as justifying ideology. That is why, just now, we can most easily specify the unity and the shape of the power elite in terms of the military ascendancy.

But we must always be historically specific and open to complexities. The simple Marxian view makes the big economic man the *real* holder of power; the simple liberal view makes the big political man the chief of the power system; and there are some who would view the warlords as virtual dictators. Each of these is an oversimplified view. It is to avoid them that we use the term "power elite" rather than, for example, "ruling class."

In so far as the power elite has come to wide public attention, it has done so in terms of "military clique." The power elite does, in fact, take its current shape from the decisive entrance into it of the military. Their presence and their ideology are its major legitimations, whenever the power elite feels the need to provide any. But what is called the "Washington military clique" is not composed merely of military men, and it does not prevail merely in Washington. Its members exist all over the country, and it is a coalition of generals in the roles of corporation executives, of politicians masquerading as admirals, of corporation executives acting like politicians, of civil servants who become majors, of vice-admirals who are also the assistants to a cabinet officer, who is himself, by the way, really a member of the managerial elite.

Neither the idea of a "ruling class" nor of a simple monolithic rise of "bureaucratic politicians" nor of a "military clique" is adequate. The power elite today involves the often uneasy coincidence of economic, military, and political power.

. . .

◎ The Composition of the Power Elite

Despite their social similarity and psychological affinities, the members of the power elite do not constitute a club having a permanent membership with fixed and formal boundaries. It is of the nature of the power elite that within it there is a good deal of shifting about, and that it thus does not consist of one small set of the same men in the same positions in the same hierarchies. Because men know each other personally does not mean that among them there is a unity of policy; and because they do not know each other personally does not mean that among them there is a disunity. The conception of the power elite does not rest, as I have repeatedly said, primarily upon personal friendship.

As the requirements of the top places in each of the major hierarchies become similar, the types of men occupying these roles at the top—by selection and by training in the jobs—become similar. This is no mere deduction from structure to personnel. That it is a fact is revealed by the heavy traffic that has been going on between the three structures, often in very intricate patterns. The chief executives, the warlords, and selected politicians came into contact with one another in an intimate, working way during World War II; after that war ended, they continued their associations, out of common beliefs, social congeniality, and coinciding interests. Noticeable proportions of top men from the military, the economic, and the political worlds have during the last fifteen years occupied positions in one or both of the other worlds: between these higher circles there is an interchangeability of position based formally upon the supposed transferability of "executive ability," based in substance upon the co-optation by cliques of insiders. As members of a power elite, many of those busy in this traffic have come to look upon "the government" as an umbrella under whose authority they do their work.

As the business between the big three increases in volume and importance, so does the traffic in personnel. The very criteria for selecting men who will rise come to embody this fact. The corporate commissar, dealing with the state and its military, is wiser to choose a young man who has experienced the state and its military than one who has not. The political director, often dependent for his own political success upon corporate decisions and corporations, is also wiser to choose a man with corporate experience. Thus, by virtue of the very criterion of success, the interchange of personnel and the unity of the power elite is increased.

Given the formal similarity of the three hierarchies in which the several members of the elite spend their working lives, given the ramifications of the decisions made in each upon the others, given the coincidence of interest that prevails among them at many points, and given the administrative vacuum of the American civilian state along with its enlargement of tasks—given these trends of structure, and adding to them the psychological affinities we have noted—we should indeed be surprised were we to find that men said to be skilled in administrative contacts and full of organizing ability would fail to do more than get in touch with one another. They have, of course, done much more than that: increasingly, they assume positions in one another's domains.

The unity revealed by the interchangeability of top roles rests upon the parallel development of the top jobs in each of the big three domains. The interchange occurs most frequently at the points of their coinciding interest, as between regulatory agency and the regulated industry, contracting agency and contractor. And, as we shall see, it leads to co-ordinations that are more explicit, and even formal.

The inner core of the power elite consists, first, of those who interchange commanding roles at the top of one dominant institutional order with those in another: the admiral who is also a banker and a lawyer and who heads up an important federal commission; the corporation executive whose company was one of the two or three leading war material producers who is now the Secretary of Defense; the wartime general who dons civilian clothes to sit on the political directorate and then becomes a member of the board of directors of a leading economic corporation.

Although the executive who becomes a general, the general who becomes a statesman, the statesman who becomes a banker, see much more than ordinary men in their ordinary environments, still the perspectives of even such men often remain tied to their dominant locales. In their very career, however, they interchange roles within the big three and thus readily transcend the particularity of interest in any one of these institutional milieux. By their very careers and activities, they lace the three types of milieux together. They are, accordingly, the core members of the power elite.

These men are not necessarily familiar with every major arena of power. We refer to one man who moves in and between perhaps two circles—say the industrial and the military—and to another man who moves in the military and the political, and to a third who moves in the political as well as among opinion-makers. These in-between types most closely display our image of the power elite's structure and operation, even of behind-the-scenes operations. To the extent that there is any "invisible elite," these advisory and liaison types are its core. Even if—as I believe to be very likely—many of them are, at least in the first part of their careers, "agents" of the various elites rather than themselves elite, it is they who are most active in organizing the several top milieux into a structure of power and maintaining it.

. . .

The outermost fringes of the power elite—which change more than its core—consist of "those who count" even though they may not be "in" on given decisions of consequence nor in their career move between the hierarchies. Each member of the power elite need not be a man who personally decides every decision that is to be ascribed to the power elite. Each member, in the decisions that he does make, takes the others seriously into account. They not only make decisions in the several major areas of war and peace; they are the men who, in decisions in which they take no direct part, are taken into decisive account by those who are directly in charge.

On the fringes and below them, somewhat to the side of the lower echelons, the power elite fades off into the middle levels of power, into the rank and file of the Congress, the pressure groups that are not vested in the power elite itself, as well as a multiplicity of regional and state and local interests. If all the men on the middle levels are not among those who count, they sometimes must be taken into account, handled, cajoled, broken or raised to higher circles.

. . .

◉ The Interests of the Power Elite

The conception of the power elite and of its unity rests upon the corresponding developments and the coincidence of interests among economic, political, and military organizations. It also rests upon the similarity of origin and outlook, and the social and personal intermingling of the top circles from each of these dominant hierarchies. This conjunction of institutional and psychological forces, in turn, is revealed by the heavy personnel traffic within and between the big three institutional orders, as well as by the rise of go-betweens as in the high-level lobbying. The conception of the power elite, accordingly, does *not* rest upon the assumption that American history since the origins of World War II must be understood as a secret plot, or as a great and co-ordinated conspiracy of the members of this elite. The conception rests upon quite impersonal grounds.

There is, however, little doubt that the American power elite—which contains, we are told some of the greatest organizers in the world—has also planned and has plotted. The rise of the elite, as we have already made clear, was not and could not have been caused by a plot; and the tenability of the conception does not rest upon the existence of any secret or any publicly known organization. But, once the conjunction of structural trend and of the personal will to utilize it gave rise to the power elite, then plans and programs did occur to its members and indeed it is not possible to interpret many events and official policies of the fifth epoch without reference to the power elite. "There is a great difference," Richard Hofstadter has remarked, "between locating conspiracies in history and saying that history *is*, in effect, a conspiracy. . . . "

The structural trends of institutions become defined as opportunities by those who occupy their command posts. Once such opportunities are recognized, men may avail themselves of them. Certain types of men from each of the dominant institutional areas, more far-sighted than others, have actively promoted the liaison before it took its truly modern shape. They have often done so for reasons not shared by their partners, although not objected to by them either; and often the outcome of their liaison has had consequences which none of them foresaw, much less shaped, and which only later in the course of development came under explicit control. Only after it was well under way did most of its members find themselves part of it and become gladdened, although sometimes also worried, by this fact. But once the co-ordination is a going concern, new men come readily into it and assume its existence without question.

So far as explicit organization—conspiratorial or not—is concerned, the power elite, by its very nature, is more likely to use existing organizations, working within and between them, than to set up explicit organizations whose membership is strictly limited to its own members. But if there is no machinery in existence to ensure for example, that military and political factors will be balanced in decisions made, they will invent such machinery and use it, as with the National Security Council. Moreover, in a formally democratic polity, the aims and the powers of the various elements of this elite are further supported by an aspect of the permanent war economy: the assumption that the security of the nation supposedly rests upon great secrecy of plan and intent. Many higher events that would reveal the working of the power elite can be withheld from public knowledge under the guise of secrecy. With the wide secrecy covering their operations and decisions, the power elite can mask their intentions, operations, and further consolidation. Any secrecy that is imposed upon those in positions to observe high decision-makers clearly works for and not against the operations of the power elite.

There is accordingly reason to suspect—but by the nature of case, no proof—that the power elite is not altogether "surfaced." There is nothing hidden about it, although its members often know one another, seem quite naturally to work together, and share many organizations in common. There is nothing conspiratorial about it, although its decisions are often publicly unknown and its mode of operation manipulative rather than explicit.

· · ·

❧ *C*onclusion

The idea of the power elite rests upon and enables us to make sense of (1) the decisive institutional trends that characterize the structure of our epoch, in particular, the military ascendancy in a privately incorporated economy, and more broadly, the several coincidences of objective interests between economic, military, and political institutions; (2) the social similarities and the psychological affinities of the men who occupy the command posts of these structures, in particular the increased interchangeability of the top positions in each of them and the increased traffic between these orders in the careers of men of power; (3) the ramifications, to the point of virtual totality, of the kind of decisions that are made at the top, and the rise to power of a set of men who, by training and bent, are professional organizers of considerable force and who are unrestrained by democratic party training.

Negatively, the formation of the power elite rests upon (1) the relegation of the professional party politician to the middle levels of power, (2) the semi-organized stalemate of the interests of sovereign localities into which the legislative function has fallen, (3) the virtually complete absence of a civil service that constitutes a politically neutral, but politically relevant, depository of brainpower and executive skill, and (4) the increased official secrecy behind which great decisions are made without benefit of public or even Congressional debate.

As a result, the political directorate, the corporate rich, and the ascendant military have come together as the power elite, and the expanded and centralized hierarchies which they head have encroached upon the old balances and have now relegated them to the middle levels of power. Now the balancing society is a conception that pertains accurately to the middle levels, and on that level the balance has become more often an affair of intrenched provincial and nationally irresponsible forces and demands than a center of power and national decision.

. . .

ℰndnote

[1]Hofstadter, R. op. cit., pp. 71–72.

☙ ☙ ☙

Questions

1. Define the power elite.

2. According to Mills, which three domains (i.e., institutions) make up the core of the power elite?

3. Of the three domains, which takes precedence? Explain the interplay among the three institutions. How do the interests of these three groups conflict? How are their interests similar?

4. To what degree does Mills rely on a "conspiracy theory" to explain the existence and continued prominence of the power elite?

5. Mills's thesis was first presented some four decades ago to explain a historical pattern that may or may not be applicable today. Which groups do you think make up the power elite in contemporary American society? Which groups constitute the power elite in other societies? Speculate as to why these groups might differ across cultures or societies.

Mate Selection and Marriage Around the World

Bron B. Ingoldsby

Most people in Western societies choose to marry because they have fallen in love with someone. However, choice is just one of several approaches to mate selection that are practiced around the world. For example, the Yanomama of Venezuela use a combination of arranged marriage and marriage by capture to provide young people with mates. This article explores why various routes to marriage were historically preferred and why they are practiced today.

• • •

*H*istorically, there have been three general approaches to choosing one's mate: marriage by capture, marriage by arrangement, and free-choice mate selection. I examine each of them in turn.

☺ Marriage by Capture

Although it has probably never been the usual method of obtaining a wife, men have taken women by force in many times and places. This typically occurred in patriarchal societies in which women were often considered property. Often women were seized as part of the spoils of war, and other times a specific woman was forced into marriage because the man wanted her and could not afford the brideprice or

"Mate Selection and Marriage Around the World," by Bron B. Ingoldsby, reprinted from *Families in Multicultural Perspectives*, 1995, Guilford Press. pp. 143–151.

obtain the permission of her parents. The capture and marriage of a woman was legal in England until the reign of Henry VII, who made it a crime to abduct an heiress (Fielding, 1942).

The ancient Hebrews would seize wives under certain circumstances. A dramatic example is recounted in the Old Testament (Judges, Chapter 21), where it was arranged for young women to be kidnapped from two different areas to serve as wives so that the tribe of Benjamin would not die out after a war that they had lost.

There was also a formal procedure for dealing with wives captured in warfare:

> When thou goest forth to war against thine enemies, and the Lord thy God hath delivered them into thine hands, and thou hast taken them captive; And seest among the captives a beautiful woman, and hast a desire unto her, that thou wouldest have her to thy wife; Then thou shalt bring her home to thine house; and she shall shave her head, and pare her nails; And she shall put the raiment of her captivity from off her, and shall remain in thine house, and bewail her father and her mother a full month: and after that thou shalt go in unto her, and be her husband, and she shall be thy wife. And it shall be, if thou have no delight in her, then thou shalt let her go whither she will; but thou shalt not sell her at all for money, thou shalt not make merchandise of her, because thou hast humbled her. (Deuteronomy 21:10–14)

At least she was given time to get used to the idea and never sold into slavery! Fielding (1942) cites a number of different cultures, including the Australian aborigines, who frequently resorted to marriage by capture in the recent past. The Yanomama of Venezuela (an Amazonian tribe) are reported (Peters, 1987) to use capture as one of their mate selection options. One village is often raided by another for the specific purpose of finding wives. If a man captures a young, attractive female, he must be careful as other men from his own village will try to steal her from him.

In the popular musical *Seven Brides for Seven Brothers,* the concept of marriage by capture is acted out, and one of the songs is based on the historical incident of the rape of the Sabine women. There are many cultures that still have remnants of the old practice of marriage by capture in their wedding ceremonies. In each of them, the match is prearranged, but the husband pretends to take his bride by force, and she feigns resistance.

One example are the Roro of New Guinea. On the wedding day, the groom's party surrounds the bride's home and acts out an assault on it. The bride attempts to run away but is caught. Then a sham battle ensues, with the bride's mother leading the way and crying at the loss of her daughter when she is taken off to the groom (Fielding, 1942).

◉ Marriage by Arrangement

It appears that the most common method of mate selection has been by arrangement. Typically, the parents, often with the aid of certain relatives or professional matchmakers, have chosen the spouse for their child. This form of mate choice is more common when extended kin groups are strong and important. Essentially, marriage is seen as of group, rather than individual, importance, and economics is often the driving force rather than love between the principles.

Arranged marriages have been considered especially important for the rulers of kingdoms and other nobility. Care had to be taken to preserve bloodlines, enhance wealth, and resolve political issues. It is believed, for instance, that the majority of King Solomon's 700 wives and 300 concubines were acquired for the purpose of political alliances.

Stephens (1963) identifies four major reasons that determine mate choice in societies in which marriages are arranged. The first is *price*. The groom's family may need to pay for the bride, with either money or labor. In some cultures, the situation is reversed, with the bride's family paying a dowry to the husband. In other cases, there is a direct exchange, where both families make payments to each other or simply trade women for each other's sons.

The second consideration is *social status*. That is, the reputation of the family from which the spouse for one's child will come is very important. A third determinant is any *continuous marriage arrangement*. This refers to a set pattern for mate selection, which is carried on from generation to generation. For instance, cousin marriages are preferred in many societies.

The final criteria for mate choice are *sororate and levirate* arrangements, which refer to second marriages and tend to be based on brideprice obligations. These terms are more fully explained later. . . . Stephens also notes 19 societies (including, for example, some large ones such as China and Renaissance Europe) that have practiced child betrothals or child marriages. This means that the marriage is arranged before puberty and can even be worked out before the child is born.

In addition to marriage by capture, the Yanomama also practice variety within arranged marriages. The ideal match is between cross-cousins, and the majority of unions fall into this category. Most betrothals are made before the girl is three years of age. Men initiate these arrangements at about the time they become hunters, which is shortly after they turn 15. Another acceptable form of mate selection is sister exchange. Two unrelated single males wish to acquire wives and have sisters who are not promised to anyone, so they simply trade sisters (Peters, 1987).

Some societies have provided an "out" for couples who have strong personal preferences that go against the arrangement of their families. This is to permit elopement. Stephens (1963) gives this account of the Iban of Borneo:

> When a young woman is in love with a man who is not acceptable to her parents, there is an old custom called *nunghop bui,* which permits him to carry her off to his own village. She will meet him by arrangement at the waterside, and step into his boat with a paddle in her hand, and both will pull away as fast as they can. If pursued he will stop every now

and then to deposit some article of value on the bank, such as a gun, a jar, or a favor for the acceptance of her family, and when he has exhausted his resources he will leave his own sword. When the pursuers observe this they cease to follow, knowing he is cleared out. As soon as he reaches his own village he tidies up the house and spreads the mats, and when his pursuers arrive he gives them food to eat and toddy to drink, and sends them home satisfied. In the meanwhile he is left in possession of his wife. (p. 200)

Following is a detailed look at some of the specific mechanisms of arranged marriages.

Brideprice

Throughout much of human history, marriage has been seen as chiefly an economic transaction. As an old German saying goes, "It is not man that marries maid, but field marries field, vineyard marries vineyard, cattle marry cattle" (Tober 1984, p. 12). The purpose of a brideprice is to compensate the family of the bride for the loss of her services. It is extremely common and is indicative of the value of women in those societies. Stephens (1963) reports that Murdock's World Ethnographic Sample yields the following breakdown on marriage payments:

Brideprice—260 societies
Bride service—75 societies
Dowry—24 societies
Gift or woman exchange—31 societies
No marriage payment—152 societies

This means that in 62% of the world's societies, a man must pay in order to marry a woman. The price is usually paid in animals, shell money, or other valuable commodities and often exceeds one's annual income. Some cultures prefer payment in service, often many years of labor to the bride's parents, or at least permit it for suitors who cannot afford to pay in goods. One famous example from the Old Testament is that of Jacob, who labored seven years for each of Laban's two daughters, Leah and Rachel.

Dowry

The dowry appears to be an inducement for a man to marry a particular woman and therefore relieve her family of the financial burden of caring for her. Although relatively rare, it is a sign of a culture that places a low value on women. Actually, the key purpose of a dowry is probably to stabilize a marriage, because it is not given to the husband but is something that the bride brings with her into the marriage. For example, in Cyprus before the time of English influence, the expected dowry was often a house. If the husband divorced his wife or mistreated her and she left him, the dowry went with her. Like modern-day wedding gifts, or the bride's trousseau, it was an investment in the marriage and intended to reduce the chances of a breakup (Balswick, 1975).

The dowry has been around for a long time. The Babylonian code of Hammurabi (1955 B.C.) clearly stated that the wife's property stayed with her if her husband divorced her and passed on to her children when she died. Ancient Greece and Rome also considered the dowry to be essential in any honorable marriage (Fielding, 1942).

Recent research in the southern Indian state of Kerala (Billig, 1992) differentiates between the traditional dowry and an actual "groomprice." Groomprice is money paid by the bride's family directly to the husband to use as he sees fit. In the 1950s and 1960s, rapid population growth resulted in more younger women looking for husbands a few (average of seven) years older than themselves. This surplus of potential brides increased the value of husbands. Popular revulsion for the groomprice has resulted in a decrease in the age difference (now five years), women lowering their social status expectations for their husband or increasing their own education, and a government outlawing of the practice.

Sororate and Levirate

These terms refer to marriage practices designed to control remarriages after the death of the first spouse. In cultures that practice the sororate, a sister replaces a deceased wife. Assume that a man has paid a good brideprice for his wife but some time later she becomes ill and dies. He has lost his wife and the brideprice. Therefore, to make good on the original bargain, the parents who received the brideprice provide the man with a new wife. This new wife is an unmarried sister or other close relative of the first wife. Here we see how marriage is often more of an economic transaction than it is a personal relationship.

Much more widely practiced has been the levirate. Under this system, it is the husband who dies, and his wife must be married to a brother of the deceased man. There are various reasons for this practice. One is that the wife belonged to her husband as part of his property and as such would be inherited along with the other possessions by a near relative. Another is that it is presumed that women need someone to take care of them, and brothers-in-law (which is the meaning of the Latin word *levir*) should assume that responsibility. It has been reported that the levirate has been practiced by the New Caledonians, the Mongols, the Afghans, the Abyssinians, the Hebrews, and the Hindus, as well as certain Native American and African tribes (Fielding, 1942).

The chief reason that the Hindus and Hebrews practiced the levirate was religious and had to do with the importance of having a son in the family. Hindu men needed a son to perform certain sacrifices, so if a man died before having one, a boy born to his former wife and brother would carry out those ceremonies in his name (Fielding, 1942).

For the Hebrews, it was also important that every man have a son, so that his name would not die out. There was a ritualized penalty for men who refused to marry their brother's widow and rear a son in his name:

And if the man like not to take his brother's wife, then let his brother's wife go up to the gate unto the elders, and say, My husband's brother refuseth to raise up unto his brother a name in Israel, he will not perform the duty of my husband's brother. Then the elders of his city shall call him, and speak unto him: and if he stand to it, and say, I like not to take her; Then shall his brother's wife come to him in the presence of the elders, and loose his shoe from off his foot, and spit in his face, and shall answer and say, So shall it be done unto that man that will not build up his brother's house. (Deuteronomy 25:7–9)

The punishment for refusing to practice the levirate used to be more severe than the above-quoted ritual. In Genesis, Chapter 38, we read of Judah's son Onan and how he was killed by the Lord for refusing to impregnate his dead older brother's wife. The book of Ruth in the Old Testament is also an excellent example of how the levirate worked. It is an account of how Naomi has no more sons for her daughter-in-law Ruth to marry, so she arranges for another male relative, Boaz, to take on the responsibility.

Matchmaking

There are various ways in which two young people can be brought together. Typically, the parents of both boys and girls will work out the details among themselves and then announce it to their children. The initial go-between in Turkey has been the boy's mother, who would inspect possibilities at the public baths and then give reports to her son (Tober, 1984). The popular musical *Fiddler on the Roof* is about father-arranged marriages. Often, hired go-betweens, or matchmakers, assist in making the arrangement. They might act as intermediaries between the families or suggest potential spouses. Checking for astrological or other religious signs and requirements could also be part of their job.

In the 1800s, bachelor pioneers in the American West would sometimes find a wife by ordering one from a mail-order catalog.

Even today, many Asian families publish matrimonial want ads in search of a respectable spouse for their child (Tober, 1984). I recently found the following in the classified section of a Philippine newspaper:

> FOREIGNERS: video match a decent friendship marriage consultant office introducing a beautiful single educated Filipina view friendship to marriage.

> LADIES: Australian European businessmen newly arrive in town sincerely willing to meet decent Filipina view friendship to marriage. Ambassador Hotel suite 216.

Computer dating services in the United States, Japan, and elsewhere manifest the continued utility of professional matchmaking, even in societies in which the individuals involved make the final decisions themselves. There are also magazines designed for singles that include matrimonial or relationship want ads.

There are immigrants to Western societies who are not comfortable with love-based unions and prefer to have their marriages arranged by their parents or through a mediator. It is estimated, for instance, that up to 90% of the marriages in the East Indian community in Edmonton, Alberta, are to some degree arranged (Jimenez, 1992). Some ethnic Indians return to the Indian subcontinent to find a spouse, whereas others allow their parents to find a match locally for them. Some place ads in newspapers such as *India Today* or *India Abroad,* which focus on desired background characteristics such as education, religion, and age. In deference to Western customs, the young people can veto any match that does not appeal to them, and a dowry is rarely accepted.

◎ Free-Choice Mate Selection

. . . Love gradually became the principal criterion for marriage in the Western world after the Renaissance. The shift from kinship and economic motives to personal ones in mate selection led to the conclusion that the individuals themselves, rather than their parents or others, were best qualified to make the decision. In societies in which the basic family unit is nuclear, both romantic love and free mate choice are more common. This is because extended kin groups are not important enough to see marriage as needing to be group controlled.

Even though free choice is the mate selection method of the modern United States, one should not conclude that it is the most common approach in the world. In a survey of 40 societies, Stephens (1963) found only five in which completely free mate choice is permitted. An additional six allowed the young people to choose their spouse, but subject to parental approval. Twelve other cultures had a mix of arranged marriages and free-choice (usually subject to approval) unions, and the final 16 allowed only arranged marriages.

Moreover, even free choice does not mean that one can marry anyone. All societies have marital regulations. The rule of *exogamy* declares that a person must marry outside his/her group. Typically, this means that certain relatives are unavailable as marriage partners. Exogamous rules are generally the same as the incest taboos of the society, which prohibit sexual intercourse between close blood relatives. Others go beyond that, however. In classical China, two people with the same surname could not marry even if there was no kinship relation (Hutter, 1981).

The rule of *endogamy* declares that a person must marry within his/her group. This rule applies social pressure to marry someone who is similar to oneself in important ways, including religion, race, or ethnic group; social class; and age. These factors have been found to be related to marital compatibility and are precisely the kinds of things considered by parents in arranged marriages. One reason why the divorce rate seems to be higher in free-choice societies may be that many couples ignore endogamy issues and allow romantic love to be practically the sole consideration in mate selection. There is a tendency for marriages to be fairly homogenous, however, even in free-mate-choice societies.

A final factor is *propinquity* (geographical nearness). It is, of course, impossible to marry someone who lives so far away from you that you never meet. At another level, however, this principle refers to a human tendency to be friends with people with whom it is convenient to interact. Let us say that you leave your hometown to attend college elsewhere. You left a boyfriend or girlfriend back at home and you also meet someone new at college. All other things being equal, which one will you marry? Generally, it will be the one at school simply because it is easier.

Some Examples

Free mate choice is on the rise in China today. However, it is very different from the courtship pattern in North America. Young people gather information about each other first and check for mutual suitability before going public with their relationship. In fact, dating follows, rather than precedes, the decision to marry. Typically, the couple knows each other for well over two years before marrying. This cautious approach is paying off, as the quality of these marriages seems to be higher than that of arranged unions (Liao & Heaton, 1992).

The Igbo are a people living in present-day Nigeria (Okonjo, 1992). About 55% of the Igbo have their marriages arranged, while the remaining 45% are in free-choice unions. Most of the latter are younger, indicating a move from arranged to free choice, which we see occurring throughout much of the world today. Regardless of type, premarital chastity is very highly valued among the Igbo.

As the Igbo move to free mate choice based on love, their various arranged practices are falling into disfavor. Customs that are quickly disappearing include *woman-to-woman* marriage. In this situation, an older childless woman pays the brideprice to marry a younger female, usually a cousin. A male mate is chosen for the "wife" to have children with, but they belong to the older female spouse, who has the legal role of "husband."

Another way of securing an heir is *father-to-daughter* marriage. If a man has no sons, he may prohibit a daughter from marrying. She has children from a male mate (not the father) but her sons are considered her father's. Women whose husbands turn out to be impotent are allowed to have a lover from whom to have children, who are considered to be the legal husband's. Other arranged practices seldom practiced anymore are the levirate and child marriages.

❂ Courtship and Sex

One final issue in the area of mate selection is premarital sexuality in courtship. There is considerable variation across cultures concerning the acceptability of premarital sexual relations. Most are fairly permissive, however. Of 863 societies in Murdock's Ethnographic Atlas, 67% impose little restriction on premarital sex. The largest proportion of permissive societies are found in Pacific regions, and the most restrictive are the Arab and Muslim nations (Wen-Shing & Jing, 1991).

In the Marshalls of Micronesia, sexual activity begins around puberty. It is common to have many different partners, to cohabit with a few, and eventually to marry a more permanent mate. There is no stigma to being an illegitimate child or an unwed mother, and having children does not seem to reduce a woman's chances of finding a future mate (Wen-Shing & Jing, 1991). In this culture, sexuality is just seen as part of life, with no special taboos or significance attached to it.

The Hopi also included sexuality as part of their courtship procedure. A girl was allowed to receive suitors in her late adolescence. The boys would sneak into her house at night and sleep with her, and the parents would pretend not to notice if he was considered a good marriage prospect. Eventually, she would become pregnant and then select her favorite lover as her husband. The families involved would then arrange the marriage. As a result, a Hopi boy would never have intercourse with a girl whom he was not willing to marry (Queen, Habenstein, Quadagno, 1985).

In the United States today, one estimate is that about 80% of college men and 63% of women in college have had premarital intercourse (Kephart & Jedlicka, 1991). The "sexual revolution" of the

1960s and 1970s had a major impact on premarital behavior: In the 1930s, only 15% of U.S. women had experienced premarital coitus. In spite of fairly high rates of sexual experience, there is still widespread disapproval of premarital coitus in U.S. society. In comparison, other Western countries appear to be more relaxed about it. Much of today's caution has to do with the dangers associated with sexually transmitted diseases and unwanted pregnancies.

. . .

References

Balswick, J. (1975). The function of the dowry system in a rapidly modernizing society: The case of Cyprus. *International Journal of Sociology and the Family, 5*(2), 158–167.

Billig, M. (1992). The marriage squeeze and the rise of groomprice in India's Kerala state. *Journal of Comparative Family Studies, 23*(2), 197–216.

Fielding, W. (1942). *Strange customs of courtship and marriage.* New York: New Home Library.

The Holy Bible. King James Version.

Hutter, M. (1981). *The changing family: Comparative perspectives.* New York: Wiley.

Jimenez, M. (1992, July 26). Many Indo-Canadians follow age-old custom. *The Edmonton Journal,* p. B3.

Kephart, W., & D. Jedlicka. (1991). *The family, society, and the individual.* New York: HarperCollins.

Liao, C., & T. Heaton. (1992). Divorce trends and differentials in China. *Journal of Comparative Family Studies, 23*(3), 413–429.

Okonjo, K. (1992). Aspects of continuity and change in mate-selection among the Igbo west of the River Niger. *Journal of Comparative Family Studies, 23*(3), 339–360.

Peters, J. (1987). Yanomama mate selection and marriage. *Journal of Comparative Families Studies, 18*(1), 79–98.

Queen, S., R. Habenstein, & J. Quadagno. (1985). *The family in various cultures.* New York: Harper & Row.

Stephens, W. (1963). *The family in cross-cultural perspective.* New York: Holt, Rinehart & Winston.

Tober, B. (1984). *The bride: A celebration.* New York: Harry N. Abrams.

Wen-Shing, T., & H. Jing. (1991). *Culture and family: Problems and therapy.* New York: Haworth Press.

◉ ◉ ◉

Questions

1. What are the three primary approaches to choosing a mate? Explain why one approach is most commonly used in a society.

2. What is the rule of endogamy? What is the rule of exogamy? Explain how these rules limit who would make an appropriate mate for you.

3. How are computer dating services and personal ads in newspapers and on the Internet forms of matchmaking? Do you know anyone who has used one of these services? What was the result? Would you ever use these services? Why or why not?

4. Do a search for Internet dating services. How many sites did you find? Did you find any specialized sites? In what ways were they specialized? What does this specialization suggest to you about the advantages and disadvantages of free-choice mate selection?

Women and Islam

JANE I. SMITH

Since September 11, 2001, much about terrorism has been reported and writ-
ten about in popular media. Along with this information, a direct connection
has been made between terrorist activities and the Islamic faith. Unfortu-
nately, most people who are not Islamic know very little about the Islamic
faith aside from the information that the media has presented.

We "think we know" that Islamic women are uniformly oppressed and
exploited in a world controlled by men. In this selection, Jane Smith provides
a historical overview of the Islamic women's role, including such topics as
marriage, divorce, inheritance and ownership of property, and veiling. In
some ways, this article will undoubtedly challenge stereotypical beliefs.

To attempt to talk about women in Islam is of course to venture into
an area fraught with the perils of overgeneralization, oversimplifica-
tion, and the almost unavoidable limitations of a Western bias. The first
problem is simply one of raw numbers. There are perhaps close to half a bil-
lion Muslim women inhabiting all major areas of the world today. Is it possible to say anything that holds true for all of them, let alone for their sisters
over the past fourteen centuries of Islam?

Then one must consider all the various elements that comprise the picture of Islamic womanhood. Many of these elements are directly related to
the religion of Islam itself, such as past and present legal realities, roles permitted and enforced as a result of Muslim images of women, and the variety
of Islamic and hetero-Islamic rites and practices in which Islamic women
have traditionally participated. Other elements contributing to the full picture of women in Islam—such as education, political rights, professional
employment opportunities, and the like—have less to do with the religion
per se but are still influenced by it.

The Holy Qur'ān (sometimes transliterated as "Koran") still forms the
basis of prevailing family law in most areas of the Muslim world. It has
always been and still is considered to be the last in a series of divine revela-
tions from God given in the seventh century C.E. to humanity through the

vehicle of his final prophet Muhammad. The Qur'ān is therefore the literal and unmitigated word of God, collected and ordered by the young Muslim community but untainted with the thoughts and interpretations of any persons, including Muhammad himself. It is obvious, then, why the regulations formulated by the Qur'ān in regard to women have been adhered to with strictness and why changes in Muslim family law are coming about only very slowly in the Islamic world.

The circumstances of women in pre-Islamic Arabia are subject to a variety of interpretations. On the one hand, certain women—soothsayers, priestesses, queens, and even singular individuals—did play powerful roles in society.[1] On the other hand, whatever the earlier realities for women in terms of marriage, divorce, and inheritance of property, it is clear that the Qur'ān did introduce very significant changes that were advantageous for women. Contemporary Muslims are fond of pointing out, quite correctly, that Islam brought legal advantages for women quite unknown in corresponding areas of the Western Christian world.[2] What, then, does the Qur'ān say about women?

The earliest messages of the Qur'ān, and the twin themes that run through all the chapters, are of the realities of the oneness of God and the inevitability of the day of judgment.[3] All persons, men and women, are called upon to testify to those realities. (Tradition has it that Umm Salama, one of the wives of the Prophet, reminded him that he was saying "men" only, after which he clearly identified both believing men and believing women as fully responsible for their religious duties and fully accountable at the time of the final resurrection and judgment.)[4] Religiously speaking, then, men and women are fully equal in the eyes of God according to the Qur'ān.

Before looking at the specifics of the legal injunctions for women, it is necessary to consider two verses that have caused a great deal of consternation to Westerners. One is 2:228, which says literally that men are a step above women, and the other is 4:34, clarifying that men are the protectors of women (or are in charge of women) because God has given preference to one over the other and because men provide support for women. Perhaps because these verses have been so troublesome for non-Muslims (especially feminists), they have been subject to an enormous amount of explanation and interpretation by contemporary Muslim apologists eager to present a defense of their religion. These writers, men and women, affirm that it is precisely because men are invested with the responsibility of taking care of women, financially and otherwise, that they are given authority over the females of their families. And that, affirm many Muslim women today, is exactly the way it should be. We will return to this perspective later, particularly in light of what a desire for liberation means—and does not mean—for many Muslim women.

Turning then to the Qur'ānic legal injunctions for women, we find that they are clustered around four major issues: marriage and related topics, divorce, inheritance and ownership of property, and veiling and seclusion. These form what is called the "personal and family law" part of the total complex of legal realities in Islam. Islamic law (the *sharī'a*) is based primarily on the Qur'ān, secondarily on those things that the Prophet is supposed to have said and done (chronicled in a body of literature called the *hadīth*), and to a lesser extent on analogy and legal reasoning. The four major schools of law in the Sunni tradition (which makes up 85 percent of the Muslim population) are in general agreement on most aspects of the law and differ only on relatively minor points in personal and family law. Elements comprising personal law are more specific in the Qur'ān than many other aspects of the sharī'a and so have been more resistant to change in contemporary times. Of the non-Communist Islamic countries, only Turkey now has a secular law including family and personal law. In most other countries there is a kind of dual system of a secular civil and a religious family code.

According to the Qur'ān, a man may marry up to four wives, so long as he is able to provide for each equally.[5] He may marry a Muslim woman or a member of the Jewish or Christian faith, or a slave woman.[6] A Muslim woman, however, may marry only one husband, and he must be a Muslim. Contemporary Muslim apologists are quick to point out that these restrictions are for the benefit of women, ensuring that they will not be left unprotected. In Islam, marriage is not a sacrament but a legal contract, and according to the Qur'ān a woman has clearly defined legal rights in negotiating this contract. She can dictate the terms and can receive the dowry herself.[7] This dowry (mahr) she is permitted to keep and maintain as a source of personal pride and comfort.

Polygamy (or more strictly polygyny, plurality of wives) is practiced by only a small percentage of the contemporary Muslim population, and a man with more than two wives is extremely rare. Many countries are now taking steps to modify the circumstances in which a husband may take more than one wife, although only in two countries, Turkey and Tunisia, are multiple marriages actually illegal. Other countries have made such moves as requiring the husband to have the permission of the court (as in Iraq and Syria) or to get the permission of the first wife (as in Egypt), or permitting the wife to write into her marriage contract that she will not allow a cowife (as in

Morocco and Lebanon). It seems reasonable to expect that other countries will make changes and modifications. It is interesting to note that while for some finances have dictated monogamy—most husbands have simply not been able to afford more than one wife—changing economic realities may again dictate that a man contemplate the possibility of having several wives to work and supply income for the family.

Muslim women traditionally have been married at an extremely young age, sometimes even before puberty. This practice is related, of course, to the historical fact that fathers and other male relatives generally have chosen the grooms themselves, despite the guarantee of the Qur'ān that marriage is a contract into which male and female enter equally. While it is true that technically a girl cannot be forced into a marriage she does not want, pressures from family and the youth of the bride often have made this prerogative difficult to exercise. Today, the right of a male member of the family to contract an engagement for a girl against her wishes has been legally revoked in most places, although it is still a common practice, especially in rural areas.

In the past, the members of an engaged couple have not been allowed to see each other until the wedding. This practice is now changing even in the most conservative places. Saudi Arabian *ulema* (religious leaders), for example, are realizing that the divorce rate can be lowered if both parties know more clearly what they are getting into. In most Muslim countries today the minimum age for marriage is around 18 for young men and somewhere between 15 and 17 for young women.

On the basis of some rather obscure references in the Qur'ān, birth control has generally been frowned upon by Muslim religious leaders, and abortion and sterilization are strictly forbidden. However, a number of family-planning efforts are now taking place to halt the rise in the high fertility rate (the average Muslim woman has around seven children). Among Middle Eastern countries, Egypt, prerevolutionary Iran, Tunisia, and Morocco officially have adopted population control policies, and a number of the ulema are attempting to show that birth control is permissible in Islam.[8] Western images of Muslim men divorcing wives with abandon by issuing the dreaded triple statement "I divorce thee" have blurred the clear Qur'ānic discouragement of divorce except as a last resort, although they may reflect what has been the painful reality for many women through the ages. It is said that for the Prophet divorce was a thing to be detested. The Qur'ān does have some specific words for those cases in which separation is absolutely necessary,[9] and on the basis of these words Islamic law has traditionally understood two specific kinds of divorce, *talaq* and *khul'*.

Talaq, divorce taken at the initiative of the man, is the most frequent form of separation. One kind of *talaq* is fully acceptable under the law; it can be either a single repudiation after the waiting period of three months to ensure that a wife is not pregnant, or three successive repudiations in three months. The triple repudiation, which is the utterance of the talaq three times in succession without the three-month waiting period, is technically legal although so undesirable as to be classed as sinful according to the five-fold division of deeds in Islamic law. It is fair to say that this kind of divorce has been used far too often, making the Western stereotype in this case not too far from the truth.

Divorce initiated by the wife is called *khul'*. While technically possible, this form of divorce has not been effected nearly as often in any Near Eastern country as has repudiation by the male, both because women often have not been informed of its possibility or have been prevented from carrying it out, and because, unlike *talaq,* it requires either a special stipulation in the marriage contract or must be made on the basis of specific grounds such as desertion, physical abuse, lack of maintenance by the husband, insanity, impotence, and the like.

In the contemporary Islamic world, divorce rates vary considerably from one country to the next. Muslim apologists insist that divorce is not nearly as common in Islamic countries as it is, for example, in the United States. This statement is generally true, although in some countries, such as Morocco, the rate is high and continues to grow. Often what is really only the breaking of the engagement contract is included in divorce statistics, skewing the measure. Many countries are now considering serious changes in divorce procedures. The simultaneous triple repudiation generally has been declared illegal, and in many countries divorce initiated by either party, the man or the woman, must take place in the court of law. Other countries add special stipulations generally favorable to the woman. It remains true, however, that men can divorce for less cause than women, and often divorces hung up in courts with male judges can prove enormously difficult for women to gain.

In accordance with Islamic law, custody of the children traditionally has gone to the father at some time between the age of 7 and 9 for boys and between 7 and puberty for girls, depending on the legal school. This practice too is slowly changing, and in most areas women who have been divorced by their husbands are allowed to keep their sons until puberty and their daughters until they are of an age to be married.

It is considered one of the great innovations of the Qur'ān over earlier practices that women are permitted to inherit and own property. Non-Muslims have generally found great difficulty with the Qur'ānic stipulation that a woman is allowed to inherit property but that the inheritance should be only half that of a male.[10] According to the Islamic understanding, however, the rationale is precisely that which applies to the verse saying that men are in charge of women. Because women are permitted to keep and maintain their own property without responsibility for taking care of their families financially, it is only reasonable that the male, who must spend his own earning and inheritance for the maintenance of women, should receive twice as much.

Despite this rationale, it is true that women have not always been permitted to have access to the financial resources that the Qur'ān makes available to them. As in other areas of family law, such as the possibility of writing specific stipulations into the marriage contract for women, the failure to assume financial responsibility often has come through ignorance or willful cheating by male members of the family. Again we find that in many parts of the Muslim world attempts are being made to equalize the procedure for inheritance between men and women, particularly since women are playing an increasing role in the labor force.[11] To date, however, only Turkey in the non-Communist world and Albania and the Soviet Union among the Communist countries have discarded this Qur'ān-based law of inheritance.

According to the Qur'ān, women should not expose themselves to public view with lack of modesty.[12] It does not say that they should be covered specifically from head to toe, nor that they should wear face veils or masks or other of the paraphernalia that has adorned many Islamic women through the ages. The Qur'ān also suggests that the wives of the Prophet Muhammad, when speaking to other men, should do so from behind a partition, again for purposes of propriety.[13] It has been open to question whether this statement is meant to apply to all women. In the early Islamic community, these verses were exaggerated and their underlying ideas elaborated and defined in ways that led fairly quickly to a seclusion of women which seems quite at odds with what the Qur'ān intended or the Prophet wanted. When the community in Medina was established, women participated fully with men in all activities of worship and prayer. Soon they became segregated, however, to the point where an often-quoted hadīth (no doubt spurious) attributed to Muhammad has him saying that women pray better at home than in the mosque, and best of all in their own closets.[14] Today a number of contemporary Muslim writers are urging a return to the practices of the young Muslim community, with women no longer segregated from the mosque or relegated to certain rear or side portions as they generally have been, but participating fully in worship with men.[15]

The practice of veiling women, which still continues in many parts of the Islamic world, began during the period of the early conquests, when Muslims came into contact with the lands of Byzantium. Veiling was observed at that time in such places as Syria, Iraq, and Persia, and was taken into Islam particularly for urban and upper-class women. In general, veiling has not been common among Muslim village women, partly because they generally do not encounter strangers in that context, and partly because it would hinder them from various kinds of work in which they have traditionally been engaged.

Veiling and seclusion have been major factors in the lives of Muslim women, then, since the early days of the growth of the Muslim empire. Western observers of the Muslim world for centuries have been fascinated and horrified at stories of the harems (literally, "forbidden places") where women have been cut off from the social lives of males. Life in these female enclaves has provided material for studies of female compensation and lines of authority and power. For the most part, the kind of enforced seclusion that characterized so much of the Muslim world for centuries is dying out, the economic realities of women in the labor force being one of the primary reasons. It must be recognized that for many Muslim women, seclusion was not entirely an evil. With freedom inevitably comes responsibility, and while some female voices in the Islamic world are crying loudly for an end to the kind of isolation and segregation that they see as demeaning,[16] others are recognizing that an end to seclusion can also mean assuming a major part of the burden of providing for the family, a worry that formerly rested primarily on the shoulders of the males.[17] Again, it should be stressed that this kind of seclusion has mainly characterized city rather than rural women.

What is popularly known as "veiling" is part of the general phenomenon of the segregation of women and yet is also distinctly apart from it. The two are increasingly seen as separate by contemporary Islamic women seeking to affirm a new identity in relation to their religion. Veils traditionally have taken a number of forms: a veil covering the face from just below the eyes down; a *chador* or *burka* covering the entire body, including the face, often with a woven screen in front through which women can see but not be seen; and a full face mask with small slits through the eyes, still worn in some areas of the Arabian Gulf. These costumes, so seemingly oppressive to Western eyes, at least have allowed women to observe without being observed, thus affording their wearers a degree of anonymity that on some occasions has proven useful.

The general movement toward unveiling had its ostensible beginning in the mid-1920s, when the Egyptian feminist Huda Sha'rawi cast off her veil after arriving in Egypt from an international meeting of women. She was followed literally and symbolically by masses of women in the succeeding years, and Egyptian women as well as those in other Middle Eastern countries made great strides in adopting Western dress. At the present time in the history of Islam, however, one finds a quite different phenomenon. Partly in reaction against Western liberation and Western ideals in general, women in many parts of the Islamic world are self-consciously adopting forms of dress by which they can identify with Islam rather than with what they now see as the imperialist West. Islamic dress, generally chosen by Muslim women themselves rather than forced upon them by males, signals for many an identification with a way of life that they are increasingly convinced represents a more viable alternative than that offered by the West.

This new form of dress, sometimes called *shar'i* (literally, "legal"), differs somewhat from country to country. In general, it is highly conservative, with arms covered to the wrists, legs covered either with a long skirt or with loose pants over which hangs a kind of tunic, and a scarf (not over the face) or a wimplelike covering on the head.[18] This dress is by no means universal, and when traveling across the Muslim world one still finds many women wearing local versions of very traditional dress and many continuing to dress as their Western sisters do. But modern Islamic dress is in evidence in Egypt, Turkey, Palestine, Syria, and even parts of the Arabian Gulf states such as North Yemen, a traditionally very conservative Islamic state. In Iran, the Islamic revolution under Imam Khomeini has reemphasized the chador, banned long ago by the Westernized government. To what extent the chador is approvingly chosen by Iranian women and to what extent it is an enforced product of the revolution remains to be seen.

We see, then, that while legal circumstances for women have undergone some significant changes in the past half-century, the dictates of the Qur'ān continue to be enormously influential in the molding of new laws as well as in the personal choices of Muslim men and women. It has been suggested that while the Qur'ān itself clearly improved circumstances over what they were for pre-Islamic Arabian women and in fact did establish a structure in which women were both protected and given clear rights and responsibilities, this situation changed for the worse in succeeded centuries. Contemporary Muslims are generally quick to point out that many of the hadīths describing the inferiority of women are spurious, that developments in the male-oriented community which led to the severe domination and seclusion of women were contrary to the dictates of the Qur'ān and the desires of the Prophet Muhammad for his community, and that the only way to establish a truly Islamic community with equal (if different) roles for women and men is to return to the Qur'ān and to hold as closely as possible to its formulations. This is not to say, however, that some Muslim women are not advocating radical changes for women of the sort that would be applauded by most Western feminists. I will return to that question shortly.

I have stressed here the insistence of the Qur'ān on the religious and spiritual equality of men and women. And aside from some unfortunate hadīths with very weak chains of authority suggesting that the majority of women will be in the Fire on the Day of Judgment because of their mental and physical inferiority,[19] religious literature in general, when talking about human responsibility and concomitant judgment, makes women full partners with men under the divine command to live lives of integrity and righteousness.[20] Nonetheless, as was suggested, early in the development of the community women began to find the mosque, the common place of worship, less and less accessible. As segregation became increasingly the pattern, it is not surprising to find that women, squeezed out of the more formal aspects of the Islamic faith, developed their own forms of religious response. Since God was conceived of as male and males generally were persons with whom women did not and could not interact in their everyday social lives, they often chose intermediary forms of religious response that were apparently more appropriate to their needs and conditioning.

One area in which this substitution took place was in healing and semimagical practices. Women have always been, and continue to be, primary agents in the relationship of humans to the world of spiritual powers. It is they who know how to ward off evil *jinn,* to cajole the spirits of the rivers and fields, to apply special formulae, and to appropriately display blue beads to challenge the power of the evil eye. These unorthodox practices served both to further isolate women from the formal rituals of the Islamic community and to give them an arena in which they could feel comfortable and in control. Despite periodic efforts to "clean up" such heterodox practices, they have been and continue to be a powerful part of the lives of many Muslims, especially women.

Of course, women do participate in many of the activities and duties considered incumbent on all good Muslims, but generally these practices have a somewhat different function for them than for men. Prayer for women, as we have said, is usually in the home rather than in the mosque, and does not necessarily follow the pattern of the regularized five times a day. Participation in the fast itself is normally the same as for the men (except when women are pregnant, nursing, or menstruating), but the particular joys of preparing the fast-breaking meals are for the women alone. While the husband determines the amount of money or goods to be distributed, for almsgiving, another responsibility of all Muslims, it is often the wife who takes change of the actual distribution.

The last duty incumbent on Muslims after the testimony to the oneness of God and prophethood of his apostle Muhammad, the prayer, the fast, and paying the almstax is the pilgrimage once in a lifetime to the holy city of Mecca. Women do participate in this journey, and as transportation becomes easier and the care provided for pilgrims in Saudi Arabia becomes more regularized with modernization, increasing numbers of females join the throngs which gather to circumambulate the Kaaba at Mecca each year. For many women, however, this singular event may be only part of the meaning of pilgrimage. Yearly or more often, they make shorter journeys to the tombs and resting places of various persons considered to be among the saints of Islam. For Shi'ite Muslims, this journey may be to Kerbala or other shrines of Muslim leaders venerated as members of the household of the Prophet, while Sunnis visit innumerable large and small shrines to revere and talk with the deceased in their tombs.

Visitation of saints' shrines by longer pilgrimage or local visits is certainly not exclusive to women in Islam. Many men include such practices along with their observation of the more formalized aspects of the Muslim faith. This particular kind of religious experience has had a special meaning for women, however, and across the Islamic world one can find women spending long periods of time at shrine tombs, relaxing in a space in which none of the demands of their regular lives are put upon them. The shrine is a place in which women can be together, or alone can be in communication with a personage considered in some senses to be able to help them with the kinds of personal problems in which the high God may seem too remote to be interested.

Saints in Islam are both male and female. One is normally recognized as a saint not by any process of canonization but because of some miraculous deed(s) performed or through a dream communication after death with a living person requesting that a shrine be erected over his or her tomb. Often a woman is favored with these dreams and after the construction of the shrine she becomes the carekeeper of the tomb, a position of some honor and responsibility. Saints form a special category of person in the general Islamic understanding; unlike ordinary mortals, they are awake and very much conscious in their tombs after death. They are reported to be carrying on activities such as praying, reciting the Qur'ān, and responding to the greetings of their visitors. They are not actually worshipped, for that would be anathema in monotheistic Islam, but are considered to have a kind of special authority from God to help answer the requests of persons who come to them for assistance.[21]

While a man may be more likely to ask a saint for his or her intercession with God on the day of judgment or for strength in carrying out religious duties, women are more specifically interested in solving the immediate problems that trouble them in their daily lives. A study revealed that in Egyptian Nubia, for example, the problems more often brought to a saint were finding a husband for one's daughter, keeping one's husband from wanting to take another wife, illness or physical problems, retribution on another woman in the community who has been cruel or gossiping, and the like.[22]

The practice of saint veneration has been the object of puritanical scorn and wrath since the early days of Islam. Despite periodic efforts to purge it from the faith, however, it has continued to be a powerful force in the private and personal lives of countless Muslims. Even with the increasing numbers of women today who are consciously acknowledging their roles in the more formal structure of Islam by adopting Islamic dress and participation in the structured rituals, it seems clear that for many Islamic women relationships with saints and reliance on their assistance with the problems of life still plays a crucial role.

In addition to these more generalized practices, Muslim women in various parts of the world participate in certain activities that can be characterized as religious and which are more or less peculiar to women. In Egypt, the Sudan, and a few other areas, women (particularly middle- and lower-middle-class women) occasionally hold what are called "zār ceremonies," rituals designed to rid them of supposed spirit possession. Men may scoff at these activities, but generally are forced to come up with the money necessary for their wives to participate.[23] In most Muslim areas, activities related to spirit possession involve women generally or even exclusively. In Iraq some women enjoy hereditary positions as mollas (religious teachers). They receive money for such responsibilities as holding public sessions (qrayas) in which stories are read about the life of Hussain, the martyred grandson of the Prophet.[24] As with visitation to the tombs and the attendance at zārs, these are opportunities for women to meet together away from the home under the cloak of a traditionally sanctioned activity.

While women in the Islamic world have been segregated and secluded, and historically have been considered second-class citizens by the vast majority of males in the community, they have not been totally without power. They have been able to maintain a degree of control over their own lives and over the men with whom they live through many of the religious practices described above. The fact that they alone have the ability to bear children, the influence they continue to play in the lives of their sons, and the power they have over their son's wives are subtle indications that there are certain checks and balances on the obvious authority invested by the Qur'an in men. From sexuality to control of the network of communications in the family to manipulation of such external agencies as spirits and super-natural beings, women have had at their control a variety of means to exert their will over the men in their families and over their own circumstances.[25] The subtle means of control available to women throughout the world have of course been exploited: withholding sexual favors (a questionable but often-quoted had̄ith says that if a woman refuses to sleep with her husband, the angels will curse her until the morning),[26] doing small things to under-mine a husband's honor such as embarrassing him in front of guests, indulging in various forms of gossip and social control, and the like.

In the Islamic world today, as was suggested in the beginning, there are an enormous number of currents going in various directions. Along with the kinds of comfort and power women achieve in more traditional ways and running parallel with some of the changes in the legal realities for women are rapid advances in education and employment opportunities. On the one hand, what is true for Muslim women in terms of education and entry into the work force in many ways is incidental to the fact of their being Muslim. On the other hand, male attitudes conditioned by the tradition of Islam, although not necessarily supported by the Qur'an itself, have been and con-tinue to be influential in determining what opportunities are available for women.

Until fairly recently, education for women in the Muslim world has been minimal. Girls were given the rudiments of an Islamic education, mainly a little instruction in the Qur'an and the traditions so as to be able to recite their prayers properly. Beyond that their training was not academic but domestic. In the late nineteenth and early twentieth century, Islamic leaders awoke with a start to the reality that Muslims were significantly behind the West in a variety of ways, including technology and the education necessary to understand and develop it. Many of these leaders recognized that if Islamic nations were to compete successfully in the contemporary world, it had to be with the aid of a well-educated and responsible female sector. Thus, this century has seen a number of educational advances for women, and in some countries, such as Egypt, Iraq, and Kuwait, women constitute very significant numbers of the university population. Nonetheless, illiteracy in many Muslim nations continues to be high, and the gap between male and female literacy rates is even increasing in some areas. In Saudi Arabia, where at present the economic resources are certainly available, large numbers of Saudi girls are receiving a full education, though separated from boys, and are taught either by men through television transmission or by women.

In education as in most areas of life, the male understanding of women as encouraged by certain parts of the Islamic tradition continues to play an important role. The Qur'ān does state, along with the stipulation that women can inherit only half of what men inherit, that the witness (in the court of law) of one man is equal to that of two women. This unfortunately has been interpreted by some in the history of Islam to mean that women are intellectually inferior to men, unstable in their judgment, and too easily swayed by emotion.[27] Such perspectives are certainly not shared by all but nonetheless have been influential (and in some places are increasingly so today) in making it difficult for a woman to have access to the same kinds of educational opportunities that are available to men. Certain subjects are deemed "appropriate" for a woman to study, particularly those geared to make her the best and most productive wife, mother, and female participant in the family structure.

The prevalent view, confirmed by the Qur'ān, is that women should be modest and should neither expose themselves to men nor be too much in public places, where they will be subject to men's observation or forced to interact with males not in their immediate families. This view obviously has contributed to the difficulties of receiving a full education and of securing employment outside the home. More employment opportunities are open to women today than in the past, however, and in many countries women hold high-level positions in business, government, civil service, education, and other sectors. Statistics differ greatly across the Islamic world and are difficult to assess because they often fail to take into account the rural woman who may work full-time in the fields or other occupation outside the house but does not earn an independent salary.

It is also true that the economic realities of the difficult present time are coming hard against the traditional attitudes that the woman should remain in the home and not be part of the public work force. Increasing numbers of women are having to work to help support the family, often in factories and other heavy labor industries. Such realities are certainly not always liberating for women, of course, who have to struggle with home maintenance along with the pressures of the job. Day-care facilities for children are generally unavailable, and the extended family system which used to afford ready baby-sitting for all the children in the larger family is tending to break up. Fuller participation of women in the work force probably will lead to a raising of the traditionally low marriage age for young women.

While some Islamic women, then, are receiving a university education and are able to learn new skills and enter interesting and fulfilling professions, most of them are certainly not so fortunate. And the tightening economic realities may actually work against female advancement. As the need to go to work increases, many girls may in fact have to quit school. For many women, work does not mean the opportunity to have training in new areas because they are often channeled into professions which use their home-oriented skills as maids, food and textile industry workers, and the like.[28]

Saudi Arabia presents an interesting case study of the confrontation of Islamic ideas with contemporary reality. Women are greatly inhibited in the labor arena; because of conservative religious attitudes they must be veiled and covered, are not permitted to drive or even ride in a taxi with a strange man, and in general are unable to participate on the social and professional level with males. However, in a country in which production is both necessary and economically possible and which suffers from a lack of manpower, the use of women in the work force or increased importation of foreign labor seem the only two (both undesirable) alternatives. Thus more Saudi women are working, and because of their right to inherit, are accumulating very substantial amounts of money. It is interesting to note the rapid rate of construction of new banks exclusively for women in places like Jiddah and Riyadh.

The aforementioned Qur'ān verse about the witness of two women being equal to that of one man and the supporting literature attesting to female intellectual, physical (and in fact sometimes moral) inferiority have made it difficult for Muslim women to achieve equal political rights. In most Arab countries (except Saudi Arabia and certain of the Gulf States), as well as in most other parts of the Islamic world, women have now been given the vote. Centuries of passivity in the political realm, however, have made it difficult for women to take advantage of the opportunities now available to them. In some countries, such as Egypt, women are playing major political roles, but generally women politicians find little support from men or even from other women for their aspirations. This is not to underestimate the strong current in Islamic thinking which encourages the full participation of women in politics, as well as in the educational and professional fields.

Like an intricate and complex geometric pattern on a Persian rug or a frieze decorating a mosque, the practices, roles, opportunities, prescriptions, hopes, and frustrations of Islamic women are woven together in a whole. The colors are sometimes bold and striking, at other times muted and subtle. Some contemporary Muslim women are progressive and aggressive, no longer content to fit the traditionally prescribed patterns. Others are passive and accepting, not yet able to discern what new possibilities may be open to them, let alone whether or not they might want to take advantage of such opportunities. Some are Westernized as their mothers and grandmothers were and have every intention of staying that way, while others are increasingly clear in their feelings that the West does not have the answers and that Islam, particularly the Islam of the Qur'ān and the community of the Prophet Muhammad, is God's chosen way for humankind. For the latter, their dress, their relationships with their husbands and families, and their verbal assent to Islamic priorities reflect this conviction that the time has come to cease a fruitless preoccupation with things Western and to reaffirm their identity as Muslim women.

It is difficult for Western feminists to grasp exactly what the Muslim woman may mean by "liberation." For many Islamic women, the fruits of liberation in the West are too many broken marriages, women left without the security of men who will provide for them, deteriorating relations between men and women, and sexual license that appears as rank immorality. They see the Islamic system as affirmed by the Qur'ān as one in which male authority over them ensures their care and protection and provides a structure in which the family is solid, children are inculcated with lasting values, and the balance of responsibility between man and woman is one in which absolute equality is less highly prized than cooperation and complementarity.

The new Islamic woman, then, is morally and religiously conservative and affirms the absolute value of the true Islamic system for human relationships. She is intolerant of the kind of Islam in which women are subjugated and relegated to roles insignificant to the full functioning of society, and she wants to take full advantage of educational and professional opportunities. She may agree, however, that certain fields of education are more appropriate for women than others, and that certain professions are more natural to males than to females. She participates as a contributor to and decisionmaker for the family, yet recognizes that in any complex relationship final authority must rest with one person. And she is content to delegate that authority to her husband, father, or other male relative in return for the solidarity of the family structure and the support and protection that it gives her and her children.

That not all, or even most, Muslim women subscribe to this point of view is clear. And yet, at the time of this writing, it seems equally clear that, if Western observers are to understand women in the contemporary Islamic world, they must appreciate a point of view that is more and more prevalent. The West is increasingly identified with imperialism, and solutions viable for women in the Islamic community are necessarily different from the kinds of solutions that many Western women seem to have chosen for themselves. For the Muslim the words of the Qur'ān are divine, and the prescriptions for the roles and rights of females, like the other messages of the holy book, are seen as part of God's divinely ordered plan for all humanity. Change will come slowly, and whatever kinds of liberation ultimately prevail will be cloaked in a garb that is—in one or another of its various aspects—essentially Islamic.

Endnotes

[1]Nabia Abbott, "Pre-Islamic Arab Queens," *The American Journal of Semitic Languages and Literatures* 17 (January 1941) 1–22. See also, A. F. L. Beeston, "The Position of Women in Pre-Islamic South Arabia," *International Orientalists' Congress* 22, 2 (1951), 101–06.

[2]See, for example, Gamal A. Badawi, "Woman in Islam," in *Islam: Its Meaning and Message,* ed. Kurshid Ahmad and Salem Azzam (Leicester: The Islamic Foundation, 1975), 131–35.

[3]"Say: He is God, the One and the Only, God the Eternal, Absolute" (Surah 112:1–2). "Then, when one blast is sounded on the Trumpet, and the earth is moved, and its mountains, and they are crushed to powder at one stroke—on that Day shall the Event come to pass" (69:13–15).

[4]Sadīq Hasan Khān, Husn al-uswa (Cairo: Matba'ah al-Imām, n.d.), 117.

[5]Surah 4:3.

[6]Surah 5:6.

[7]Surah 65:4.

[8]See Nadia H. Youssef, "The Status of Fertility Patterns of Muslim Women" in *Women in the Muslim World,* ed. Lois Beck and Nikki Keddi (Cambridge: Harvard University Press, 1978), 69–99.

[9]Surah 2:226–30; 65:1–2.

[10]Surah 4:11–12, 177.

[11]It is estimated, for example, that women in Saudi Arabia now own somewhere between 25 and 50 percent of the property in major cities such as Jiddah and Riyadh.

[12]Surah 24:31.

[13]Surah 33:53–59.

[14]Ahmad Galwash, *The Religion of Islam,* vol. 1 (Qatar: Education and Culture Ministry, 1973), 155–56.

[15]See, for example, Ahmad Sakr, *al-Khutab* (Ann Arbor: Taleemul Islam Publications, 1977).

[16]See, for example, Fatima Mernissi, *Beyond the Veil* (New York: Schenkman Publishing Company, 1975).

[17]See, for example, B. Aisha Lemu and Fatima Heeren, *Women in Islam* (Islamic Council of Europe, 1978), 13–18.

[18]John A. Williams, "A Return to the Veil in Egypt," *Middle East Review 11,* 3 (1979), 49–59.

[19]Ahmad Ibn Hanbal, Musnad, vol. 1 (Cairo: al-Matba'ah al-Maymanīyah, 1895), 137.

[20]See Jane I. Smith and Yvonne Haddad, *The Islamic Understanding of Death and Resurrection* (Albany: State University of New York Press, 1981), Appendix B.

[21]Farīd Māhir, *Karmāmāt al-awliyā'* (Cairo: al-Matba'ah al- Ālimīya, 1971), 85–90.

[22]Nawal al-Messiri, "The Sheikh Cult in Dahmit," in *Nubian Ceremonial Life,* ed. John Kennedy (Berkeley: University of California Press, 1978), 61–103.

[23]Lucie Wood Saunders, "Variants in Zar Experience in an Egyptian Village," in *Case Studies in Spirit Possession,* ed. Vincent Crapanzano and Vivien Garrison (New York: John Wiley and Sons, 1977), 177–91.

[24]Robert A. and Elizabeth W. Fernea, "Variations in Religious Observance among Islamic Women," in *Scholars, Saints and Sufis,* ed. Nikki R. Keddie (Berkeley: University of California Press, 1972), 391–95.

[25]See, for example, Daisy Hilse Dwyer, "Women, Sufism and Decision-Making in Moroccan Islam," in Beck and Keddie, *Women in the Muslim World,* 585–98.

[26]Yvonne Haddad, "Traditional Affirmations Concerning the Role of Women," in *Women in Contemporary Muslim Societies,* ed. J. I. Smith (Lewisburg: Bucknell University Press, 1980), 70.

[27]See, for example, "Al-Azhar, Islam, and the Role of Women in Islamic Society," *The Islamic Review 40,* 8 (August 1952), 2–4.

[28]See Fatima Mernissi, "The Patriarch in the Moroccan Family: Myth of Reality," in *Women's Status and Fertility in the Muslim World,* ed. James Allman (New York: Praeger Publishers, 1978), 312–32.

◉ ◉ ◉

Questions

1. In what ways have verses in the Qur'ān highlighting the superiority of men over women contributed to gender inequality in Islamic communities?

2. What does the Qur'ān say about modesty? Can you rationalize this view with the insistence in conservative Islamic communities that women wear Burkas?

3. How prevalent are gender differences in Islamic communities? List as many areas as you can where women are "less than equal" to men.

4. In what ways do Islamic women maintain power and control?

5. What are some implications for modern people of the Islamic faith returning to a stricter interpretation of the Qur'ān?

6. How might Western feminists' views of liberation differ from liberal Islamic women's views of liberation?

Canadian and American Culture: The Garden and the Jungle

MICHAEL ADAMS

> *Sociologist Michael Adams has researched Canadian values for over twenty-five years. He recently expanded that research to include the United States and compare the values, beliefs, attitudes, and practices of Canadians and Americans. In this excerpt from* Sex in the Snow: Canadian Social Values at the End of the Millennium, *he examines the roles that both countries ascribe to the social institutions of religion, family, state, and the marketplace. He reveals why countries that share the same continent have cultures that are so different.*

*A*s countless commentators—most prominently the eminent sociologist Seymour Martin Lipset—have pointed out, historically, Canadians have been much more deferential to institutional authority than was the case among Americans. However, in the space of a single generation, Canadians have, for better or worse, by necessity and by choice, become much less deferential. On many registers we are now even more critical of institutional authority and of our élites than Americans are of theirs. Canadians can be likened to children on the last day of school, running and squealing in the schoolyard, free at last from the rules and discipline imposed by tradition. A nation of "repressed hedonists"—an apt description of our longest serving prime minister, quoted above—has decided that "peace, order, and good government" is not enough, and, like citizens around the world, we want some of the "life, liberty, and happiness" promised in America's founding declaration. For a very long time, Canadians lived under the not-always-benign rule of the church, the state and the large institutions of the industrial era—corporations, state monopolies and labour unions. Now we are freer to call the shots.

Since the 1960s, the widespread questioning of authority has become a fact of civic life in much of the Western world. However, Canada's evolution in this respect has been particularly rapid, to the point of being characterized as a "revolution" by Canada's pre-eminent journalist Peter C. Newman in his book *The Canadian Revolution: From Deference to Defiance.* Perhaps one reason for this is the Canadian surfeit of geography and dearth of history, as Mackenzie King observed half a century ago. As a result, no historical ideology has the sort of grip on our souls that the myth of the American Dream has south of the border. Even the Conquest (of Quebec by General Wolfe in 1759) has lost much of its resonance for Quebec francophones, thirty-five years after the Quiet Revolution. Instead, Canadians have a sort of flexible "geophilosophy," more pragmatic and rooted less in history and more in the multicultural, multimedia reality of their everyday existence. In today's wired world, both history and geography have lost most of their relevance for Canadians, in spite of the valiant efforts of the Charles R. Bronfman Foundation's Heritage Moments series of mini-docudramas. Today we have too much of neither, but perhaps instead have too little imagination to see ourselves as the world does—as the best place on earth.

Arguably, the relative lack of historical and ideological baggage has allowed Canadians to adapt rapidly to changing conditions both within our borders and around the world. It has also resulted in pronounced sociocultural differences between Canadians and Americans in the roles they ascribe to the fundamental institutions of religion, state, family, and the marketplace.

Despite their mythological adherence to the ideal of personal freedom, Americans, in fact, harbour a far greater confidence in many institutions than do Canadians. In general, Americans have a greater faith in the family, the state (that is, "America"), religion, and the market.

For example, Americans express far greater confidence in big business. Part of this difference can be attributed to the fact that "big business" in the United States usually means *American* big business. In Canada, "big business" is often a foreign-owned corporation, typically an American branch plant. In America, anti-trust laws force fierce competition. In Canada, public-sector monopolies and private-sector oligopolies have dominated many markets; the result was a culture of *ressentiment*—resentful dependence—which began to unravel in the late 1980s.

But now, Canadians have become "masters of suspicion," with both the positive and negative aspects that come with such a posture. In spite of our historical reputation for deference to elites, Canadians, who were once more religious than Americans, are now less so. Although mere church attendance figures fail to do justice to the phenomenally greater religiosity in the United States, they do illustrate important differences between the two countries. In the 1950s, 60 per cent of Canadians attended church every Sunday; today, that number is 30 per cent. In the United States, attendance continues to hover around 40 per cent, little changed from the level in the 1930s and '40s.

Even Quebecers, whose motto is *Je me souviens* (or "I remember"), have come to forget or reject a great deal of their sociocultural inheritance. With the exception, of course, of the French language itself, almost every other institution in that centuries-old society has been turned upside down. In the space of a single generation, people who came from families of ten children are today having only one child, or sometimes none. The decline in weekly church attendance among Quebec Catholics has been even more precipitous than in the rest of the country.

One factor that initially contributed to greater *Canadian* religiosity and deference to authority was the historical role played by the major Christian denominations. Historically, in Canada, the Catholic and Anglican churches, both very hierarchical organizations, played a dominant role. And they did so with explicit or tacit government sanction, in part through the constitutional provisions that protected Catholic and Protestant denominational schools. In contrast, the American constitution separated church and state. Evangelical or populist sects had to compete for the attention and adherence of their American flocks, thereby giving religion a less institutional focus.

Historically, this difference favoured greater religiosity in Canada. However, with faith in institutions declining in both countries, the more heterarchical orientation of religion in the United States has proven the more resilient and "market sensitive." In Canada, most mainstream Judeo-Christian denominations are losing their grip on the population. Moreover, many of the values traditionally associated with them have come under critical scrutiny, if they have not been largely discarded. These include deference to state authorities ("render unto Caesar"), patriarchal definitions of family, guilt, duty, and fear of divine retribution.

Not only does our research show that Canadians are far weaker than Americans on the dimension of religiosity, but that the secularization of our country shows no signs of abating. If anything, this trend is accelerating. Despite a nominal separation of church and state in the United States, religion continues to play a major role in American politics, but virtually no role here. In this respect, the 49th parallel is a veritable "de-mystification zone." American politicians wear their religion on their sleeves; here, even the most devout politicians, including Reform Party leader Preston Manning, seldom mention their religious affiliation and Christian values.

Even Canadians who say they believe in God—still a majority—tend not to let this belief influence their lifestyle on a day-to-day basis. When it comes to their religious practices, they are more likely to apologize than proselytize. Reginald Bibby, the foremost sociologist of religion in this country, comments that "The vast majority of Canadians still call themselves Christian, but they're grasping bits and pieces of the traditional creed—'the fragmented god.' We now see a high level of belief in almost anything imaginable, but there's no rhyme or reason to it. And when we try to measure the sort of guidance these private beliefs play in people's lives, there's really nothing there. There's no ultimate moral authority. So it really doesn't hold up to anything."[1]

On the other hand, four out of five Americans believe in life after death, a virgin birth and miracles. Almost all Americans (95%) believe in God, and a World Values survey conducted in 1992–93 found that more than four in five Americans consider themselves to be "a religious person."

In the United States, social or values issues can still play an important role in elections, inspiring US author Ben Wattenberg to recently write the influential *Values Matter Most*.[2] In Canada, it is unemployment and the deficit that are top public priorities in the late 1990s—both pragmatic economic issues. With tongue planted firmly in cheek, some Canadians have said the ultimate Canadian destiny is to redeem America. If this were ever to happen, it would be a secular redemption, a redemption from Redemption.

Just as Canadian religious institutions have suffered a greater decline in public confidence than have their American counterparts, so, too, has there been a greater decline in confidence in government here. Traditionally, Canadians had far greater faith in the state than did their American cousins. Much of this phenomenon can be traced to the very different origins of the two countries. In several books, most recently *American Exceptionalism*, Lipset examines the historical and cultural differences between Canada and the United States in the founding myths of each country: the revolutionary and individualistic tradition of the United States, contrasted with the counter-revolutionary and communal tradition of Canada; the American rags-to-riches myth of Horatio Alger versus the Canadian theme of surviving adversity; the American promise of life, liberty, and the pursuit of happiness in contrast to the Canadian bargain of peace, order, and good government. In terms of political ideology, Canada inherited strong strains of Toryism, liberalism, and socialism. The United States has known only various trains of liberalism qualified by religious moralism.

Traditionally, Canada was very much a communitarian, or group-oriented society. According to Lipset, Canada's "organizing principle," our decision not to join the American Revolution in 1776 and break with England, left us with the values and priorities of the Old World, and an essentially Tory and conservative world-view. To restate the old joke: America was founded on the principle of the people against the government; Canada, on the other hand, was founded on the principle of the government against the people.

Old World Tory conservatism, which takes an organic, "Hegelian" view of society, sees the whole as greater than the sum of its parts and, as such, values group rights over individual rights. This particular world-view, along with the nation's climate, geography, and smaller population, has made Canadians generally accepting of state intervention in many aspects of their daily lives. Many observers have remarked that Canada was traditionally a very "Hegelian" society, a label that applies to the country's pre-eminent political philosopher, Charles Taylor.

This organic view was reflected in Canadians' constantly trying to accommodate competing interests within the framework of existing social institutions, a profoundly reformist (rather than revolutionary) ambition. However, it has now become apparent to Canadians that traditional institutions can no longer deliver the goods: the church can no longer deliver everlasting life, the state can no longer provide security from the cradle to the grave, and employers can no longer guarantee life-long employment.

As these formerly unassailable institutions crumble, Canadians are forced to forge new links and networks with communities of choice and of mutual interest, rather than looking to government or other élites to lead them through life. With the growth of social-values tribalism and the underground economy, Canadians have moved from an organic model of society to a rhizomatic one, where personal networking replaces a reliance on representatives, institutions or an idealized notion of the country.

Our research shows that Americans, in addition to a greater religiosity, are characterized by a strong belief in the importance of national superiority, a romantic need to demonstrate to the world the exceptionalism of their country and culture. American Republicans have distilled these values into their purified essence.

The summer blockbuster of 1996, *Independence Day*, starts out as just such a paean to American exceptionalism. However, by the end of the film it has become an exhortation to global unity in a common cause, with everyone included, from the First Lady to a stripper with a heart of gold, from a black soldier to a Jewish intellectual, with a sympathetic portrayal of a gay character tossed in for good measure. In the end, the entire world unites, under American leadership, to defeat the aliens from outer space. It's appealing, because this sort of ecumenism is so obviously absent from the US body politic these days.

Unfortunately, the tendency of Americans to identify themselves as simply "Americans" rather than "hyphenated" Americans appears to have done little to strengthen the social fabric in the United States. Indeed, as we can see from our synthesis map of values, the attitudinal differences between Canada's "distinct society" Quebec and the rest of the country pale in comparison to those that exist among the major regions of the United States. It may be argued that Canadians' institutional recognition of social pluralism, including state-sponsored bilingualism and multiculturalism, has provided a vehicle for the expression of *some* aspirations of ethnic communities. This has not made them any less Canadian: in fact, it has helped to make them *quintessentially* Canadian. It is not an exclusive disjunction, in which one is *either* ethnic or Canadian: one can comfortably be both, and the very Canadian trend toward more flexible personalities and a diffused sense of identity suggests that the recognition of a multicultural, fluid, and flexible reality need not encourage an ossified ethnic tribalism. Twenty-five years of public-opinion polling in Canada has taught me a seemingly paradoxical truth: Canadians feel *strongly* about their *weak* attachments to Canada, its political institutions and their fellow citizens. In other words, they feel strongly about the right to live in a society that allows its citizens to be detached from ideology and critical of organizations, and not to feel obliged to be jingoistic or sentimentally patriotic. Canadians' *lack of* nationalism is, in many ways, a distinguishing feature of the country. In the 1950s we said, "better dead than red." If you believe in an afterlife, maybe it's better to be dead, but Canadians are now too pragmatic to jeopardize their lives for any ideology.

Until recently more deferential to politicians, Canadians have been rejecting the authority of political office in much more dramatic ways than have Americans. Witness the near annihilation of the federal Conservatives in the 1993 election, and the introduction of the parvenu Bloc Québecois and the Reform Party as the second and third parties in the House of Commons. Canada has maintained a turnout rate of around 75 per cent in elections. The United States, on the other hand, is becoming increasingly plutocratic, with the rich and vested interests presiding over a nation where fewer than half the citizens exercise their franchise in presidential elections. In the Congressional elections of 1994, fewer than one in five Americans actually voted for the Republicans, who nevertheless took this "victory" as a mandate for sweeping change.

Despite their sometimes brutal individualism, Americans revere institutions as anchors for their values; Canadians are coming to see many of their institutions as ineffective or irrelevant. For example, Americans revere the office of President and consider it a "crisis of confidence" when the incumbent's approval rating falls below 40 per cent. For an extended period of time, former prime minister Brian Mulroney had an approval rating hovering around 10 per cent, a situation unheard of in the United States.

As I mentioned earlier, a frequently cited characteristic distinguishing Canada from other countries is our institutionalized tolerance of diversity. However, this policy, along with other sacred cows of government, has come under increasing scrutiny. In an attack on Canada's policy of multiculturalism, Neil Bissoondath writes, "It may be that one of the unstated desires behind the institution of multiculturalism was a wish to mark ourselves as different from the United States: if they have a melting pot, then we'll have a mosaic. If they ask immigrants to shrug off their past and assume a new identity, we'll ask immigrants to conserve their past and make it their only identity."[3] Mr. Bissoondath goes on to charge that a failure to accept each other "as simply Canadian" weakens the social fabric.

However, I believe that Canada's more receptive attitude to ethnic diversity is *not* a case of an individual pretending to be what he/she was in the past, but rather, the simple recognition of differences that exist in the present. This hypothesis is supported by the fact that, in Canada, there is a correlation between support for multiculturalism and modern trends (such as equality of the sexes) rather than traditional trends (such as religiosity). Multiculturalism is a "modern" trend, located in the lower half of the map, rather than a "traditional" one that would be found near the top of the map. And perhaps the most modern of Canadians, the New Aquarians, are also the most supportive of ethnic diversity.

As in so many other areas, multiculturalism in Canada will likely evolve from a government program to some sort of "market multiculturalism" that's more voluntaristic and pragmatic than the current approach. For example, schools might emphasize their racial and ethnic diversity to attract students. Companies might promote multiculturalism in order to retain and attract both employees and customers. The average Canadian can savour the gastronomic and cultural diversity of Canada's global village.

Clearly, when compared to our hot-blooded cousins to the south, we conform to the shy and deferential stereotype: except when playing hockey, we are non-violent and courteous. We raise the tone at the end of sentences, transforming assertions into hypotheses so as not to give offence, often adding "eh" to emphasize our politeness. We will stop at Stop signs, even if no cars are in sight, and even if the sign says *Arrêt*.

Given these differences, is it any surprise that an international survey by a major condom manufacturer found that Americans have sex more often than any other people in the world, but that Canadians were most likely to say that the pleasure of their partner was very important? If Americans are hot Dionysians having sex in the sun, Canadians are cool Apollonians having sex in the snow, with the need for pragmatism that entails: blankets, mukluks and a realization that we are in this together.

Many Canadians believe that the 1990s have witnessed a steadily increasing income gap between the "haves" and the "have-nots"; in fact, this is only true for *earned* income. When transfers to lower-income individuals in the form of unemployment insurance, welfare, and old-age security are factored in, the overall income gap has remained fairly constant, but at a growing and unsustainable cost to government and the taxpayer. Therefore, as the *Globe and Mail's* Bruce Little observes, even though the market will probably continue to produce an inequitable distribution of earned income, governments will be increasingly unwilling and unable to offset this chilling trend.[4] However, in spite of the general retreat of governments, most Canadians continue to cling, however tenuously, to the principle of a kinder, gentler society. This stands in stark contrast to the social Darwinistic ideology that is dominant in the United States. Theirs is a world in which the fittest flourish while others languish. It is government by *triage*, in which resources are allocated to those deemed most worthy of being saved, or, more likely, those who have enough political clout to make their voices heard—older, well-off Americans being at the top of the list.

Despite these fundamental differences, there are indications that Canadian politics are replicating some American—or rather, some international—trends. The Ontario election of 1995, which saw a massive legislative majority accorded Mike Harris's Conservatives, witnessed a revolt by largely white, middle-class voters against an NDP government that they saw as "squandering" their tax dollars on policies of "overly generous" state welfare and employment equity (affirmative action). They voted in favour of a tax cut for the wealthy and middle class, with little concern for the plight of the poor. As columnist Allan Fotheringham put it, "Score one for the angry white guys." Canadians may still believe that the quality of our social programs distinguishes us from the United States, but a significant proportion of the population has come to question the price we pay for this benefit.

There are heated debates as to whether the cuts currently under way across the country are the solution to our economic problems, or an ideological reaction to market pressures. James Laxer, a political science professor at York University, argues that while the Harris government is *for the rich*, it is not a government *of the rich* and was not elected by the rich.[5] While those in the highest income-tax brackets will benefit most from tax cuts, middle-class conservative supporters will benefit from "cultural benefits," i.e., hot button issues such as a hard line on punishing young offenders, and the scrapping of photo radar (the latter may have inspired David Cronenberg's latest film *Crash*).

Part of the cultural benefits accruing to people opposed to multiculturalism and alternative family structures is a feeling of ethnic and moral superiority. As *The Globe and Mail* put it in an article about the United States, but that could be equally applied to sentiments now evident in neo-conservative Ontario, "the big dogs are suddenly fed up with blacks, gays, immigrants and everyone else that isn't them. Throughout the land can be heard the creaking sound of drawbridge politics, as the no-longer-silent majority try to isolate themselves in the duchies of suburbia."[6] For his part, Laxer suggests that the Harris agenda reflects the theory wittily and ironically summed up by John Kenneth Galbraith that, "the problem with our society is that the poor have too much money, and the rich don't have enough."

In my opinion, analyzing the election of the Ontario Conservatives in terms of the Americanization of Canadian politics is only telling part of the story. I interpret this vote as an effort by Ontarians to reverse some of the excesses—however well-intended—of state intervention, and to restore fiscal responsibility to the public sector. The mid-1990s have seen governments of all political stripes—Liberal in Ottawa, New Democratic in Saskatchewan, Conservative in Alberta, and the PQ in Quebec—adopt many of the same fiscal and social policies. In 1996, in British Columbia, a slightly more interventionist New Democratic government was re-elected. Sure, there is some evidence of the Americanization of Canadian politics—after all, the plurality did vote in favour of free trade in 1988—but there is just as much evidence that all Canadian governments are reducing services *reluctantly* and with little of the ideological fervour of the American right.

Canadians, I am convinced, are pragmatic, not ideological, people. They want a sustainable social-welfare state, perhaps not the social-democratic paradise envisioned by the Canadian left, but one that will still leave Canada a more egalitarian place than the republic to the south. It is no accident that other social-welfare states reacted to globalization in much the same manner as Canada: look at Germany or New Zealand or what was once socialist heaven on earth—Sweden. They all bit the fiscal bullet.

The sociocultural differences between Canada and the United States, like the differences between Quebec and the rest of Canada, or even between men and women, may be diminishing over time, but the differences that remain will, in my view, be significant and meaningful for many generations to come.

It is clear from the sociocultural data that, in spite of the many obvious similarities between the two countries, there are a number of significant differences in the values that guide and give meaning to the lives of people in each society. The first is in the flexibility we allow ourselves in terms of self-identity.

We Canadians are not without national pride. However, we question the assumption that national identity is the defining characteristic of community. This has afforded us a greater acceptance of diversity in each other's sense of self, and in the attachments people have with various communities. Here you are allowed, not only to be a hyphenated Canadian, but also to decide which side of the hyphen best describes and defines you from moment to moment. A sort of pragmatic tolerance is the rule, rather than a clearly defined identity dictated by tradition. America, on the other hand, has a firm tradition of rejecting, or ghettoizing, hyphenated identities, in favour of one strong national identity.

Is this because America was conceived, torn asunder, and then reunited within a crucible of violence? In Canada, we negotiated our independence from Mother England. After their conquest in 1759, the British accommodated the French, starting with the Quebec Act in 1774. Allowing Quebecers to keep their language and customs, rather than pursue the course of assimilation, set a precedent for the non-violent accommodation of successive waves of immigrants. More recently, and thanks partly to the Charter of Rights and Freedoms, this same inclusiveness has opened up new possibilities for women, gays and lesbians, people with disabilities, and others wishing to "immigrate" into the mainstream of society.

Canadians' recent questioning and criticism of their institutions has also resulted in more flexible and open personal relationships than is the norm in the United States. In my opinion, our questioning of the family has not resulted in its devaluation, but rather in an assault on patriarchy, and a greater belief in the equality of women and young people. It has also resulted in a more flexible definition of family, including a greater acceptance of non-Scriptural relationships, such as sex outside of marriage, and gay and lesbian relationships. Now one-third of children in Canada are born to parents who are living together but not married, and less than half of Canadian families conform to the traditional model of married-parents-with-kids. Jean Dumas, an analyst at Statistics Canada remarked, "There is a real change, not only in the size of the family, but in the concept of the family. The flexibility with which the cell of society adapts to societal change is amazing. All the talk about the death of the family is nonsense."[7]

In America, common-law marriage and the birth of children out of wedlock is interpreted as a sign of moral decay and the disintegration of society. The religious and political right inveigh against such trends with routine moralizing. In Canada overall, the trend goes essentially unnoticed in politics and is as much a marketing challenge as a moral threat to mainstream churches. North of the border, unmarried couples are becoming the norm, with formerly Catholic Quebec in the vanguard. However, there is antagonism among some of Canada's older-values tribes on these questions.

In the United States, gender is now a major factor in Americans' political ideology and party choice. Women tend to support "kinder and gentler" policies that preserve the social-welfare state, and have thus become the backbone of the Democratic party. Men opt for a more competitive free-market economic model and Darwinistic social policies and are making the Republicans into a stag party. In America, it seems, "Men are from Mars and Women are from Venus."

In Canada, the ideological and partisan gap is far less pronounced. Yes, we see the tendency of women to be more on "the left" and men on "the right" of the political spectrum, but only a tendency. Canada's governing party, the Liberals, are slightly more popular among women than among men, but only slightly. Both the "left-wing" NDP, and the "right-wing" Progressive Conservatives draw similar levels of support from men and women. The further right-of-centre Reform Party is disproportionately male, but in Canada, unlike the United States, this positioning has served to limit Reform's appeal among mainstream male voters.

Further evidence of the advanced evolution of Canadian social values in the area of institutionalized gender stereotyping is the fate of the Miss Canada Beauty Pageant. Though nearly every US state, county, and town continues the ritual display of nubile female pulchritude, culminating in the annual Miss America and the redundant Miss Universe contests, Canada's CTV television network cancelled the Miss Canada contest in 1992 due to

171

lack of interest on the part of sponsors and the general public. Meanwhile, in Texas, a related parody of Americana was played out when the mother of a would-be cheerleader, Wanda Webb Holloway, was convicted of plotting the death of the mother of her daughter's rival.

In addition to allowing for common-law and same-sex relationships, the Canadian redefinition of the family has resulted in a greater respect for the opinions of young people. One of the differences that distinguishes Canadian values from American is Canadians' greater adherence to the idea of an equal relationship with youth. Canadians are more egalitarian than Americans and more inclined to believe that young people are capable of making their own decisions, and should be accorded the same rights and responsibilities as any other member of society.

Americans, on the other hand, are more likely than Canadians to believe that young people do not really know what is in their best interest, and that they should let their elders tell them what to do. It is significant that in Canada, there is a positive correlation between rejection of authority and belief in an equal relationship with youth; in the United States these trends are independent of each other. Certainly it makes intuitive sense that a rejection of hierarchical relationships in general would include those based on age. So, why has this not happened in the US? Our data suggest that the answer may lie in the fact that in both countries people fear that permissive attitudes toward young people may facilitate criminal behaviour. The greater fear of crime in the US is reflected in a much harsher, more authoritarian attitude toward the young, one now realized in public curfews for youth and/or other exclusionary measures.

Another distinguishing characteristic of Canadians is our tendency toward nonviolence. Canadians value peace and order and will likely continue to do so, even without a Mountie standing over their shoulder. Americans value freedom of the individual more than peace and order.

Despite public perceptions to the contrary, Canadian statistics show a decline in rates of violent crime that parallels a decline found in the United States. Statistics Canada reported that in 1995 the overall crime rate fell by 1 per cent, a decline for the fourth year in a row. Violent crime declined by 4.1 per cent in 1995, the largest drop since the agency started gathering such statistics in 1962.[8] In 1995, the homicide rate also hit a 26-year low. Despite this overall decline, Statistics Canada reported that there was an increase in the number and proportion of murders committed by youth.

The decline in overall crime rates in Canada and the US are due, at least partly, to the demographic reality of aging populations. This same demographic factor also helps explain why there is a higher hysteria over crime—older people tend to have a much greater fear of violence than do the young.

For their part, Americans express somewhat contradictory views on the topic of violence. On the one hand, they are more likely than Canadians to accept violence as normative, and even exciting, and are reluctant to institute the most modest of gun-control measures. At the same time, crime has long been one of the main issues of concern to the American public.

Violent-crime rates peaked in the United States in 1990, with the arrival of crack cocaine. In more recent years, there has been a decline in the rate of violent crime in the US. This can be attributed to a number of factors, including lower rates of crack use, the death or imprisonment of many of the worst offenders, and, as I just pointed out, an aging population. Nonetheless, the United States is far from being out of the woods, especially in view of recent social program cuts and an imminent "echo boom" of teenagers and young adults, the age groups most likely to commit crimes. In the United States (and, to a lesser extent, in Canada) it is expected that violent crime will increase in the years ahead, simply because of a significant rise in the 15-to-24-year-old population. Demography may not be destiny, but in this instance it is a wake-up call of sorts, especially in the United States.

In the United States, people who murder strangers have an 80 percent chance of getting away with it. It is a small step from recognition of this to a cost/benefit analysis on the part of those who, economically and socially, have little to lose by taking a chance on a life of crime.

And despite recent declines, the violent-crime rate in the United States remains many times higher than in Canada. Tom Pollock, head of Universal Pictures, pointed to Canada as evidence that there is not a correlation between onscreen violence and real-life violence. "We have a perfect control group," he said. "It's called Canada. They get all our records, movies and TV, yet their rate of violent crime is one-tenth that of the US. Toronto is on the other side of the lake from Buffalo but a world apart. What Canada has that we don't is strict gun control . . . as well as less racial polarization and multi-generational poverty. Those are the real causes of violence."[9]

Both American and Canadian value systems are being shaped by the globalization of technology, trade, travel, finance, communications, and culture. Some people believe that these broad contextual trends are acting to homogenize our values and lifestyles, and it is true that Canadians consume massive amounts of American popular culture. But we are not alone in this: on the other side of the Atlantic, even the proud and ethnocentric French now watch more American movies than those made in their own country.

The similarities in the way we live are legion, from the food we eat to the cars we drive, and in our social-values research we see broad similarities in the evolution of our values from conformity to traditional codes (order, authority, Judeo-Christian morality, and attendant guilt) to more personal-ized, experiential values, with no theological pretensions or claims to univer-sal validity. This pattern is particularly pronounced among the youth tribes.

In each country, baby boomers were in the vanguard of the new values: the quest for personal autonomy and self-fulfilment, the values most associ-ated with the "Me Generation." Feminism, which was part of this search for autonomy and self-fulfilment, continues to be a strong trend in both coun-tries, despite a backlash by those seeking to turn back the clock. So, too, is the trend away from asceticism and deferred gratification to hedonism and immediate gratification. On both sides of the border, people want to join the party, and have as much fun as possible on the roller coaster of life. They are less willing to wait for their ultimate reward in the next life (though Ameri-cans, much more than Canadians, continue to find comfort in the prospect of a more exalted world beyond death's door).

Individualism has been a growing trend in both the United States and Canada since the 1950s. However, our data indicate an important difference between the American and Canadian orientations to individualism: the American orientation can be characterized as "rugged individualism" and the Canadian version is more "responsible" than rugged. American individualism is more competitive. Our values research finds that Americans are much more likely than Canadians to embrace a sense of personal and national vital-ity and the stimulation of personal challenge; they are also more likely to admit to feelings of stress in the pursuit of success.

North of the 49th parallel, we treasure equality; south of it, they treasure freedom. Lipset points out that, historically, the United States also laid claim to being the land of equality of opportunity, with Canada being the land of élite accommodation of group interests. However, it appears to me that Canada is now more egalitarian than the United States, and that Americans continue to cling tenaciously to a myth of social mobility that, in reality, holds for only a small proportion of their population. For example, in Canada the richest 1 per-cent of the population holds about 25 percent of the nation's wealth; in the United States the richest 1 percent holds over 40 per cent of the wealth.[10]

Despite many signs that the United States is fast becoming a hereditary oligarchy, the ideal of social mobility—the belief that through education and hard work, anyone can rise to the top—remains a key component of the American Dream. There is insufficient recognition that growing proportions of Americans are born, not only into poverty, but also into hopelessness. To borrow Lord Durham's description of Canada in 1840, the United States is once again becoming two nations "warring within the bosom of a single state," only this time it is the rich versus the poor, with levels of violence approaching that of America's Civil War in the 1860s.

Even among the disadvantaged echelons of society, the American orientation to life is more judgmental and moralistic than is the Canadian. The American moral code is more firmly rooted in Judeo-Christian doctrine, a Manichean world of good and evil, right and wrong, good guys and bad guys, Eve created out of man's rib, and Adam created in the image of God and given dominion over the natural world. Canadian morality transcends traditional religious definitions; it can be characterized as a secular, pluralistic, and ecological morality, a greater responsibility for the other. The Canadian emphasis on egalitarian values goes beyond the equality of human beings—whatever their sex, age, race, ethnicity, or sexual orientation—to the consideration of non-human species and the natural environment. I expect this principle will be codified in the preamble the next time we amend the Canadian constitution. Canada's global village is a global garden.

It is my opinion that, although economic integration continues apace, there has been much less sociocultural assimilation of Canada by the United States than is often feared. In important ways, Canadians and Americans live different sorts of lives. Moreover, I predict such assimilation will not take place for many generations to come, if ever. Though our economic axis has become north-south, our cultural axis has become, like our population, cybernomadic. Whereas television was initially a force that helped create mass society and popular culture, the new technologies of VCRs, satellite TV, and the Internet all contribute to a sociocultural fragmentation of mass society in favour of personal choice and empowerment. Common ideals and even "common sense" are increasingly hard to maintain, and the American national motto—"*e pluribus unum*"—or "*out of many, one*"—has turned out to be a tragic joke. It is truly ironic that Canada, a country that historically accommodated and even celebrated differences, has actually ended up creating a culture where a broad range of values unites us, and differentiates us significantly from Americans. On the other hand, the United States, in its drive to create a melting pot that disparages cultural and linguistic diversity, has, in fact, developed into a country of mutually exclusive identities and many warring factions. They have become a nation of god-fearing Darwinists, we have become a collection of tolerant social democrats.

Many people see social fragmentation and tribalism on the rise around the world, and the United States reverting to the *ethnic* tribalism of the past. Others, like Francis Fukuyama and Gwynne Dyer see more sanguine, hopeful trends. If my reading of Canada is correct, this country may be the harbinger of a more utopian future, as we experience an evolution from traditional ethnic tribalism to a postmodern tribalism based on social values.

In fact, despite tribal differences, French and English Canadians have far more in common with each other in terms of values than either group has with the Americans (however offensive this observation might be to political ideologues of the "distinct society"). Notwithstanding the Quiet Revolution in Quebec and the Values Revolution in Canada as a whole, Canadians themselves are not revolutionaries: they are rebels and reformers. And in spite of our growing intimacy with American commerce and culture, Canada remains a distinct society on the northern half of the North American continent.

Even in the face of powerful international forces favouring integration, our roots, our history, our size, our degree of secularization, our institutions, and, yes, even our climate have created two very different sociocultural environments on this continent. If we are the kinder, gentler society of level playing fields, then America is the land of shining cities, each surrounded by a walled moat outside of which roams a marauding and dangerous underclass. In their own minds, most Canadians have decided which model they prefer: an overwhelming majority say they would choose to remain in Canada even if they had equal opportunities in the United States.

Notes

[1]Reginald Bibby, quoted in *Western Report*, June 10, 1996.

[2]Ben Wattenberg, *Values Matter Most* (New York: The Free Press, 1995).

[3]Neil Bissoondath, *Saturday Night*, October 1994, p. 20.

[4]Bruce Little, *The Globe and Mail*, July 10, 1995.

[5]James Laxer, *The Toronto Star*, July 16, 1995.

[6]Graham Fraser, headline of *The Globe and Mail*, July 15, 1995.

[7]Jean Dumas quoted by Fabrice Taylor, *The Globe and Mail*, July 8, 1995.

[8]Elaine Carey, *The Toronto Star*, July 31, 1996.

[9]*The Toronto Star*, July 11, 1995.

[10]Carol Goar, *The Toronto Star*, May 14, 1995.

◉ ◉ ◉

Questions

1. Adams makes many comparisons between Canadian and American culture. Select and summarize the two comparisons that are most meaningful to you, and explain why you selected them.

2. What does Adams mean when he says Canadians have moved from an "organic model of society to a rhizomatic one."

3. What is multiculturalism? Why do Canadians and Americans experience it so differently? What are the costs and benefits of these different experiences?

4. What themes in this piece might have led Adams to subtitle it "The Garden and the Jungle?"

5. Which country's culture is most consistent with your values, and why? Have your views about Canada or the United States changed after reading this article? Explain.

Cross-Cultural Patterns in Mobile-Phone Use: Public Space and Reachability in Sweden, the USA and Japan

NAOMI S. BARON, AMERICAN UNIVERSITY, WASHINGTON, DC, USA
YLVA HÅRD AF SEGERSTAD, UNIVERSITY OF GOTHENBURG, SWEDEN

The use of mobile phones has grown tremendously over the last decade. Moreover, as cell phones become increasingly sophisticated, the way we use them has also changed. In this article, the authors examine attitudes toward quiet in public spaces, personal use of public space, tolerance of self-expression, and the appropriateness of cell-phone use in Sweden, Japan, and the United States. After you have read this article, you should understand the ways in which cultural differences shape how and where we use cell phones.

*I*t was a glorious September day. One of the authors was walking up Aveny in Gothenburg, nearing the statue of Poseidon. As an American, she had been struck by how quiet Swedes seemed to be in public places. People talked on their mobile phones, but you rarely heard them. Suddenly she was assaulted by a booming voice from across the broad street. She spied a man striding quickly and talking on his mobile phone. Surprised by the volume (though unable to discern actual words), she crossed the street and unobtrusively came up behind this violator of the Swedish mold. He turned out to be Italian.

Reprinted from *New Media & Sociology* 12, no. 1 (2010), by permission of Sage Publications.

This article draws upon data from a cross-national study of mobile phone use by university students to examine correlations between cultural variables and mobile phone usage. Our empirical focus is on Sweden, the USA and Japan. We begin by laying out some of the cultural considerations we will be taking into account.

Cultural Issues and Mobile-Phone Use

Do national cultural profiles exist?[1] In the early 19th century, Alexis de Tocqueville thought so. He described Americans as being strong individualists (de Tocqueville, 2000: 482–8) and as always chasing after new pleasures (pp. 511–14). Today we speak of taciturn Finns and loquacious Italians. Obviously, not all members of a cultural group fit national stereotypes, and there is cultural diversity within nation-states. Nonetheless, most societies can be characterized by parameters allowing us to predict, at least statistically, how members of those groups are likely to behave in many circumstances.

Do cultural patterns shape the way people use mobile phones? The Introduction to this themed section (Baron, 2010) reviews some of the literature on cross-cultural comparisons of information and communication technologies (ICTs). Granted, both handsets and telecommunications services vary somewhat between countries. For example, US mobile phones (unlike those in most of the world) generally do not use pre-paid SIM cards; as of early 2008, Swedes could pay bus fares with their mobiles while Italians and Japanese could not. Yet on balance, the technology is becoming increasingly similar internationally.

It hardly follows, of course, that everyone with a mobile phone—even within a single national or cultural context—uses it the same way. Some keep their phones on at all times, while others only switch them on to make a call. Males and females may differ in their use of ICTs (Baron, 2004). In many countries, text messaging is rampant among teenagers and young adults, while older adults do more talking. How much expendable income you have may shape usage patterns (compare, for instance, rural farmers in Africa with wealthy urban Angolans; or consider Cubans, for many of whom talking on a mobile is far too expensive–Booth, 2009). Usage also may follow fashion: One year, having dozens of ring tones is *de rigueur*, while the next, no one cares. In the same way, even nations sharing cultural similarities (such as the Nordic countries) report differences in mobile phone practices (TeliaSonera, 2004a, 2004b; Textually.org, 2004).

Our goal in this article is heavily empirical: to sample mobile-phone usage patterns in three countries, looking for similarities and differences. Ultimately, the purpose of cross-cultural analysis is to explain which differences might result from cultural distinctions. Such analysis is fraught with challenges. Differences might, for example, result from cost, amount of experience with the technology, or gender. Even more challenging is identifying legitimate cultural traits to measure. Large-scale cross-cultural comparisons of national cultures exist (Hofstede, 1997), but they may not accurately measure the cultural variables in which one is interested. They may also be out-of-date.

While it is important to avoid cultural stereotypes, social science field work has taught us that participant observation and examination of popular culture can lead to useful hypotheses about cultural folkways. For the purposes of this study, our selection of cultural traits to compare with mobile-phone practices has been somewhat informal, relying upon a combination of published literature and knowledge of everyday practices. While we do not claim methodological rigor for these selections, we suggest they give us a reasonable starting place for thinking about empirical correspondences between culture and mobile phones.

Sweden, the USA and Japan

The sociologist Åke Daun (2006) has explored how Swedes see themselves culturally, and how others perceive them. Among the traits he highlights are being taciturn, being punctual, avoiding conflict and offering many 'thank you's'.

Daun also observed similarities between Swedish and Japanese cultural patterns. For instance, he describes the implicit Swedish injunction not to stick out in a crowd or to promote one's own abilities. In Sweden, discussions of this point commonly lead to mention of Aksel Sandemose's fictional town of Jante, which lived by such commandments (*Jante-lagen*) as 'Thou shalt not fancy thyself better than *we*' (Sandemose, 1936: 77). Daun notes that Japanese share similar attitudes regarding the importance of humility (Daun, 2006: 176).[2]

Outsiders to both cultures quickly notice other similarities. In Japan and Sweden, you remove shoes upon entering someone's home. In neither country do you commonly utter the equivalent of 'Excuse me' when maneuvering past another person on a busy street. (Instead, you work your way around, in silence. By contrast, Americans are constantly saying 'Excuse me'.) Yet there are strong socio-political distinctions between Sweden and Japan: Sweden is a welfare state while Japan is not; there is much less social conformity in Sweden than in Japan and so on.

Consider notions of appropriate behavior in public space in Sweden, the USA and Japan:

	Sweden	USA	Japan
quiet in public space	yes	no	yes
public space is for personal use	yes	yes	no
tolerance of self-expression	yes	yes	no

First: the issue of quiet in public space. Compared with many other cultures, both Swedes and Japanese are relatively quiet in public places. Americans tend to be noisier.

Next: making personal use of public space. Sweden (like other Nordic countries) tends to view outdoor areas as public space, even if legally owned by specific individuals. By *allemansrätten* ('every man's right', meaning 'right to roam'), individuals have the right, for example, to cross someone's backyard to reach their destination without seeking permission. In Japan, such behavior would be unthinkable. American attitudes offer something of a contradiction. In many states, Americans have the right to shoot if you trespass on their property. Yet the USA is also committed to preserving vast tracks of land for public use.

Finally, tolerance of self-expression: Sweden is highly tolerant (e.g. of dress, in sexual matters), while Japan (at least traditionally) is more conformist. The USA, like Sweden, is generally broadminded regarding individual self-expression. This American attitude, often bolstered by appeals to the US Constitution's First Amendment (guaranteeing freedom of speech) is reflected in the ways that many Americans conduct themselves in public space. They discuss private issues in the hearing distance of others; they ignore traffic signals; they litter with impunity. Since quiet in public space, personal use of public space and tolerance of self-expression all potentially involve behavior while in the presence of others, we encompass all three with the term 'public space'.

❀ Research Questions

We have identified four research questions (RQs) that might reveal cultural differences in mobile-phone use:

RQ1: Are there differences in the frequency with which Swedish, American and Japanese university students use their mobile phones for talking and for texting?[3]

RQ2: Are there differences among Swedish, American and Japanese students regarding use of mobile phones in public space?

RQ3: Are there differences in what Swedish, American and Japanese students like most and like least about having a mobile phone?

RQ4: Are there differences in the attitudes of Swedish, American and Japanese university students regarding the fact that mobile phones make it easy to engage in communication but also difficult to avoid such communication?

Methodology

General Research Design

Data were collected between November 2007 and May 2008 from 18–24-year-old university students in Sweden, the USA and Japan.[4] These countries were selected because of cross-national diversity in their experience with ICTs, cultural differences and the availability of research sites in each location.

Students were recruited to complete an online questionnaire (using advertisements, word-of-mouth, information posted on course websites), resulting in a convenience sample. The questionnaire was constructed in English but then translated into Swedish and Japanese. The 10-minute survey was administered through a URL link to the professional version of Survey Monkey, an online survey tool that can be implemented in multiple languages and scripts. In addition, focus groups were conducted in each country, though findings are not generally reported here.

Subjects

A total of 1223 university students completed the online questionnaire. Subjects were drawn from two universities (in different cities) in each country (Sweden: Gothenburg and Karlstad; USA: Washington, DC and East Lansing, MI; Japan: Kyoto and Tokyo). The subject pool is summarized in Table 1.[5]

TABLE 1 *Subjects Completing Online Questionnaire from Sweden, the USA and Japan*

| Country | Total Subjects | Gender Distribution | | Mean Age |
		M	F	(Years)
Sweden	171	38.6%	61.4%	21.5
USA	523	26.8%	73.2%	19.8
Japan	529	29.1%	70.9%	19.8

Survey Questions

The full survey (excluding demographic information) consisted of 54 quantitative (or scalar) questions, a word-association task and five open-ended questions. The present study focuses on the following subset of questions.

RQ1: Frequency of Use

Two questions were asked to provide a usage baseline:

- Talking: 'Yesterday, what was the combined total number of voice calls you made and received on your mobile phone? Include voice-mails you left for other people and that you received.'

- Texting: 'Yesterday, what was the combined total number of text messages you sent and received on your mobile phone?'

For both talking and texting, respondents were asked to select from a range of intervals (e.g. 0, 3–4, more than 30). Some intervals were later collapsed for purposes of analysis.

RQ2: Public Space

One set of questions involving public space asked subjects to judge the acceptability of talking or texting on mobile phones in five venues:[6]

- eating dinner at home with your family
- sitting with people you know in an informal café
- paying at the cash register at a convenience store
- walking in public
- riding a local bus, tram or subway

For each scenario, subjects were asked to select 'always', 'usually', 'occasionally' or 'never'.

A second cluster of questions involved issues of loudness and topic of conversation. The first two questions were:

- 'In your perception, do *you* speak more loudly on a mobile phone than when speaking with someone standing next to you?'

- 'In your perception, do *other people* speak more loudly on a mobile phone than when speaking with someone standing next to them?'

Subjects were asked to select 'always', 'usually', 'occasionally' or 'never'. The third and fourth questions probed whether subjects were bothered by other people's behavior:

- 'Are you bothered when other people are talking on their mobile phones and they are talking loudly?'
- 'Are you bothered when other people are talking on their mobile phones and they are talking about personal affairs?'

Subjects were asked to select 'very much', 'some', 'a little' or 'not at all'.

RQ3: 'Like Most'/'Like Least'
Subjects were asked two open-ended questions:

- 'What is the *one* thing you like *most* about having a mobile phone?'
- 'What is the *one* thing you like *least* about having a mobile phone?'

RQ4: Reachability
To analyze 'reachability', we extracted data from the 'like most' and 'like least' responses.

❧ Results

RQ1: Frequency of Use

Findings for the frequency of using voice and texting functions on the mobile phone are summarized in Table 2. Swedes had the lowest overall mobile-phone usage. This finding is consonant with research conducted in 2004 by the telecommunications operator TeliaSonera, which reported that Swedes used their mobile phones less than some of their Nordic neighbors. While Finns averaged 249 minutes of talk-time per month, for Swedes the average was only 130 minutes. For text messaging, the Norwegian monthly average was 76, while Swedes averaged only 17 a month (Textually.org, 2004).

Table 3 focuses on high-frequency (≥ 11) compared with low-frequency (≤ 4) usage. Americans were most likely to make heavy use

TABLE 2 *Percentage of Mobile-Phone Voice Calls (Made and Received) and Text Messages (Sent and Received) on Previous Day**

		0–2	3–4	5–10	11–20	>20
Sweden	Voice	36.3	25.7	31.6	5.8	0.6
(N = 171)	Texts	34.5	21.6	30.1	9.9	2.9
US	Voice	22.0	26.6	38.4	10.5	2.5
(N = 523)	Texts	27.0	13.4	26.8	15.1	17.8
Japan	Voice	62.4	23.1	12.7	1.3	0.6
(N = 529)	Texts	8.5	9.8	29.5	25.3	26.8

*Because of rounding, several rows do not sum to 100%.

TABLE 3 *Percentage of High- and Low-Frequency Voice Calls and Texting*

	≥11 Voice Calls	≥11 Texts
High		
Sweden	6.4	12.8
USA	13.0	32.9
Japan	1.9	52.1
	≤4 Voice Calls	≤4 Texts
Low		
Sweden	62.0	56.1
USA	48.6	40.4
Japan	85.5	18.3

(≥11 per day) of voice functions, twice that of Swedes and more than six times than that of Japanese counterparts. The Japanese subjects made up for their paucity of voice calls by texting. Japanese were four times as likely as Swedes to be high-frequency texters, with Americans falling between them. For low-frequency texting, Swedes were three times more likely than Japanese to be low-volume users of texting, with Americans in between.

RQ2: Public Space

Considerations regarding use of mobiles in public space were clustered into two groups: appropriate places for use, and issues of loudness or being bothered.

Appropriate Places for Use

Subjects evaluated the acceptability of talking or texting in five different venues. Each venue can be viewed in cultural perspective, drawing upon our earlier cultural characterization of Sweden, the USA and Japan:

eating dinner at home with your family	tolerance of self-expression
sitting with people you know in an informal café	tolerance of self-expression
paying at the cash register at a convenience store	public space is for personal use
walking in public	public space is for personal use
riding local bus, tram or subway	public space is for personal use

Table 4 summarizes the percentage of subjects from each country who judged each of the five venues to be 'always' or 'usually' acceptable places to talk on their mobile phone, while Table 5 reports data on texting.

The first two venues (eating at home, in an informal café) both involve the physical presence of familiar people. Swedish subjects were four times as likely as Americans (Sweden 14.6%; USA 3.5%) (p < .01) to accept talking on a mobile phone while eating at home. Swedes were twice as comfortable as Americans talking in a café while with friends (42.7% and 22.6%, respectively) (p < .01). In fact, several American focus group participants noted feeling left out if they were eating with someone who made or received a call. Apart from Swedes talking on their phones in an informal café, none of these percentages is particularly high. Therefore, another way of viewing these data is to say that the majority of Swedish, American and Japanese subjects found it inappropriate to use voice functions under these two circumstances, with Swedes being the most tolerant.

TABLE 4 *Percentage of Subjects Reporting 'Always' or 'Usually' Acceptable to* Talk *on Mobile Phone (by Venue)*

Venue	Sweden (N = 171)	USA (N = 523)	Japan (N = 529)
Eating dinner at home with your family	14.6	3.5	13.0
Sitting with people you know in an informal café	42.7	22.6	13.8
Paying at the cash register at convenience store	57.3	22.4	31.6
Walking in public	97.7	94.6	73.7
Riding local bus, tram or subway	89.5	67.1	4.0

TABLE 5 *Percentage of Subjects Reporting 'Always' or 'Usually' Acceptable to* Text *on Mobile Phone (by Venue)*

Venue	Sweden (N = 171)	USA (N = 523)	Japan (N = 529)
Eating dinner at home with your family	35.7	22.8	22.7
Sitting with people you know in an informal café	64.9	59.7	26.7
Paying at the cash register at convenience store	48.0	34.2	47.3
Walking in public	95.3	84.3	76.2
Riding local bus, tram or subway	98.2	94.3	83.7

While both Swedes and Americans were more comfortable talking on their mobile phones in a café than at home with family, Japanese responses for the two venues were nearly the same (13.8% and 13.0%). One explanation may be that Japanese cafés are often fashionable places that people perceive as being more public than Swedes or Americans view comparable spaces.[7]

Text messaging while eating at home or in a café with friends was more acceptable across the board. Again, Swedish participants led those comfortable with the practice at home (Sweden 35.7%; USA 22.8%; Japan 22.7%) (p < .01). Swedes were far more comfortable texting in an informal café than were Japanese (64.9% and 26.7%, respectively) (p < .01) and slightly more comfortable than Americans

(64.9% and 59.7%). Americans were far more comfortable texting than talking on their mobiles at the family dinner table (texting 22.8%; talking 3.5%) (p < .01).

The discrepancy between American and Japanese acceptance of texting in cafés when sitting with friends is stark. Americans were twice as likely as Japanese (USA 59.7%, Japan 26.7%) (p < .01) to approve of the practice. Again, the explanation probably lies in the fact that Americans are more likely to perceive a venue such as Starbucks as casual space (inviting personal use), while Japanese may see the coffee shop as public space requiring public behavior.

Collectively, these data are largely consonant with the cultural description of Swedes and Americans being more tolerant of self-expression (here, communicating with non-present others) than Japanese. The low figure for Americans talking on their phones while at the family dinner table might partly reflect the fact that many American families rarely eat dinner together.[8] When they do, the occasion becomes, by default, more formal.

The next three questions involved use of mobile phones while in general public space. Swedish subjects were nearly three times as likely as Americans (Sweden 57.3%; USA 22.4%) (p < .01) and almost twice as likely as Japanese (31.6%) (p < .01) to talk on their phones while paying at a convenience store cash register. Regarding texting, Swedes and Japanese were essentially on par (Sweden 48.0%; Japan 47.3%), followed by Americans (34.2%).

The fact that one out of three Japanese subjects accepted talking on a mobile while paying at a cash register (compared with just over one out of five Americans) may reflect more generally the public behavior of many Japanese towards people they do not know. For example, during morning and evening rush hour, many Japanese shove their way onto commuter trains, ignoring the social decorum for which the Japanese are famous in face-to-face interactions. People on trains are, by contrast, silent strangers. Perhaps university-aged Japanese students view convenience-store clerks as silent strangers as well.

Among Swedish subjects, while 57.3% felt it was appropriate to talk while conducting a financial transaction, only 48.0% indicated texting was appropriate. Focus groups suggested the problem with texting was more physical than social: it is easier to multi-task between talking on the phone and paying than between texting and paying. Some subjects may have taken the word 'acceptable' to mean 'physically reasonable', not 'socially appropriate'. As for discrepancies in perceptions of texting, the Americans had the lowest average experience in texting (Sweden 6.8 years; Japan 5.5 years; USA 3.5 years), perhaps making it more challenging to text (i.e. than for Swedes or Japanese) while conducting a financial transaction.

When walking in public, Swedish and American subjects overwhelmingly judged it acceptable to talk on their mobile phones (Sweden 97.7%; USA 94.6%). The Japanese trailed significantly behind (73.7%) (Sweden compared with Japan, USA compared with Japan: $p < .01$). (Note that when a similar question was asked by Misa Matsuda of Japanese 18–24-year-olds several years ago, the approval response was only 48%: Baron, 2008: 136). These findings are consonant with our initial cultural observation that in both Sweden and the USA it is more socially acceptable to make private use (here, talking on the phone) of public space than in Japan.

Finally, we considered the acceptability of talking or texting while riding local public transportation. The starkest difference for talking was between Sweden and Japan: 89.5 percent acceptance compared with 4.0 percent ($p < .01$). The Swedish data offer one more example of the perception of feeling comfortable conducting private business in public space. In Japan, the finding directly reflects explicit social pressure not to speak on a mobile phone while riding on public transportation.[9] In both subway cars and buses, ubiquitous signs admonish riders not to speak on their phones (Ito et al., 2005).

The US situation is interesting for a different reason. More than half the US data were collected in Washington, DC, which is served by a well-used subway network. While there are no social strictures against using mobile phones on the subway (either for talking or texting), reception is often poor. The comparatively low percentage of Americans (67.1%) who found it acceptable to talk on their mobile phones while on local transportation may reflect the fact that calls are commonly dropped while moving through subway tunnels.

Swedish, American and Japanese subjects all found it more acceptable to text on local transportation than to talk. The difference between talking and texting is sharpest for Japan (talking 4.0%; texting 83.7%), reflecting social norms.

Loudness/Being Bothered

Our second set of attitudinal measures involved voice modulation and conversational topics in public space. All questions correlate with cultural parameters:

Do *you* speak more loudly on a mobile phone?	Quiet in public space
Do *other people* speak more loudly on a mobile phone?	Quiet in public space
Are you bothered when others speak loudly?	Tolerance of self-expression
Are you bothered when others talk about personal affairs?	Tolerance of self-expression

Table 6 presents findings about quiet in public space. Swedish and American students had similar perceptions. While one-quarter of each cohort judged themselves to speak more loudly on a mobile phone than face-to-face, half the subjects passed such judgment on other speakers. Japanese respondents were less prone to perceive themselves or others as speaking more loudly on mobile phones (self 9.3%; others 10.0%).

We earlier suggested that both Swedes and Japanese are generally quieter in public space than Americans. While the Japanese data

TABLE 6 *Percentage of Subject Responding 'Always' or 'Usually' to Questions Regarding Loudness on Mobile Phone*

Venue	Sweden (N = 171)	USA (N = 523)	Japan (N = 529)
Do *you* speak more loudly on a mobile phone?	24.0	23.9	9.3
Do *other people* speak more loudly on a mobile phone?	50.3	54.5	10.0

support this characterization, Swedish subjects perceive themselves and others to be noisy on their mobile phones (paralleling the Americans). Several factors are relevant in interpreting our findings. First, we did not ask subjects to rate (nor did we independently measure) the overall volume level of face-to-face conversations. If these baselines are lower in Sweden than in the USA, mobile-phone volume in Sweden could be lower as well. Second, anecdotal evidence suggests that over the past decade, as Americans have become increasingly comfortable using mobile phones, their overall volume level has decreased.

Table 7 summarizes data on the tolerance of self-expression by others with respect to loudness and topic. Swedish subjects were the least bothered by other people's mobile phone conversations, either because of volume or topic. Only 33.9 percent of Swedes indicated being bothered 'very much' when other people spoke loudly, compared with 61.0 percent of Americans and 71.6 percent of Japanese. Similarly, only 19.3 percent of Swedes were very bothered by hearing others talk about personal affairs. These findings are consonant with the description of Swedes as tolerant of self-expression.

Americans, often described as tolerant of self-expression, were bothered nearly twice as much as their Swedish counterparts in both situations. This disparity between ideology and practice has many analogues in everyday life: Americans may believe in the Bill of Rights yet support book censorship or wiretapping without search warrants. While free speech is a cherished American right, many subjects were bothered when others spoke freely and loudly on their mobile phones.

TABLE 7 *Percentage of Subjects Indicating Being Bothered 'Very Much' by Others' Mobile-Phone Behavior*

Venue	Sweden (N = 171)	USA (N = 523)	Japan (N = 529)
Are you bothered when others speak loudly?	33.9	61.0	71.6
Are you bothered when others talk about personal affairs?	19.3	34.4	23.1

Japanese students were most bothered (71.6%) when others around them spoke loudly on mobiles. Recall that Japanese are least likely to talk on their mobile phones in general, especially in public. Moreover, Japan values quiet in public space (including in face-to-face conversation). From an early age, Japanese children are trained not to engage in *meiwaku* behaviour, that is, behavior bothersome to others. Speaking loudly in public is one form of *meiwaku* behavior, as is speaking at all on a mobile while riding local public transportation. Thus, Japanese subjects were probably more sensitive than Swedes or Americans to loud mobile-phone conversations.

However, this logic seems not to hold when considering the number of Japanese who were very bothered when others discussed personal affairs on mobile phones. About one-quarter (23.1%) found such conversations very bothersome, compared with 19.3 percent of Swedes and 34.4 percent of Americans. The explanation may lie in another aspect of Japanese culture, which is that you ignore people you do not know. As noted earlier, Japanese subjects were more likely than Americans to talk or text while paying at a cash register. We hypothesized that since the Japanese did not know the check-out clerk, there was a diminished need to engage in polite behavior. On buses and commuter trains, Japanese turn social avoidance into a fine art, fiddling with non-voice functions of their mobile phones or pretending to sleep, thereby isolating themselves from the crowd. Just so, Japanese students may be more skilled than American counterparts at ignoring other people's mobile-phone conversations. By contrast, Swedes are probably less likely to care, given that Swedish participants were the most comfortable speaking on their phones in public space.

RQ3: 'Like Most'/'Like Least'

RQ3 probed what subjects liked *most* and liked *least* about their mobile phone. Responses were coded into six major categories (Physical attributes/functions, Communication, Evaluation, Cost issues, Safety issues, No comment), as well as divided into subcategories. Table 8 presents categories and examples.

TABLE 8 *Coding for 'Like Most'/'Like Least' Open-Ended Questions*

Major Category	Sample Subcategories
Physical attributes/functions	LIKE MOST: multipurpose device (e.g. 'I have everything I need in my hand'), entertainment (e.g. 'music') LIKE LEAST: ring tones (e.g. 'annoying ring tones'), voice-mail (e.g. 'I absolutely hate voicemails')
Communication	LIKE MOST: contact (e.g. 'connected to the world'), I contact others (e.g. 'contact people anywhere'), others contact me (e.g. 'can be reached no matter where I am'), written language (e.g. 'able to send SMS') LIKE LEAST: contact (e.g. 'can't be out of touch'), I contact others (e.g. 'I have a hard time calling the people I probably shouldn't call'), others contact me (e.g. 'want to be undisturbed'), written language (e.g. 'texting is stupid'), disruption of the social order (e.g. 'people are on the phone too often and too loud', 'ringing at times it should not have rung')
Evaluation	LIKE MOST: mobility (e.g. 'the freedom'), convenience ('easy to use'), general evaluative terms (e.g. 'It is practical') LIKE LEAST: mobility (e.g. 'have to carry it around'), dependency (e.g. 'constantly and obsessively checking'), equipment issues (e.g. 'easily breaks', 'remembering to charge it'), transmission issues (e.g. 'bad connection'), general evaluative terms (e.g. 'annoying', makes my life more complicated')
Cost issues	LIKE MOST: affordability (e.g. 'can call for free on nights/weekends') LIKE LEAST: affordability (e.g. 'costs too much')
Safety issues	LIKE MOST: general issues (e.g. 'security', 'feel safer driving long distances') LIKE LEAST: safety of handset (e.g. 'theft', 'the risk of losing it'), radiation (e.g. 'causes brain tumors')
No comment	LIKE MOST: [no examples] LIKE LEAST (e.g. 'N/A', 'no disadvantages')

195

Table 9 summarizes responses regarding what subjects liked *most* and liked *least* about having a mobile phone.

For 'like most', topping the list in all three countries was communication. Swedish subjects significantly outnumbered Americans (Sweden 81.9% of all responses; USA 65.5%) (p < .01), but both significantly outnumbered Japan (47.1%) (p < .01). Swedish subjects were less likely to express positive evaluative judgments than Americans or Japanese (Sweden 8.2%; USA 18.6%; Japan 20.2%). A striking cross-cultural anomaly concerned subjects reporting that

TABLE 9   *Open-Ended Responses to 'Like Most' and 'Like Least' Questions**

	Sweden (N = 171)		USA[10] (Like Most: N = 521; Like Least: N = 522)		Japan[10] (Like Most: N = 529; Like Least: N = 525;	
	N	%	N	%	N	%
LIKE MOST						
Physical attributes/funcs	5	2.9%	25	4.8%	151	28.5%
Communication	140	81.9%	341	65.5%	249	47.1%
Evaluation (positive)	14	8.2%	97	18.6%	107	20.2%
Cost issues	0	0.0%	2	0.4%	5	0.9%
Safety issues	12	7.0%	56	10.7%	17	3.2%
No comment	0	0.0%	0	0.0%	0	0.0%
LIKE LEAST						
Physical attributes/funcs	5	2.9%	22	4.2%	76	14.5%
Communication	81	47.4%	259	49.6%	143	27.2%
Evaluation (negative)	44	25.7%	150	28.7%	184	35.0%
Cost issues	17	9.9%	57	10.9%	95	18.1%
Safety issues	17	9.9%	7	1.3%	11	2.1%
No comment	7	4.1%	27	5.2%	16	3.0%

*Because of rounding, not all columns sum to 100%.

they 'liked most' a physical attribute or function of their mobile phone. While responses for both Swedes and Americans were less than 5%, Japanese responses were 28.5 percent. Examining the physical attributes/functions data by subcategories revealed that Japanese subjects focused on the fashionable nature of the phone (9.5% of all 'like most' responses'), size of the handset (2.8%) and online connectivity (3.2%), while these combined categories garnered less than a 1 percent response rate from either Swedish or American respondents. While we cannot conclude from these data that Japanese students are less enamored with communication functions than their Western counterparts, it is clear that the Japanese focus on other features of the phone as well.

For the 'like least' question, communication again dominated in the Swedish and American data (Sweden 47.4%; USA 49.6%), with no significant difference between the two countries. But once again, the Japanese were anomalous in a number of ways. The most striking concerned 'like least' judgments about communication: While nearly 50 percent of Swedes and Americans found communication to be what they 'liked least' about mobile phones, only half that number (27.2%) of Japanese offered this response (p < .01). Japanese subjects were also most likely to voice negative evaluations (Sweden 25.7%; USA 28.7%; Japan 35.0%). The overwhelming majority of Japanese concerns involved feeling dependent upon their phones, which is not surprising, given their high volume of text messaging (see Tables 2 and 3). Finally, Japanese subjects complained about the physical attributes of their phones (14.5%) and cost (18.1%). Note that pricing plans in Japan can be quite complex, involving not only voice and text messaging but internet allocations.

One subcategory of communication yielded an interesting cross-country comparison of the use of phones in social space. Japanese respondents complained the most about mobile phones disrupting the social order (e.g. 'people disregard manners because of mobile phones'). While 7.8 percent of Japanese subjects voiced such complaints, only 1.8 percent of Swedes and 4.2 percent of Americans did so. These findings are consonant with our earlier quantitative data (Table 7) that Americans were twice as likely as Swedes to be bothered when other people were speaking loudly, but Japanese were even more bothered than Americans.

RQ4: Reachability

Our final question asked whether students evidenced conflicts over the reachability that mobile phones afforded them: seeking communication with others, while disliking the fact that phones made them reachable. To explore reachability, we re-coded the relevant 'like most' and 'like least' responses (drawing upon the communication and evaluation categories) into a single 'reachability' category that included comments about being able to reach others (e.g. 'talking to whomever I like'), about others being able to reach them (e.g. 'can always be found') and comments where directionality of contact was not specified (e.g. 'text messaging'). Table 10 summarizes the findings.

Consider first Sweden and the USA. Reachability issues accounted for the majority of 'like most' judgments in both countries, with responses slightly stronger in Sweden (Sweden 88.4%; USA 83.3%). Since Swedes in the study were also more likely than Americans to mention communication issues in their 'like most' responses (Table 9), the disparity between countries is not surprising. However, in Sweden and the USA, reachability proved a double-edged sword. More than half the respondents from both countries (Sweden 56.7%; USA 56.7%) identified some aspect of reachability as what they 'liked

TABLE 10 *'Like Most' Judgments Regarding Reachability*

	Sweden (N = 171)		USA[10] (Like Most: N = 521; Like Least: N = 522)		Japan[10] (Like Most: N = 529; Like Least: N = 525;	
	N	%	N	%	N	%
Total 'like most' responses related to reachability	151	88.4%	434	83.3%	341	64.5%
Total 'like least' responses related to reachability	97	56.7%	296	56.7%	193	36.8%

least' about having a mobile phone. As with the communication scores for the 'like least' question (Table 9), these negative responses were matched across countries.

Our Japanese data for reachability present a different profile. While 83–88 percent of the Swedish and American subjects 'liked most' issues concerning reachability, the Japanese response was only 64.5 percent (p < .01). Similarly, while 57 percent of Swedish and American subjects liked reachability least, for Japanese subjects that number was only 36.8 percent (p < .01).

✆ Discussion

This study has presented a first look at cross-cultural data on mobile-phone use by a sample of 18–24-year-old university students in Sweden, the USA and Japan. Our central question has been the extent to which cultural issues shape differential use of largely the same technology. We analyzed quantitative and scalar data, as well as open-ended responses regarding what subjects liked most and least about their mobile phones, including reachability. Table 11 aggregates major findings with respect to the four research questions.

TABLE 11 *Summary of Major Findings*

Frequency of Use (RQ1)	• American subjects talked the most on their mobile phones and Japanese the least.
	• Japanese were the most prolific texters.
	• Swedes were moderate users of both voice and texting functions.
Public Space (RQ2, RQ3) Appropriate places to talk/text	• Swedish subjects were the most comfortable talking and texting on mobile phones when in the company of people they knew (eating dinner with family at home, with friends at a café) or in public space with strangers (paying at a cash register, walking in public, riding local transportation).
	• Japanese were most reticent to talk while riding local transportation, but also hesitant to talk or text while among friends at a café.

(Continued)

TABLE 11 *Continued*

	• Japanese were comparatively comfortable talking and texting while walking in public, but less so than Swedes or Americans.
Loudness/being bothered	• Swedes and Americans were twice as likely to judge other people as speaking louder (on mobile phones than face-to-face) than they judged themselves to do so. Japanese saw less difference—both for themselves and others.
	• Japanese (followed by Americans) were most bothered when others spoke loudly.
	• Americans were most bothered when others discussed personal affairs.
Communication Issues (RQ1, RQ2, RQ3) Importance of communication	• Communication was the most prominent category for the 'like most' question in all three countries, but lowest in Japan. Communication was the most prominent category for 'like least' in Sweden and the USA, but not in Japan.
Disturbing the social order	• Americans were more likely than Swedes to judge mobile phones as disruptive of the social order, though Japanese were twice as concerned as Americans.
	• Americans were twice as likely as Swedes to be bothered by other people speaking loudly, but Japanese were even more bothered than Americans.
Reachability (R4)	• Comments on reachability accounted for 83–88% of what Swedish and American subjects 'liked most' about their mobile phones, but only 65% of what Japanese 'liked most'.
	• Americans and Swedes had equal negative mentions of reachability (57%), while only 37% of what Japanese 'liked least' referred to reachability.

Building upon the summary in Table 11, we focus the remainder of our discussion on three issues:

- a re-examination of public space usage in light of our earlier cultural characterizations

- the evolving status of mobile phone domestication in America
- the reachability conundrum

Public Space

At the outset of this article, we suggested a cultural categorization of how Swedes, Americans and Japanese use public space. Table 12 integrates evidence from our mobile-phone study into this earlier framework.

Overall, the mobile-phone data are largely consistent with our original cultural profiles. However, the apparent exceptions bear further comment. In Sweden, for example, subjects judged others to speak more loudly on mobile phones than face-to-face. In fact, half the Swedish participants voiced this sentiment, roughly the same proportion as American subjects. However, as noted earlier, the problem in evaluating this finding is that we have no empirical baseline for face-to-face volume levels in either country.

Additional support for our Swedish findings comes from other studies of Swedish mobile phone behavior. TeliaSonera (2004a) reported that 24.6 percent of Swedish respondents (age not specified) judged it was always acceptable to talk on their mobile phones during a family dinner. In another study, TeliaSonera (2004b) found that 81.6 percent of Swedes (again, age not specified) felt it was always acceptable to talk on their mobile phone in a shop. More recently, Tele2 (2008) reported that less than 3 percent of Swedes (age not specified) reported they would prefer public transport to be mobile-phone-free zones. The vast majority of Swedes (89%) found it appropriate to talk on a mobile in a restaurant. And only 19% minded hearing about other people's problems in their private relations.[11]

The American data were also generally consistent with our profile, except with regard to being bothered by the use of mobile phones by others in public space. Americans complained about other people speaking loudly, discussing personal affairs or more generally disrupting the social order. As we suggested earlier, Americans (perhaps like people in many cultures) sometimes espouse values (here, freedom of speech) that they do not consistently condone in the behavior of others.

TABLE 12 *Summary of Findings Regarding Use of Mobile Phones in Public Space*

Trait	Sweden		USA		Japan	
	Prediction	Mobile Evidence	Prediction	Mobile Evidence	Prediction	Mobile Evidence
Quiet in public space	Yes	Moderate number of voice calls (BUT: judge others to speak more loudly on phone than F2F)	No	Largest number of high-volume voice calls Judge other people to speak more loudly on phone than F2F	Yes	Smallest number of voice calls Don't speak more loudly on phone than F2F and don't judge others to speak more loudly
Public space is for personal use	Yes	Most talkers at cash register, walking, riding local transportation	Yes	Talk while walking, riding local transportation (BUT: not at cash register)	No	Fewest talkers while walking, riding local transportation (BUT: talk at cash register)
Tolerance of self-expression	Yes	Most talkers at home dinner, in café Least bothered when others speak loudly or discuss personal affairs	Yes	Text at home dinner (BUT: don't talk at home dinner) Some talk, much texting at café (BUT: bothered when others speak loudly or discuss personal affairs; judged mobile phone to disrupt social order)	No	Fewest talkers or texters in café (BUT: some talking and texting at home dinner) Bothered when others speak loudly or use mobile phone to disrupt the social order

Finally, the Japanese data also generally follow our initial profile. Two unexpected findings were the amount of talking when paying at a cash register and amount of both texting and talking when eating dinner at home. An understanding of these results will need to be embedded within a more fine-grained analysis of contemporary Japanese culture.

Americans and Domestication of Mobile Phones

The American data (collected between January and March 2008) are of particular interest because they reflect a technology still being domesticated. In a study conducted in 2005, American university students were asked to weigh the amount of talking compared with texting they did on mobile phones. Subjects reported engaging in seven voice calls for every three text messages. Moreover, the average number of text messages they sent per day was between three and six, depending upon the subject population (Baron, 2008: 143). Since 2005, use of text messaging in the USA has been skyrocketing. In September 2008, Nielsen Mobile reported that Americans were sending or receiving more text messages than voice calls on mobile phones. (The age cohort 18–24 averaged 265 calls and 790 texts per month—see Cellsigns Mobile Marketing, 2008). By June 2009, the number of texts sent overall in the USA had grown 80 percent since June 2008 (Mindlin, 2009).

As part of the domestication process, Americans may be getting quieter when they speak on mobile phones in public space. Perhaps Americans simply need to believe that their voice will transmit without needing to raise their volume. (A century ago, George Bernard Shaw complained about the 'stentorian efficiency' with which the first London telephones broadcast private messages: Briggs, 1977: 61.) To discern whether our findings reflect the domestication process or a conflicted attitude towards free speech, we may need to wait several years until Americans are as comfortable with mobile phones as counterparts in Europe or Asia.

Reachability as a Growing Conundrum

Our data suggest that Swedish, American and Japanese university students in our sample largely thought of their mobile phones as communication devices. For the 'like most' question, 47–82 percent of responses referred to communication. And for the reachability re-analysis of the 'like most' data, 65–88 percent of responses involved reachability.

Yet when asked what they 'liked least' about their mobile phones, 37–57 percent spoke of reachability. Discomfort with always being reachable is hardly unique to subjects in this study. In addition to a growing litany of anecdotal complaints, the Pew Internet & American Life Project reported in September 2008 that 49 percent of working Americans judged that 'ICTs make it harder for them to disconnect from their work when they are at home and on weekends' (Madden and Jones, 2008).

Besides the reachability conundrum itself, there is the additional question of whether conflicting feelings about reachability span across cultures. Our data suggest that while Swedish subjects displayed greater enthusiasm for reachability than American, both groups were equally negative about being reachable by others. Japanese subjects were least effusive about reachability, but also least bothered by it. In their theory of *Apparatgeist*, Katz and Aakhus (2002) suggest that the logic informing personal communication technologies is that of perpetual contact. Our study indicates that while the logic of mobile phones drives users to seek communication with others, people are uncomfortable about always being reachable. However, the conundrum seems strongest for the two Western countries compared with Japan, where, perhaps, social politeness conventions mitigate against individuals complaining about others attempting to communicate with them.

It is instructive to compare our current findings with results from a recent Eurobarometer study, charting attitudes towards mobile phones among citizens from 27 EU countries (Eurobarometer Flash Report 241, 2008). When asked to judge the statement 'People who do not use a mobile phone have less stress in their lives', 52 percent either 'strongly' agreed or 'rather' agreed. Among Swedes, the percent of respondents offering one of these two responses was 68 percent (pp. 64, 67).

Concluding Remarks

The data presented in this article lend substantial support for correlating cultural variables with mobile-phone practices. Admittedly, our data are limited (a convenience sample from a restricted age group and educational cohort in three countries), and our cultural analysis has not been methodologically detailed. However, by using a uniform research tool (the same online questionnaire, though translated), we were able to tap into subtle attitudinal issues, enabling us to probe more deeply than some of the other ICT cross-cultural analyses available.

Our study revealed several dimensions of mobile-phone use by university students that held constant across cultural contexts. The first was how strongly subjects thought about their mobile phones as essentially communication devices. While mentioning other multi-purpose functions (such as a radio, an organizer or a tool for accessing the internet), communication still predominated, especially in Sweden and the USA. In the coming years, it will be interesting to see how this balance plays out, particularly with the proliferation of internet-friendly smart phones.

Second, our study documented a clear conflict between the desire to be in communication with others and the desire not to be reached. As ICTs increasingly lead us to being 'always on',[12] it will be important to understand whether the proliferation of mobile phones is magnifying a social conundrum already in place or generating a new kind of social pressure. Research will obviously need to include voice calls and texting via mobile devices and also internet-based communication functions, such as instant messaging, blogs and social networking sites that have traditionally operated on computers.

Future cross-cultural research efforts might involve a broader cultural sampling (including, for example, Africa and the Middle East), more age groups and more varied educational backgrounds, along with a fine-grained analysis of the role of cost in determining mobile phone usage patterns and attitudes. Random (rather than convenience) sampling will make for more robust data, as will independent cultural analyses of the sort we were not able to undertake here.

Undoubtedly, mobile-phone practices will continue to evolve. It remains to be seen whether, with time, cultural differences will diminish or persist. The more closely we chart the individual and collective trajectories of mobile phones in diverse cultural settings, the better prepared we become both to design phones that fill our needs and to cope with the unanticipated consequences of mobile telephony.

Endnotes

[1]While mindful of pitfalls in equating culture with nation-state (Baron, 2010), we use the terms 'nation' (or 'country') and 'culture' here interchangeably. Our research included only university students aged 18–24, themselves a subset of national populations, and loosely sharing some cultural affinities.

[2]For more on Japanese behavioral patterns, see Doi, 1971; Lebra, 1976; Yamada, 1997. For analysis of Japanese mobile phone (keitai) behavior and its cultural underpinnings, see Ito et al., 2005. Also see Ohmori and Harata, 2008.

[3]Henceforth, when we speak of 'Swedes', 'Americans' and 'Japanese', we are referring to study participants residing in those countries, not to citizenship or to the entire country's population.

[4]As part of the larger research project, data were also collected in Italy and Korea.

[5]In Gothenburg, subjects came from two universities. Due to space limitations, gender analyses are not reported here. As for age discrepancies between samples, it was difficult to find younger subjects in Sweden, since Swedes tend to begin university studies at an older age than Americans or Japanese.

[6]Because of translation problems in the Japanese survey, we have excluded data from additional questions regarding 'sitting with people you know in a formal restaurant' and 'riding a [long-distance] train'.

[7]We are grateful to Misa Matsuda and Kumi Iwasaki for discussion of these issues.

[8]In 2003, ConAgra estimated that 40 percent of American families ate together only three or four times a week (http://findarticles.com/p/articles/mi_m4PRN/is_2003_May_30/ai_n2774 3326).

[9]On longer-distance Japanese trains, riders may speak on their mobile phones in the space between train cars.

[10]Invalid and uncodable responses were eliminated, therefore slightly reducing the sample size in the USA and Japan.

[11]Additional confirmations appear in the ongoing Swedish Mobile Barometer project (see Axelsson, 2010).

[12]For broader discussion of the ramifications of being 'always on', see Baron (2008).

References

Axelsson A-S (2010) Perpetual and personal: Swedish young adults and their use of mobile phones. *New Media & Society* [reference to be completed]

Baron NS (2004) 'See you online': gender issues in college student use of instant messaging. *Journal of Language and Social Psychology* 23(4): 397–423.

Baron NS (2008) *Always On: Language in an Online and Mobile World.* New York: Oxford University Press.

Baron NS (2010) Introduction to themed section: mobile phones in cross-cultural context: Sweden, Estonia, the USA and Japan. *New Media & Society* [reference to be completed]

Booth W (2009) In Cuba, cellphone calls go unanswered. *Washington Post* (3 January): A1.

Briggs A (1977) The pleasure telephone: a chapter in the prehistory of the media. In: Pool I (ed.) *The Social Impact of the Telephone.* Cambridge, MA: MIT Press, 40–65.

CellSigns Mobile Marketing (2008) More SMS than calls: phone calls take backseat to text messaging. 1 October. Available at: http://www.cellsigns.com/internal/blog/?m=200810

Daun Å (2006) *Swedish Mentality.* Trans. Teeland J. University Park, PA: Pennsylvania State University Press.

Doi T (1971) *The Anatomy of Dependence.* Tokyo: Kodansha International.

Eurobarometer Flash Report 241 (2008) Information society as seen by EU citizens. November. Available at: http://ec.europa.eu/public_opinion/flash/fl_241_en.pdf

Hofstede G (1997) *Cultures and Organizations: Software of the Mind*. New York: McGraw Hill.

Ito M, Okabe D and Matsuda M, eds (2005) *Personal, Portable, Pedestrian: Mobile Phones in Japanese Life*. Cambridge, MA: MIT Press.

Katz J and Aakhus M (2002) Conclusion: making meaning of mobiles—a theory of apparatgeist. In: Katz J and Aakhus M (eds) *Perpetual Contact: Mobile Communication, Private Talk, Public Performance*. Cambridge: Cambridge University Press, 301–18.

Lebra TS (1976) *Japanese Patterns of Behavior*. Honolulu: University of Hawaii Press.

Madden M and Jones S (2008) Networked workers. Pew Internet & American Life Project, 24 September. Available at: http://www.pewinternet.org/pdfs/PIP_Networked_Workers_FINAL.pdf

Mindlin A (2009) Sending a message, again and again. *New York Times*, 8 November: B3.

Ohmori N and Harata N (2008) How different are activities while commuting by train? A case in Tokyo. *Journal of Economic and Social Geography (TESG)* 99(5): 547–61.

Sandemose A (1936) *A Fugitive Crosses His Tracks*. Trans. E. Gay-Tifft. New York: Alfred Knopf.

Tele2 (2008) Survey of Swedes' opinion of (in)appropriate use of mobile phones in public settings. July.

TeliaSonera (2004a) Swedes like to talk while they eat. Press release, 11 November. Available at: http://www.teliasonera.com/press/pressreleases/item.page?prs.itemId=123439

Textually.org (2004) Use of mobile phones more common in Finland than in Sweden, 30 August. Available at: http://www.textually.org/textually/archives/2004/08/005116.htm

TeliaSonera (2004b) OK to talk on your mobile phone while shopping. Press release, 30 November. Available at: http://www.teliasonera.com/press/pressreleases/item.page@prs.itemId=125882

Tocqueville A de (2000) *Democracy in America.* Trans., ed. and with an introduction by Mansfield HC and Winthrop D. Chicago, IL: University of Chicago Press.

Yamada H (1997) *Different Games, Different Rules: Why Americans and Japanese Misunderstand Each Other.* New York: Oxford University Press.

◉ ◉ ◉

Questions

1. Describe the cultural norms of Sweden, Japan, and the United States. In what ways are they similar? Dissimilar?

2. How did the researchers collect their data? From whom did they collect it?

3. Review Tables 1–5. What do they tell you about how people in Sweden, Japan, and the United States use their mobile phones? Is the use of mobile phones consistent with cultural norms in these countries?

4. How do you feel about the use of mobile phones in public spaces? Is your response consistent with those presented in the article?

5. Consider what you learned about the use of mobile phones. What are some of the implications for how they are used in social interaction?

Are Emily and Greg More Employable Than Lakisha and Jamal?: A Field Experiment on Labor Market Discrimination

MARIANNE BETRAND
SENDHIL MULLAINATHAN

Does your name make a difference in whether you get a job? The authors conduct a field experiment to see whether racial discrimination still exists in hiring practices. They sent out fictitious résumés and manipulated the names so that they sounded like they came from either an African American or a white American in response to help-wanted ads in Boston and Chicago newspapers. Across a number of control variables including neighborhood of residence, federal versus private employers, and employers listing Equal Opportunity Employer, résumés that used African American sounding names received fewer call-backs than applicants with white American sounding names.

☺ Introduction

Every measure of economic success reveals significant racial inequality in the US labor market. Compared to Whites, African Americans are twice as likely to be unemployed and earn nearly 25 percent less when they are employed (Council of Economic Advisers, 1998). This inequality has sparked a debate on whether employers discriminate by race. When faced with observably similar African American and White applicants, do they favor the White one? Some argue yes, citing either employer prejudice or employer perception that race signals lower productivity. Others argue that discrimination is a

Reprinted from *National Bureau of Economic Research Working Paper No. w9873*, July 2003, by permission of the authors.

relic of the past, eliminated by some combination of employer enlighten-ment, affirmative action programs and the profit-maximization motive. In fact, many in this later camp even feel that stringent enforcement of affirma-tive action programs has produced an environment of reverse discrimination. They would argue that faced with identical candidates, employers might favor the African American one.[1] Data limitations make it difficult to empiri-cally test these views. Since researchers possess far less data on workers than employers do, White and African American workers that appear similar to researchers may look very different to employers. So any racial difference in labor market outcomes could just as easily be attributed to these differences unobserved by researchers as to discrimination.

We conduct a field experiment to circumvent this difficulty. We send resumes in response to help-wanted ads in Chicago and Boston newspapers and measure the number of callbacks each resume receives for interviews. We experimentally manipulate perception of race via the name on the resume. We randomly assign very White sounding names (such as Emily Walsh or Greg Baker) to half the resumes and very African American sound-ing names (such as Lakisha Washington or Jamal Jones) to the other half. Because we are also interested in how credentials affect discrimination, we experimentally vary the quality of the resumes used in response to a given ad. Higher quality applicants have on average a little more labor market experi-ence and fewer holes in their employment history; they are also more likely to have an email address, have completed some certification degree, possess for-eign language skills or have been awarded some honors.[2] In practice, we typ-ically send four resumes in response to each ad: two higher quality and two lower quality ones. We randomly assign to one of the higher and one of the lower quality resumes an African American sounding name. In total, we respond to over 1300 employment ads in the sales, administrative support, clerical and customer services job categories and send nearly 5000 resumes. The ads we respond to cover a large spectrum of job quality, from cashier work at retail establishments and clerical work in a mailroom to office and sales management positions.

We find large racial differences in callback rates.[3] Applicants with White names need to send about 10 resumes to get one callback whereas applicants with African American names need to send around 15 resumes to get one callback. This 50 percent gap in callback rates is statistically very significant. Based on our estimates, a White name yields as many more callbacks as an additional eight years of experience. Since applicants' names are randomly assigned, this gap can only be attributed to the name manipulation.

Race also affects the reward to having a better resume. Whites with higher quality resumes receive 30 percent more callbacks than Whites with lower quality resumes, a statistically significant difference. On the other hand, having a higher quality resume has a much smaller effect for African Americans. In other words, the gap between White and African-Americans widens with resume quality. While one may have expected that improved credentials may alleviate employers' fear that African American applicants are deficient in some unobservable skills, this is not the case in our data.[4] Discrimination therefore appears to bite twice, making it harder not only for African Americans to find a job but also to improve their employability.

The experiment also reveals several other aspects of discrimination. First, since we randomly assign applicants' postal addresses to the resumes, we can study the effect of neighborhood of residence on the probability of callback. We find that living in a wealthier (or more educated or more White) neighborhood increases callback rates. But, interestingly, African Americans are not helped more than Whites by living in a "better" neighborhood. Second, the amount of discrimination we measure by industry does not appear correlated to Census-based measures of the racial gap by industry. The same is true for the amount of discrimination we measure in different occupations. In fact, we find that discrimination levels are statistically indistinguishable across all the occupation and industry categories covered in the experiment. We also find that federal contractors, who are thought to be more severely constrained by affirmative action laws, do not discriminate less; neither do larger employers or employers who explicitly state that they are an "Equal Opportunity Employer" in their ads. In Chicago, we find that employers located in more African American neighborhoods are slightly less likely to discriminate. . . .

● Prior Research on Discrimination

With conventional labor force and household surveys, it is difficult to measure racial discrimination or analyze its mechanics.[6] With survey data, researchers usually measure discrimination by comparing the labor market performance of Whites and African Americans who report a similar set of skills. But such comparisons can be quite misleading. Standard labor force surveys do not contain all the characteristics that employers observe when hiring, promoting or setting wages. So one can never be sure that the African

American and White workers being compared are truly similar from the employer's perspective. As a consequence, any measured differences in outcomes could be attributed to these unobserved (to the econometrician) factors and not to discrimination.

This difficulty with conventional data has led some authors to use pseudo-experiments.[7] Goldin and Rouse (2000), for example, examine the effect of blind auditioning on the hiring process of orchestras. By looking at the treatment of female candidates before and after the introduction of blind auditions, they try to measure the amount of sex discrimination. When such pseudo-experiments can be found, the resulting study can be very informative, but finding such experiments has been extremely difficult.

A different set of studies, known as audit studies, attempt to place comparable minority and White subjects into actual social and economic settings and measure how each group fares in these settings.[8] Labor market audit studies send comparable minority (African American or Hispanic) and White auditors in for interviews and measure whether one is more likely to get the job than the other.[9] While the results vary somewhat across studies, minority auditors tend to perform worse on average: they are less likely to get called back for a second interview and, conditional on getting called back, less likely to get hired.

These audit studies provide some of the cleanest non-laboratory evidence of labor market discrimination. But they also have weaknesses, most of which have been highlighted in Heckman and Siegelman (1992) and Heckman (1998). First, these studies require that both members of the auditor pair are identical in all dimensions that might affect productivity in employers' eyes, except for race. To accomplish this, researchers typically match auditors on several characteristics (height, weight, age, dialect, dressing style, hairdo) and train them for several days to coordinate interviewing styles. Yet, critics note that this is unlikely to erase the numerous differences that exist between the auditors in a pair.

Another weakness of the audit studies is that they are not double-blind. Auditors know the purpose of the study. As Turner et al (1990) note: "The first day of training also included an introduction to employment discrimination, equal employment opportunity, and a review of project design and methodology." This may generate conscious or subconscious motives among auditors to generate data consistent or inconsistent with racial discrimination. As psychologists know very well, these demand effects can be strong. It is very difficult to insure that auditors will not want to do "a good job." Since they know the goal of the experiment, they can alter their behavior in front of employers to express (indirectly) their own views. Even a small belief by auditors that employers treat minorities differently can result in apparent discrimination. This effect is further magnified by the fact that auditors are not in fact seeking jobs and are therefore more free to let their beliefs affect the interview process.

Finally, audit studies are extremely expensive, making it difficult to generate large enough samples to understand the nuances and possible mitigating factors of discrimination. Also, these budgetary constraints worsen the problem of mismatched auditor pairs. Cost considerations force the use of a few pairs of auditors, meaning that any one mismatched pair can easily drive the results. In fact, these studies generally tend to find significant differences in outcomes across pairs.

Our study circumvents these problems. First, because we only rely on resumes and not people, we can be sure to generate comparability across race. In fact, since race is randomly assigned to each resume, the same resume will sometimes be associated with an African American name and sometimes with a White name. This guarantees that any differences we find are due solely to the race manipulation. Second, the use of paper resumes insulates us from demand effects. While the research assistants know the purpose of the study, our protocol allows little room for conscious or subconscious deviations from the set procedures. Moreover, we can objectively measure whether the randomization occurred as expected. This kind of objective measurement is impossible in the case of the previous audit studies. Finally, because of relatively low marginal cost, we can send out a large number of resumes. Besides giving us more precise estimates, this larger sample size also allows us to examine the mechanics of discrimination from many more angles.[10]

❂ Experimental Design

Creating a Bank of Resumes

The first step of the experimental design is to generate templates for the resumes to be sent. The challenge is to produce a set of realistic and representative resumes without using resumes that belong to actual job seekers. To achieve this goal, we start with resumes of actual job searchers but alter them sufficiently to create distinct resumes. The alterations maintain the structure and realism of the initial resumes without compromising their owners.

We begin with resumes posted on two job search websites as the basis for our artificial resumes.[11] While the resumes posted on these websites may not be completely representative of the average job seeker, they provide a practical approximation.[12] We restrict ourselves to people seeking employment in our experimental cities (Boston and Chicago). We also restrict ourselves to four occupational categories: sales, administrative support, clerical services and customer services. Finally, we further restrict ourselves to resumes posted more than six months prior to the start of the experiment. We purge the selected resumes of the person's name and contact information.

During this process, we classify the resumes within each occupational category into two groups: high and low quality. In judging resume quality, we use criteria such as labor market experience, career profile, existence of gaps in employment and skills listed. Such a classification is admittedly subjective but it is made independently of any race assignment on the resumes (which occurs later in the experimental design). To further reinforce the quality gap between the two sets of resumes, we add to each high quality resume a subset of the following features: summer or while-at-school employment experience, volunteering experience, extra computer skills, certification degrees, foreign language skills, honors or some military experience. This resume quality manipulation needs to be somewhat subtle to avoid making a higher quality job applicant over-qualified for a given job. We try to avoid this problem by making sure that the features listed above are not all added at once to a given resume. This leaves us with a high quality and a low quality pool of resumes.

To minimize similarity to actual job seekers, we use resumes from Boston job seekers to form templates for the resumes to be sent out in Chicago and used the Chicago resumes to form templates for the resumes to be sent out in Boston. To implement this migration, we alter the names of the schools and previous employers on the resumes. More specifically, for each Boston resume, we use the Chicago resumes to replace a Boston school by a Chicago school.[13] We also use the Chicago resumes to replace a Boston employer by a Chicago employer in the same industry. We use a similar procedure to migrate Chicago resumes to Boston.[14] This produces distinct but realistic looking resumes, similar in their education and career profiles to this sub-population of job searchers.[15]

Identities of Fictitious Applicants

The next step is to generate identities for the fictitious job applicants: names, telephone numbers, postal addresses and (possibly) e-mail addresses. The choice of names is crucial to our experiment.[16] To decide on which names are uniquely African American and which are uniquely White, we use name frequency data calculated from birth certificates of all babies born in Massachusetts between 1974 and 1979. We tabulate these data by race to determine which names are distinctively White and which are distinctively African American. Distinctive names are those that have the highest ratio of frequency in one racial group to frequency in the other racial group.

As a check of distinctiveness, we conducted a survey in various public areas in Chicago. Each respondent was given a resume with a name and asked to assess features of the person, one of which being race. In general, the names led respondents to readily attribute the expected race for the person but there were a few exceptions and these names were disregarded.[17]

The final list of first names used for this study are reported in Appendix Table 1. The table also reports the frequency of these names in the Massachusetts birth certificates data.[18] The African American first names used in the experiment are remarkably common in the population. This suggests that by using these names as an indicator of race, we are actually covering a large segment of the African American population.[19]

Applicants in each race/sex/city/resume quality cell are allocated the same phone number. This guarantees that we can precisely track employer callbacks in each of these cells. The phone lines we use are virtual ones with only a voice mail box attached to it. A similar outgoing message is recorded on each of the voice mail boxes but each message is recorded by someone of the appropriate race and gender. Since we allocate the same phone number for applicants with different names, we cannot use a person's name in the outgoing message.

While we do not expect positive feedback from an employer to take place via postal mail, resumes still need postal addresses. We therefore construct fictitious addresses based on real streets in Boston and Chicago using the White Pages. We select up to 3 addresses in each 5-digit zip code in Boston and Chicago. Within cities, we randomly assign addresses across all resumes. We also create 8 email addresses, 4 for Chicago and 4 for Boston.[20] These email addresses are neutral with respect to both race and sex. Not all applicants are given an email address. As we explained above, the email addresses are used almost exclusively for the higher quality resumes. This procedure leaves us with a bank of names, phone numbers, addresses and e-mail addresses which we can assign to the template resumes when responding to the employment ads.

Responding to Ads

The experiment was carried on between July 2001 and January 2002 in Boston and between July 2001 and May 2002 in Chicago.[21] Over that period, we collected all employment ads in the Sunday editions of *The Boston Globe* and *The Chicago Tribune* in the sales, administrative support, and clerical and customer services sections. We eliminate any ad where applicants are asked to call or appear in person. In fact, most ads we surveyed in these job categories asked for applicants to fax in or (more rarely) mail in their resume. We log the name (when available) and contact information for each employer, along with any information on the position advertised and specific requirements (such as education, experience, or computer skills). We also record whether or not the ad explicitly states that the employer is an equal opportunity employer.

For each ad, we use the bank of resumes to sample four resumes (two high-quality and two low-quality) that fit the job description and requirements as closely as possible.[22] In some cases, we slightly alter the resumes to improve the quality of the match, such as by adding the knowledge of a specific software program.

One of the high and one of the low quality resumes selected are then drawn at random to receive African American names, the other high and low resumes receive White names.[23] We use male and female names for sales jobs, whereas we use nearly exclusively female names for administrative and clerical jobs to increase callback rates.[24] Based on sex, race, city and resume quality, we assign a resume the appropriate phone number. We also select at random a postal address. Finally, e-mail addresses are added to most of the high quality resumes.[25] The final resumes are formatted, with fonts, layout and cover letter style chosen at random. The resumes are then faxed (or in a few cases mailed) to the employer.[26] All in all, we respond to more than 1300 employment ads over the entire sample period and send close to 5000 resumes.

Measuring Responses

We measure whether a given resume elicits a callback or e-mail back for an interview. For each phone or email response, we use the content of the message left by the employer (name of the applicant, company name, telephone number for contact) to match the response to the corresponding resume-ad pair.[27] Any attempt by employers to contact applicants via postal mail cannot be measured in our experiment since the addresses are fictitious. Several human resource managers confirmed to us that employers rarely, if ever, contact applicants via postal mail to set up interviews.

*W*eaknesses of the *E*xperiment

We have already highlighted the strengths of this experiment relative to previous audit studies. We now discuss its weaknesses. First, our outcome measure is crude, even relative to the previous audit studies. Ultimately, one cares about whether an applicants gets the job and about the wage offered conditional on getting the job. Our procedure, however, simply measures callbacks for interviews. To the extent that the search process has even moderate frictions, one would expect that reduced interview rates would translate into reduced job offers. However, we are not able to translate our results into gaps in hiring rates or earnings.

Another weakness is that the resumes do not directly report race but instead suggest race through personal names. This leads to various sources of concern. First, while the names are chosen to make race salient, some employers may simply not notice the names or not recognize their racial content. As a result, our findings may under-estimate the extent of discrimination. Relatedly, because we are not assigning race but only race-specific name, our results are not representative of the average African American (who may not have such a racially distinct name).[28]

Finally, and this is an issue pervasive in both our study and the pair-matching audit studies, newspaper ads represent only one channel for job search. As is well known from the existing literature, social networks are a common means through which people find jobs and one that clearly cannot be studied here. This omission would affect our results if African Americans use social networks more or if less discriminating employers rely more on networks.[29] . . .

◉ *I*nterpretation

Two main sets of issues arise when interpreting the results above. First, does our design isolate the effect of race or is the name manipulation conveying some other factors than race? Second, what do our results imply for different models of discrimination?

Potential Confounds

Though we have interpreted our results in terms of racial differences, we actually manipulate only the name on the resume. While these names clearly signal race, perhaps they also signal some other personal characteristics. More specifically, one might be concerned that employers are inferring social background from the personal name. When employers read a name like "Tyrone" or "Latoya," they may assume that the person comes from a disadvantaged background. In the extreme form of this social background interpretation, employers do not care at all about race but are discriminating only against the social background conveyed by the names we have chosen.[30]

While plausible, we feel that some of our earlier results are hard to reconcile with this interpretation. We found that while employers value "better" addresses, African Americans are not helped more than Whites by living in Whiter or more educated neighborhoods. If the African American names mainly signal negative social background, one might have expected the estimated name-gap to be lower for the better addresses. Also, if the names mainly signal social background, one might have expected the name gap to be higher for jobs that rely more on soft skills or require more inter-personal interactions. We found no such evidence.

We however directly address this alternative interpretation by examining the average social background of babies born with the names used in the experiment. We were able to obtain birth certificate data on mother's education (less than high school, high school or more) for babies born in Massachusetts between 1970 and 1986.[31] For each first name in our experiment, we compute the fraction of babies with that name and in that gender-race cell whose mothers have at least completed a high-school degree.

We [examine] the average callback rate for each first name along with this proxy for social background. Within each race-gender group, the names are ranked by increasing callback rate. Interestingly, there is significant variation in callback rates by name. Of course, chance alone could produce such variation because of the rather small number of observations in each cell (about 200 for the female names and 70 for the male names).[32]

The row labeled "Average" contains the average fraction of mothers that have at least completed high school for the set of names listed in that gender-race group. The row labeled "Overall" contains the average fraction of mothers that have at least completed high school for the full sample of births in that gender-race group. For example, 83.9 percent of White female babies born between 1970 and 1986 have mothers with at least a high school degree; 91.7 percent of the White female babies with one of the names used in the experiment have mothers with at least a high school degree.

Consistent with a social background interpretation, the African American names we have chosen fall below the African American average. For African American male names, however, the gap between the experimental names and the population average is negligible. For White names, both the male and female names are above the population average.

But, more interestingly for us, there is substantial between-name heterogeneity in social background. African American babies named Kenya or Jamal are affiliated with much higher mothers' education than African American babies named Latonya or Leroy. Conversely, White babies named Carrie or Neil have lower social background than those named Emily or Geoffrey. This allows for a direct test of the social background hypothesis within our sample: are names associated with a worse social background discriminated against more? In the last row in each gender-race group, we report the rank-order correlation between callback rates and mother's education. The social background hypothesis predicts a positive correlation. Yet, for all four categories, we find the exact opposite. The p values indicate that we cannot reject independence at standard significance levels except in the case of African American males where we can almost reject it at the 10 percent level. In summary, this test suggests little evidence that social background drives the extent of discrimination.

Names might also influence our results through familiarity. It might be that these African American names simply appear odd to human resource managers and that any odd name faces discrimination. But as noted earlier, the names we have selected are not particularly uncommon among African Americans (see Appendix Table 1). We have also performed a similar exercise to that of Table 1 and measured the rank-order correlation between name-specific callback rates and name frequency for each gender-race group. We found no systematic positive correlation.

There is one final potential confound to our results. Perhaps what appears as discrimination is actually the result of *reverse discrimination*. If qualified African Americans are thought to be in high demand, then employers with average quality jobs might feel that an equally talented African American would never accept an offer from them and thereby never call her or him in for an interview. Such an argument might also explain why African Americans do not receive as strong of a return as Whites to better resumes, since higher qualification only strengthens this argument. But this interpretation would suggest that among the better jobs, we ought to see evidence of reverse, or at least less, discrimination. However, as we discussed [earlier], we do not find any such evidence. Discrimination does not vary across jobs with different skill requirements, nor does it vary across occupation categories. Even among the better jobs in our sample, we find quite a bit of discrimination against African American names.[33]

Relation to Existing Theories

What do the results in this paper imply for existing models of discrimination? Existing economic theories can be classified into two main categories: taste-based and statistical discrimination models. Both sets of models can obviously "explain" our average racial gap in callbacks by virtue of being discrimination models. But can these models explain our other findings? More specifically, we discuss the relevance of these models with a focus on two of these findings: (i) the lower returns to credentials for African Americans, and (ii) the relative uniformity of discrimination across occupations and job requirements and, to a lesser extent, industries.

Taste-based models differ in whose prejudiced "tastes" they emphasize: customers, co-workers or employers. Customer and co-worker discrimination models seem at odds with the lack of significant variation of the racial gap by occupation and industry categories, as the amount of customer contact and the fraction of White employees must vary across these categories. More precisely, we do not find more discrimination among jobs that explicitly require "communication skills" and jobs for which we expect either customer or co-worker contacts to be higher.

Because we do not know what drives employer tastes, employer discrimination models could be consistent with the lack of occupation and industry variation. Employer discrimination also matches the finding that Chicago employers located in more African American neighborhoods discriminate less. However, employer discrimination models would struggle to explain why African Americans get relatively lower returns to their credentials. Indeed, the cost of indulging the discrimination taste should increase as the minority applicants' credentials increase.[34]

Statistical discrimination models are the prominent alternative to the taste-based models in the economics literature. In one class of statistical discrimination models, employers use the observable race to proxy for *unobservable* skills (e.g. Phelps 1972, Arrow 1973). This class of models struggle to explain the credentials effect. Indeed, the added credentials should lead to a larger update for African Americans and hence greater returns to skills for that group.

A second class of statistical discrimination models "emphasize the precision of the information that employers have about individual productivity" (Altonji and Blank, 1999). Specifically, in these models, employers believe that the same observable signal is more precise for Whites than for African Americans (Aigner and Cain 1977, Lundberg and Startz 1983, Cornell and Welch 1996). Under these models, African Americans should receive lower returns to observable skills because employers place less weight on these skills. However, how reasonable is this interpretation for our experiment? First, it is important to note that we are using the same set of resume characteristics for both racial groups. So the lower precision of information for African Americans cannot be that, for example, an employer does not know what a high school degree from a very African American neighborhood means (as in Aigner and Cain (1977)). Second, many of the credentials on the resumes are in fact externally and easily verifiable, such as a certification for a specific software.

An alternative version of these models would rely on bias in the observable signal rather than differential variance or noise of these signals by race. Perhaps the skills of African Americans are discounted because affirmative action makes it easier for African Americans to get these skills. While this is plausible for credentials such as an employee of the month honor, it is less clear why this would apply to more verifiable and harder skills. It is equally unclear why work experience would be less rewarded since our study suggests that getting a job is prone to discrimination rather than reverse discrimination.

The uniformity of discrimination across occupation is also troubling for a statistical discrimination interpretation. Numerous factors that should affect the importance of statistical discrimination, such as the importance of unobservable skills, the observability of qualifications, the precision of observable skills and the ease of performance measurement, may vary quite a lot across occupations.

These facts suggest that perhaps other models may do a better job at explaining our findings. One simple alternative model is lexicographic search by employers. Employers receive so many resumes that they may use quick heuristics in reading these resumes. One such heuristic could be to simply read no further when they see an African American name. Thus they may never see the skills of African American candidates and this could explain why these skills are not rewarded. This might also to some extent explain the uniformity of discrimination since the screening process (i.e. looking through a large set of resumes) may be quite similar across the variety of jobs we examine.[35]

❂ Conclusion

This paper suggests that discrimination is an important factor in why African Americans do poorly in the labor market. Job applicants with African American names get far fewer callbacks for each resume they send out. Equally

Table 1
First Names Used in Experiment[α]

White Female		African American Female	
Name	Frequency	Name	Frequency
Allison	4.7%	Aisha	3.6%
Anne	5.0%	Ebony	4.3%
Carrie	3.5%	Keisha	3.7%
Emily	4.7%	Kenya	4.0%
Jill	4.2%	Latonya	4.7%
Laurie	4.0%	Lakisha	4.1%
Kristen	4.4%	Latoya	4.6%
Meredith	3.9%	Tamika	5.3%
Sarah	3.9%	Tanisha	4.2%
Fraction of all births: 3.8%		Fraction of all births: 7.1%	
White Female		**African American Female**	
Name	Frequency	Name	Frequency
Brad	1.3%	Darnell	0.9%
Brendan	1.3%	Hakim	1.1%
Geoffrey	1.2%	Jermaine	1.1%
Greg	1.0%	Kareem	1.3%
Brett	1.2%	Jamal	1.2%
Jay	1.4%	Leroy	1.3%
Matthew	1.4%	Rasheed	1.4%
Neil	1.6%	Tremayne	1.4%
Todd	1.4%	Tyrone	1.6%
Fraction of all births: 1.7%		Fraction of all births: 3.1%	

[α]Notes:
1. This table tabulates the different first names used in the experiment and the frequencies with which each of these names was used. Also reported for each race-sex category is the fraction of all births in that race-sex category with these first names (from Massachusetts birth certificates, 1974 to 1979).

importantly, applicants with African American names find it hard to fight discrimination in callbacks by improving their observable skills or credentials.

Taken at face value, our results on differential returns to skill have possibly important policy implications. They suggest that training programs alone may not be enough to alleviate the barriers raised by discrimination. For training to work, some general equilibrium force outside the context of our experiment would have to be at play. So, while a massive training program at the national level may change the structure of discrimination, small training programs may not work. In fact, if African Americans recognize how employers reward their skills, they may be rationally more reluctant than Whites to even participate in these programs.

Endnotes

[1] This camp often explains the poor performance of African Americans in terms of supply factors. If African Americans lack many basic skills entering the labor market, then they will perform worse, even with parity or favoritism in hiring.

[2] In creating the higher quality resumes, we deliberately made small changes in credentials so as to minimize the chance of over-qualification.

[3] For ease of exposition, we refer to the effects uncovered in this experiment as racial differences. Technically, however, these effects are about the racial soundingness of names. We briefly discuss the potential confounds between name and race below and more extensively later.

[4] These results contrast with the view, mostly based on non-experimental evidence, that African Americans receive higher returns to skills. For example, estimating earnings regressions on several decades of Census data, Heckman et al. (2001) show that African Americans experience higher returns to a high school degree than Whites.

[5] We also argue that a social class interpretation would find it hard to explain all of our results, such as why living a better neighborhood does not increase callback rates more for African American names than for White names.

[6] See Altonji and Blank (1999) for a detailed review of the existing literature on racial discrimination in the labor market.

[7] Darity and Mason (1998) describe an interesting non-experimental study. Prior to the Civil Rights Act of 1964, employment ads would explicitly state racial biases, providing a direct measure of discrimination. Of course, as Arrow (1998) mentions, discrimination was at that time "a fact too evident for detection."

[8] Fix and Turner (1998) provide a survey of many such audit studies.

[9]Earlier hiring audit studies include Newman (1978) and McIntyre et al (1980). Three more recent studies are Cross et al (1990), Turner et al (1991), James and Del-Castillo (1991). Altonji and Blank (1999), Heckman and Siegelman (1992) and Heckman (1998) summarize these studies. See also Neumark (1996) for a labor market audit study on sex discrimination.

[10]A similar "correspondence" technique has been used in a few U.K. studies. See Jowell and Precott-Clarke (1970), Brown and Gay (1985) and Hubbock and Carter (1980). These earlier studies have very limited sample size and focus exclusively on documenting gap in callbacks between the minority and non-minority groups. Some of these studies fail to fully match skills between minority and non-minority resumes, for example by imposing differential education background by racial origin.

[11]The sites are www.careerbuilder.com and www.americasjobbank.com.

[12]In practice, we found large variation in skill levels among people posting their resumes on these sites.

[13]We try as much as possible to match high schools and colleges on quality and demographic characteristics.

[14]Note that for applicants with schooling or work experience outside of the Boston or Chicago areas, we leave the school or employer name unchanged.

[15]We also generate a set of different fonts, layouts and cover letters to further differentiate the resumes. These are applied at the time the resumes are sent out.

[16]We chose name over other potential manipulations of race, such as affiliation with a minority group, because we felt such affiliations may especially convey more than race.

[17]For example, Maurice and Jerome are distinctively African American names in a frequency sense yet are not perceived as such by many people.

[18]We also tried to use more White sounding last names for White applicants and more African American sounding last names for African American applicants. The last names used for White applicants are: Baker, Kelly, McCarthy, Murphy, Murray, O'Brien, Ryan, Sullivan and Walsh. The last names used for African American applicants are: Jackson, Jones, Robinson, Washington and Williams.

[19]One might however wonder whether this is an atypical segment of the African American population. We discuss whether the race effect could be interpreted as a social class effect later.

[20]The e-mail addresses are registered on Yahoo.com, Angelfire.com or Hotmail.com.

[21]This period spans both tight and slack labor markets. In our data, this is apparent as call-back rates (and number of new ads) dropped precipitously after September 11th, 2001. Interestingly, however, the amount of discrimination we measure in these two periods is the same.

[22]In some instances, our resume bank does not have four resumes that are appropriate for a given ad. In such instances, we send only two resumes.

[23]Though the same names are repeatedly used in our experiment, we guarantee that no given ad receives multiple resumes with the same name.

[24]Male names were used for a few administrative jobs in the first month of the experiment.

[25]In the first month of the experiment, a few high quality resumes were sent without email address and a few low quality resumes were given email addresses..

[26]As part of the faxing process, we strip all identifiers from the outgoing fax to guarantee that employers could not see that all four faxes originate from the same locale.

[27]Very few employers used email to contact an applicant back.

[28]As Appendix Table 1 indicates, the African American names we use are however quite common among African Americans, making this less of a concern.

[29]In fact, there is some evidence that African Americans may rely *less* on social networks for their job search (Holzer, 1987).

[30]African Americans as a whole come from more disadvantaged backgrounds than Whites. For this social class effect to be something of independent interest, one must assert that African Americans with the African American names we have selected are from a lower social background than the average African American and/or that Whites with the White names we have selected are from a higher social background than the average White. We come back to this point below.

[31]This longer time span (compared to that used to assess name frequencies) was imposed on us for confidentiality reasons. When fewer than 10 births with education data available are recorded in a particular education-name cell, the exact number of births in that cell is not reported and we impute 5 births. Our results are not sensitive to this imputation. One African-American female name (Latonya) and two male names (Rasheed and Hakim) were imputed in this way. For one African American male name (Tremayne) we had too few births with education data at all and it is dropped from this analysis. Our results are qualitatively similar when we use a larger data set of California births for the years 1989 to 2000 (kindly provided to us by Steven Levitt).

[32]We formally tested whether this variation was significant by estimating a probit regression of the callback dummy on all the personal first names, allowing for clustering of the observations at the employment ad level. For all but African American females, we cannot reject the null hypothesis that all the first name effects in the same race-gender group are the same. Of course, a lack of a rejection does not mean there is no underlying pattern in the between-name variation in callbacks that might have been detectable with larger sample sizes.

[33]One might argue that employers who reverse discriminate hire through less formal channels than help-wanted ads. But this would imply that African Americans are less likely to find jobs through formal channels, which does not appear consistent with the existing evidence (Holzer, 1987).

[34]One could however assume that employer tastes differ not just by race but also by race and skill, so that employers have greater prejudice against minority workers with better credentials. But the opposite preferences, employers having a particular distaste for low-skilled African Americans, also seem reasonable.

[35]Another explanation could be based on employer stereotyping or categorizing. If employers have coarser stereotypes for African Americans, many of our results would follow. See Jones (2002) for the relevant psychology and Mullainathan (2002) for a formalization of categorization.

❂ ❂ ❂

Questions

1. Describe the different forms of discrimination discovered by the research.

2. Examine the prior research on discrimination reported by the authors. Assess how well the present study overcomes these problems.

3. List and explain the three main weaknesses of the study. Determine whether the study design overcomes these weaknesses.

4. Examine the list of names in Appendix Table 1. Locate friends, peers, acquaintances, or family members with similar names to those used in this research. Interview them about their name and any possible discrimination they may have experienced based on it. Summarize the findings of this study for them.

5. Predict whether these findings are applicable to other institutional settings such as education applications, film roles, or military promotions. What about your own children—have you or will you rethink a name for your newborn given these findings? Why or why not?

References

Aigner, Dennis J. and Glenn G. Cain, "Statistical Theories of Discrimination in Labor Markets," *Industrial and Labor Relations Review,* 1977, 30 (1): 175–187.

Altonji, Joseph G. and Rebecca M. Blank, "Race and Gender in the Labor Market," in Orley Ashenfelter and David Card eds, *Handbook of Labor Economics,* vol. 3, Elsevier Science B.V., 1999.

Arrow, Kenneth J., "What Has Economics to Say About Racial Discrimination?" *The Journal of Economic Perspectives,* 1998, 12 (2): 91–100.

Arrow, Kenneth J., "The Theory of Discrimination," in Orley Ashenfelter and Albert Rees, eds., *Discrimination in Labor Markets,* Princeton, NJ: Princeton University Press, 1973.

Becker, Gary S., *The Economics of Discrimination,* 2nd Edition, University of Chicago Press: Chicago, IL (1961).

Brown, C. and P. Gay, *Racial Discrimination 17 Years After the Act,* London, UK: Policy Studies Institute, 1985.

Council of Economic Advisers, *Changing America: Indicators of Social and Economic Well-Being by Race and Hispanic Origin,* September 1998. *http://w3.access.gpo.gov/eop/ca/pdfs/ca.pdf.*

Cornell Bradford and Ivo Welch, "Culture, Information and Screening Discrimination," *The Journal of Political Economy,* 1996, 104 (3): 542–571.

Cross, Harry, Genevieve Kenney, Jane Mell and Wendy Zimmermann, *Employer Hiring Practices: Differential Treatment of Hispanic and Anglo Job Applicants,* Washington, DC: Urban Institute Press, 1990.

Darity, William A. Jr. and Patrick L. Mason, "Evidence on Discrimination in Employment: Codes of Color, Codes of Gender," *The Journal of Economic Perspectives,* 1998, 12 (2): 63–90.

Fix, Michael and Margery Austin Turner (eds.), *A National Report Card on Discrimination in America: The Role of Testing,* 1998.

Goldin, Claudia and Cecilia Rouse, "Orchestrating Impartiality: The Impact of Blind Auditions on Female Musicians," *The American Economic Review,* 2000, 90 (4): 715–741.

Heckman, James J., "Detecting Discrimination," *The Journal of Economic Perspectives,* 1998, 12 (2): 101–116.

Heckman, James J. and Peter Siegelman, "The Urban Institute Audit Studies: Their Methods and Findings," in Michael Fix and Raymond J. Struyk, *Clear and Convincing Evidence: Measurement of Discrimination in America,* Lanham, MD: Urban Institute Press, 1992.

Heckman, James J., Lance J. Lochner and Petra E. Todd, "Fifty Years of Mincer Earnings Regressions," Mimeo, University of Chicago, Chicago, 2001.

Holzer, Harry J., "Informal Job Search and Black Youth Unemployment," *American Economic Review,* 1987, 77 (3): 446–452.

Hubbock, J. and S. Carter, *Half a Chance? A Report on Job Discrimination against Young Blacks in Nottingham,* London UK: Commission for Racial Equality, 1980.

James F. and S. W. DelCastillo, "Measuring Job Discrimination by Private Employers Against Young Black and Hispanic Seeking Entry Level Work in the Denver Metropolitan Area," Mimeo, University of Colorado at Denver, Denver, 1991.

Jones, Melinda, *Social Psychology of Prejudice,* Saddle River NJ: Pearson Education, 2002.

Jowell, R. and Prescott-Clark P., "Racial Discrimination and White-Collar Workers in Britain," *Race,* 1970, 11: 397–417.

Katz, Lawrence F. and Lawrence H. Summers, "Industry Rents: Evidence and Implications," *Brookings Papers on Economic Activity,* 1989: 209–275.

Lundberg, Shelly J. and Richard Startz, "Private Discrimination and Social Intervention in Competitive Labor Market," *The American Economic Review,* 1983, 73 (3): 340–347.

McIntyre, Shelby J., Dennis J. Moberg and Barry Z. Posner, "Discrimination in Recruitment: An Empirical Analysis: Comment," *Industrial and Labor Relations Review,* 1980, 33 (4): 543–547.

Mullainathan, Sendhil, "Thinking Through Categories," Mimeo, Massachusetts Institute of Technology, Cambridge, 2003.

Neumark, David, "Sex Discrimination in Restaurant Hiring: An Audit Study," *The Quarterly Journal of Economics,* 1996, 111 (3): 915–942.

Newman, Jerry M., "Discrimination in Recruitment: An Empirical Analysis," *Industrial and Labor Relations Review,* 1980, 32 (1): 15–23.

Phelps, Edmund S., "The Statistical Theory of Racism and Sexism," *The American Economic Review,* 1972, 62: 659–661.

Raphael, Steven, Michael A. Stoll and Harry J. Holzer, "Are Suburban Firms More Likely to Discriminate against African Americans?," *Journal of Urban Economics,* 2000, 48 (3): 485–508.

Turner, Margery A., Michael Fix and Raymond J. Struyk, *Opportunities Denied, Opportunities Diminished: Racial Discrimination in Hiring,* Washington, DC: Urban Institute Press, 1991.

Turner, Margery A., Raymond J. Struyk and J. Yinger, *Housing Discrimination Study Synthesis,* Washington DC: Urban Institute Press, 1991.

A Half Century of Class and Gender in American TV Domestic Sitcoms

RICHARD BUTSCH

Is there a pattern of persistent images in American TV sitcoms? Are The Honeymooners, The Flintstones, *and* The King of Queens *the same show with different faces? Using socioeconomic class and gender as a focus of analysis, Butsch gives a panoramic view of American television across five decades of domestic situation comedies and says, "Yes!" He compares and contrasts the wealth of imagery of social class in which men and women, adults and children are featured. He concludes that while stereotypes persist across time and space, there has been some variety added in—but it, too, suffers from stereotypic imagery.*

Over a half-century of television, domestic situation comedies have reinforced images of the middle class as better than the working class. Similar inequalities have been portrayed for men versus women, black versus white, old versus young, and for other status hierarchies. Already embedded in the larger culture, these stereotypes are used to signify character types that advance dramatic goals. Nevertheless, the pervasiveness of network television and the persistence over five decades have contributed immeasurably to reproducing these same stereotypes.

Women, for example, have been cast as main characters only where the subjects of romance or family are salient; they have been absent from rational discussions in scripts [Gerbner, 1972]. Women's presence thus signals certain themes. Similarly, traits culturally associated with a lower status, applied to a person of higher status devalues that person. Men are devalued by characterizing them as feminine. Such status inversion can then effectively con-

Reprinted by permission from *Cercles* 8, (2003).

firm other lower statuses held by the person. Female, black and lower-class adults have been devalued by characterizing them as child-like. Child-like attributions undercut their adult status, confirming their lower status as female, black or lower-class.

Scott (1988) has argued that class is symbolically coded in gender terms, so that gender becomes a means of establishing class status. That is, when a person has two contradictory status positions, such as black man or white woman, the higher status can be undercut to resolve the contradiction in favor of the lower status. De-masculinizing working-class men—i.e. applying descriptors which contradict the culturally accepted definition of masculine—devalues them not only as men but also uses gender to affirm their subordinate class status. Men may be de-masculinized by describing them as women or as boys, making them "feminine" or child-like [Baron, 1989].

This paper investigates how valuations of class on television have been constructed by manipulating gender and age traits. A wealth of studies document television images of women [Olson & Douglas, 1997; Steenland, 1995; Ferguson, 1990]; some have documented images of men [Hanke, 1990; Cantor, 1990; Craig, 1992]. An older research tradition has tabulated occupational frequencies [Smythe, 1954; DeFleur, 1964; Seggar & Wheeler, 1973, U.S. Commission on Civil Rights, 1977; Greenberg, 1980].

Few studies however have examined the pattern of images across many series and over several seasons, what we might call the historical tapestry of television culture. [Thomas, 1982; Lipsitz, 1986; Butsch, 1992]. Such analysis is needed to reveal persistent images. Character types which recur time and again over years have a special importance in the culture as stock images—the country bumpkin, the dizzy blonde—used to construct a culture's tales and even to type each other in everyday life [Klapp, 1962; Schutz, 1967]. Also few studies have examined the intersection of gender and class [Steeves & Smith, 1987]. Feminist scholars are finding this an important aspect of our cultural discourse [Ferguson, 1990]. Such analysis adds depth to our understanding of the traditional types in our culture's tales.

Butsch (1992) and Butsch & Glennon (1980, 1982, 1983) surveyed four decades of domestic situation comedies from the beginning of network television in 1946 to 1989 and found persistent patterns throughout. This paper extends the earlier work to the 1999–2000 season and emphasizes the gender-class intersection. It concentrates on how gender has been used to construct contrasting images of the working class and middle class.

☸ Persistent Cultural Types

The significance of imagery depends upon its pervasiveness and persistence. Pervasive and persistent images crystallize as cultural types and form the mainstream culture, the context within which exceptions, alternative and oppositional images, may appear and to which they must refer. Character types which recur across series and across time, and contrasts between types, which may only be evident when we look at the panorama of series taken together, are of especial importance.

The paper therefore focuses on the most pervasive medium, primetime television, and on that perennial prime time genre, the domestic situation comedy. Five decades of television families have provided a wealth of imagery of class in which men and women, adults and children are pictured in comparisons and contrasts. Literally hundreds of family series have been broadcast, different characters but repeated types and themes, an electronic tradition of oft-told tales. Domestic situation comedy series have been the mainstay of prime-time programming, and their format does not dictate any particular class. Occupation and thus the class portrayed is not an artifact of the genre as it is of police, lawyer or medical drama series. Domestic situation comedies are defined as half-hour prime-time nationally distributed series in which the main characters are members of a family and in which the major portion of action is among family members usually in the home. Excluded are series featuring singles, multiple families and households, and series not set in the twentieth century.

A list of all domestic situation comedy series was compiled from Brooks and Marsh (1999) and the annual *TV GUIDE Fall Preview* issues and each was categorized as portraying a working-class, middle-class, or upper-class family. The occupation of the head of household was used to distinguish middle from working-class families. If sources described the head as independently wealthy, that overrode occupation as the indicator of class. The occupational distinction between middle-class and working-class occupations is primarily that between mental and manual labor, an artificial—few occupations are strictly one or the other—but status-laden distinction woven through many American institutions [Braverman, 1974, 377–380]. This distinction is used to justify educational tracking, the organization of work and even class-based definitions of masculinity. Thus examining the imagery of class has broad implications for understanding our culture.

The most successful of these series—defined as those having five or more first-run seasons, the length preferred in the syndication market, or, for those series introduced less than five years ago, ranked in the top twenty of the annual Neilsen ratings—were selected from the list for further analysis of characterization. It is these series and characterizations which have become sedimented in the national culture and conversation, shows which most Americans know something about even if they haven't seen them. This analysis was based upon information gathered from viewing episodes, reading scripts at the Annenberg Library of the University of Pennsylvania, and descriptions of episodes in weekly *TV Guide* schedules as well as newspaper and magazine reviews of the programs.

Working-Class Scarcity, Middle-Class Affluence

While not absent, working-class families appeared infrequently through the four and half decades from the beginning of network broadcasts in 1946 to the 1989–1990 season. Of 262 domestic situation comedy series, only 4% featured a blue collar employee as head of house, including series which appeared only briefly before cancellation. Adding clerical and service workers, the numbers of working-class series still constituted only 14% of all series. In the 1990s, 16 additional working-class series appeared, albeit briefly, bringing the representation of the working class for the entire period 1946–2000 to 14% of 315 domestic situation comedies with heads of house portrayed as working-class, i.e. holding occupations as blue-collar, clerical or unskilled or semi-skilled service workers. Blue-collar families were most under-represented: only 8% (25 series) compared to 45% of actual American families in 1970 in the middle of the five decades.

There were three periods in which the numbers of new working-class series peaked: in the mid-1950s, in the early 1970s and in the late 1980s and the 1990s. Each of these peaks occurred during transitional periods for network television: the first during the initial years of television when networks were borrowing heavily from radio—*I Remember Mama* and *The Life of Riley* were radio shows before television—and exploring the potential of this new medium; the second in the early 1970s when Norman Lear produced *All in the Family, Good Times* and *Sanford and Sons* as part of CBS's effort to shift from an older rural audience to a younger urban audience in response to declining ratings with undesirable demographics; the most recent revival (*Roseanne, The Simpsons,* and several less successful series) has come at a time of intense competition from new networks, cable and internet. Working-class families, in other words, were given a try when "normal" fare wasn't established or sustaining ratings. But even in these peak years working-class shows remained a minority among domestic situation comedies.

By contrast, over two thirds (68%) of domestic situation comedy series presented middle-class families, representing the majority of series except almost every season. Middle-class families tended to be more than usually affluent and successful, further accenting the difference from working-class families. Glamorous, prestigious professions predominated over more mundane ones: e.g. 9 doctors to each nurse as a head of household, 4 professors to each school teacher, 10 lawyers to each accountant. And within a given profession characters were presented as great successes or young with much promise. Dick Van Dyke was a writer for a TV show; *Bachelor Father* was a lawyer living in Beverly Hills; *Life with Father* featured a Wall Street banker; *Halls of Ivy* an Ivy League president. The father of *Family Affair* was not just an engineer but president of his engineering firm. These shows pushed the upper limits of "middle-classness" without being described as independently wealthy.

Many television families had servants, another indicator of affluence. In shows introduced in the 1950s and 1960s it was common for a middle-class television family to have a maid or handyman. The high school principal father of *The Stu Erwin Show* employed a handyman. *Bachelor Father, Father of Bride, Hazel, Karen,* and *Green Acres* all featured lawyers with maid, houseboy or handyman. The new realism of the 1970s and 1980s muted some of this affluence. Servants in these decades appeared almost exclusively in wealthy families or as child-care in single-parent homes—although *The Brady Bunch* had a maid on an architect's income.

In the 1950s and 1960s working wives appeared not as indicators of economic necessity but as professional successes in their own right. The wives in *Mr. Adams and Eve, Peter Loves Mary,* and *Mona McClusky* were Broadway or movie stars. Jean Kerr, the nationally syndicated newspaper columnist, was portrayed as the wife in *Please Don't Eat the Daisies*. The wives in several series had given up careers to become housewives. Mary Tyler Moore played a wife in the *Dick Van Dyke Show* who had given up her career as a dancer. Mothers who were single parents were not shown struggling to make ends meet but typically pursuing successful and interesting careers: in *The Eve Arden Show* as an author and lecturer; in *The Doris Day Show* as a magazine reporter; in *The Partridge Family* as leading her family singing group.

Working wives or mothers appeared much more frequently in the 1980s and 1990s than in previous decades, but still often pursed successful careers.

Angela in *Who's the Boss* was an advertising executive, Claire Huxtable of *The Cosby Show* a lawyer, in *The Ellen Burstyn Show* a writer/college professor. In other words, the domestic situation comedy population has been persistently and overwhelmingly middle-class, predominantly successful professionals, with some managers, and a smattering of wealthy and manual workers. A fictional world in which success is so pervasive makes success the expected norm. When success is confined predominantly to the middle-class series, and failure to the working-class series, the failing working-class men are thereby labeled deviants and responsible for their own failure.

☺ *Working-Class Stereotypes*

Numbers indicate the scarcity of the working class. But they did appear. In fact, a remarkable percentage of blue collar series became television classics (*The Honeymooners, The Flintstones, All in the Family, The Simpsons*) and have created a vivid cultural type of the working-class man. That imagery persistently devalued the working-class male, as an inept bumbler and even a buffoon. Situation comedy is built around a humorous "situation" which is resolved during the half hour. In working-class series the character typically caught in the situation, usually of his own making, was the man. Usually his wife had to help him out of the situation. The devaluation of the working-class male operates primarily by inverting gender statuses in working-class series while sustaining them in middle-class series. Humor was built around some variant of working-class man's stereotypic ineptitude, immaturity, stupidity, lack of good sense or emotional outburst, traits that have been culturally defined as feminine or child-like. This character type of the urban working-class male has supplanted the country bumpkin in our panoply of cultural types. While television did not invent the type, it certainly has cemented its position in our culture.

The characterization is accentuated by contrasts to the wives and children in these working-class series, as well as by contrasts to the middle-class men in other series. Typically working-class wives and often the children were portrayed as more intelligent, rational, sensible, responsible, mature than their husbands. Mother, not father, typically knew best. The children were often smarter than their fathers and their successes contrasted to their fathers' failures. At best father was benign but inferior, at worst an embarrassment. The working-class man could not fulfill his "superior" status as adult male.

On the other hand in middle-class series the middle-class men fulfill their manly roles competently. They are typically intelligent, rational, mature and responsible as the culture expects a man to be and as the working-class wives are. The middle-class wives too are typically sensible, mature and responsible in their supportive roles as wives and mothers. Middle-class husband and wife formed a team of what Glennon and Butsch (1982) called super-parents. Occasionally a middle-class series was built around a fool as the source of humor. In these cases however, the fool was almost always the wife, some variant of the "dizzy blonde," rather than the husband. This devaluation is consistent with the lower status of women; it avoids undercutting the middle-class status of the family, which the culture defines in terms of the husband as head of house.

● The 1950s and 1960s

This formula was established for television in the 1950s, when these gender stereotypes were even stronger and more stark. Working-class male heads of house were consistently portrayed as dumb but lovable, i.e. they cared about their families but were bumbling, incompetent and often immature, not figures of respect, in contrast to their more sensible wives. Ralph Kramden of *The Honeymooners,* Chester Riley of *The Life of Riley,* and Lars Hansen of *I Remember Mama* were created in this mold.

Ralph Kramden was obsessed with success and modest affluence, at which he constantly schemed but invariably failed. He wanted to succeed as a husband by buying his wife, Alice the simple comforts, a television or a nicer apartment. He tried get-rich-quick schemes, such as marketing what he thought was Alice's homemade sauce, only to learn it was dog food. Alice always warned him, later quipped "I told you so," and Ralph was always repentant. He occasionally tried more conventional means such as applying for a promotion, or making a list of good and bad points for a self-improvement program—means Alice approved of, but which also got nowhere. Ralph's friend Ed Norton was true to the type as well, even dumber than Ralph whom he followed as a loyal sidekick.

Alice's logic and sarcasm invariably bested Ralph in arguments that typically ended by him saying, in angry frustration, "Just you wait Alice, one of these days, pow, right in the kisser." She recognized the foolishness of his schemes, and sometimes got him out of the messes he'd gotten them into. Chester A. Riley, the father in *The Life of Riley* was much like Ralph, without the tension and anger of *The Honeymooners.* Chester too was continually concocting schemes for his family. He attempted to fix a school election so his daughter would win, but succeeded only in embarrassing her. His incessant failures were expressed in his closing line for each episode, "What a revoltin' development this is!." Chester's friend and fellow worker, Gillis, was something of an exception to the type. Gillis was a self-assured, cocky wheeler-dealer who is continually explaining the ways of the world to Chester, often incorrectly. He once convinced Chester mistakenly that the company was planning to fire him, so that Chester considered quitting before he was fired. But Gillis' cockiness made him less attractive than the generous and well intentioned Chester. He was not bumbling, but not lovable either.

Chester's wife, Peg and the children all showed more sense than Chester. Peg was tolerant of Chester's fiascos and helped him—sometimes enlisting the children, teenager Babs and adolescent Junior, in the effort as well—to save face. The children were Chester's intellectual superiors. While Chester tripped over the English language, Junior headed for college. *I Remember Mama* was one of the few working-class series in which a working-class family was taken seriously. It was a sentimental reminiscence of family life in the 1910s. No one was the butt of humor. Yet Lars the father in this Norwegian immigrant family was an "earnest bumbler" in the words of the show's scriptwriter [Time, 1951]. Lars tried to discipline the children but frequently Mama had to conspire to help him save face. The children went to Mama for advice.

The only working-class domestic situation comedy of the 1960s, *The Flintstones* was a cartoon version of *The Life of Riley* and *The Honeymooners*. The anger and money problems of *The Honeymooners* were absent, but Fred Flintstone's loudmouth brashness is reminiscent of Ralph Kramden. Like Ralph, Fred was the leader and his friend, Barney the sidekick, although Barney was not as dumb as Ed Norton and more cautious. Fred's wife, Wilma exhibited much of the motherly tolerance of Fred's shenanigans as Peg did of Chester Riley's. When Fred persuaded Barney to play hookey from work to attend a ball game, Wilma and Barney's wife Betty caught them and for their punishment the "boys" had to take the wives to the opera. Typically Wilma was aware of Fred's surreptitious schemes from the beginning and provided both a safety net for him when he failed as well as a punishment, much as a mother would for a child. *The Flintstones* carried the inversion of adult and child status to an extreme.

❧ The 1970s

When *The Flintstones* left the air in 1966 no working-class family series appeared until *All in the Family* in January 1971. In the 1970s, Norman Lear and MTM Productions began to modify situation comedy [Feuer, 1987; Taylor, 1989], but nevertheless retained the essential qualities of these portrayals. Characters were less one-dimensional than during the 1950s and more mediating themes appeared. Norman Lear, who produced *All in the Family, Sanford and Son,* and *Good Times,* introduced real life problems such as money, racism and abortion that were non-existent in 1950s shows.

But the gender inversion of working-class males persisted. Archie of *All in the Family* and Fred Sanford of *Sanford and Son* were reminiscent of Ralph Kramden and Chester Riley; James of *Good Times* was more like Lars of *I Remember Mama.* In *All in the Family* producer Norman Lear intentionally created a character whose prejudices would be revealed as illogical and senseless. By making Archie a ridiculous figure, Lear hoped that viewers would see how stupid their own prejudices were and change their attitudes. Archie's malapropisms made him the butt of humor, just as Chester Riley's did in the 1950s. Archie also engaged in hair-brained schemes like Ralph Kramden's and Chester Riley's. Archie too was a well-intentioned, loving husband and father who simply was too inept to succeed.

Edith was not as evidently superior to Archie as the earlier wives were. She was much more hesitant in her criticism of Archie, and she only occasionally stood up to him. But she tried in her timid way to advise him against his hair-brained schemes. The foil for Archie was Mike, his son-in-law. Mike, while from a working-class Polish family clearly represented the middle class. He went to college and became a college instructor. Middle-class taste and values were embodied in him. He was the college liberal to Archie's silent majority; the high-brow to Archie's low-brow. In one episode Archie changed the television channel from a Beethoven concert which Mike was watching to midget wrestling. Mike's response was "You want to watch midgets? [. . .] What am I doing? I'm arguing culture with a man who buys a wallet and keeps the picture of Fay Wray in it." Mike was the spokesperson for the values Lear hoped to promote.

Sanford and Son was a black version of *All in the Family.* Widower Fred Sanford was as bigoted and ignorant as Archie. His foil was his son, Lamont. Like Mike of *All in the Family,* Lamont was oriented to improvement and middle-class manners. He was continually embarrassed by his father's blatant violations of middle-class decorum. *Good Times* was a black version of *I Remember Mama.* Like Mama, the mother Florida was the mainstay of the family. The father James was often unemployed and hot-tempered as well. James, like Lars of *I Remember Mama,* was not a buffoon but nevertheless unable to fulfill his role as breadwinner and father-figure which the children could look up to.

The role of fool fell to teenage J. J., the oldest son. J. J. was the one with endless get-rich-quick schemes. However, two things distinguished him from the working-class men. He was not a man but a teenager, and he was not a failure. He succeeded as a painter and was popular with girls. His success in fact contrasted to his father's inadequacies. Rather than a fool, he was an irreverent jokester; his irreverence became an attraction to some viewers in the 1970s. The other children, Thelma and Michael were model children headed out of poverty into the middle class. Thelma attended college and hoped to become a doctor. She broke off an engagement with an auto mechanic with whom she had little in common; the high brow entertainment she liked, he found boring. Michael was very bright and talked about as a future president.

❧ The 1980s

In the 1980s there was more variation in themes and character, yet the character types still persisted. While *Roseanne* modified the image, *The Simpsons* was an 1980s recreation of *The Flintstones* that continued to represent the working class through the 1990s, and *Married with Children* was a ruder version of *The Honeymooners*. Homer, the father in *The Simpsons,* barely brings home the bacon. The children's "college fund" has only $88.50 in it. They can't afford a new TV until Homer receives double his money back for guaranteed family therapy that fails to work for them. He causes a nuclear accident while waving to his son touring the nuclear power plant where he works. When he succeeds it is mostly in spite of himself.

The Simpsons repeats the tradition's negative contrasts between father and mother, father and children. Marge, the wife, reminiscent of Edith Bunker, is somewhat more levelheaded than Homer. The kids are embarrassingly smarter than their father. Second-grader Lisa betters her dad at Scrabble; Bart consistently beats him in a boxing video game. Both better him in arguments, with him resorting to shouting at the kids. *Married with Children* portrays a family of uniformly unlikable people. The show is a spoof of the typical TV family, excising the familial warmth that typified the middle-class series. The contrast is not between family members, but to the wholesomeness of other TV families. Gender is not inverted. Instead class is used directly, spoofing the affluent and successful middle class with a low income failure. The father Al Bundy, a shoe salesman, is dumb, but not lovable as in the traditional working-class type. The show is an endless stream of putdowns: Al's wife, Peg regularly complains of his lack of money and sexual inadequacy. Peg's friend describes him as having no skills and no brain. In one episode Al says life did not pass him by but sat on his head. Peg and her daughter Kelly are also depicted as dumb. Peg can't remember what channel her favorite TV show is on. Kelly does not know what it means when the neighbor calls her a simpleton. The son, Bud is the only one with any intelligence and he's an oversexed adolescent.

Family Matters features a black policeman as father, who typically bungles his efforts. He gets lost taking a shortcut, then gives the wrong directions to rescuers; he says all the wrong things when he tries to impress his boss. But he's not quite a buffoon and the children are respectful of him. In advising and discipline the parents are a team. Yet consistent with the tradition of working-class wives, Harriet the wife is the more sensible person in the family. An exception to the working-class character type is the father, Dan Conners of *Roseanne,* who is not merely well meaning and loving but also sensible. His children respect him. In one episode Dan is the voice of wisdom when he advises Roseanne not to engage in a power struggle with teenage Becky. Whereas Lisa and Bart Simpson are disappointed in Homer, the Conners' children listen with rapt attention to their parents' stories of the 1960s and are taken in by pranks the parents pull. Dan and Roseanne are content with their working-class manners. They could use more money, but they're not conflicted about behaving "properly" and don't aspire to cultural upward mobility.

❂ ℭhe 1990s

More working-class series appeared in the 1990s than in any other decade. Of 53 new domestic sitcoms from 1990 to 1999, 16 featured working-class families. Other shows for which the occupation is not blue collar or is not specified are set in working-class locales. The occupation of Hank of *King of the Hill* (1998) is unspecified, but the setting suggest a blue collar suburb. *The Torkelsons* appears working-class from the occupation of the single mother as a nanny, but the setting is not clear from descriptions. Eleven series featured black families, indicating another trend toward more representation of subordinate groups. None however achieved the classic level of *The Flintstones* or Archie Bunker. Even though relatively recent, their names are not memorable: *Dinosaurs, Roc, Thea, Joe's Life, Bless This House, That's Life, King of Queens, Costello, Jesse. Grace Under Fire* is the only one that lasted long enough to be classified as a hit.

Yet the working-class stereotypes persisted. The *Dinosaurs*'s father is a

Jurassic Archie Bunker. In *Joe's Life* the father is unemployed and takes care of the kids while the mom supports the family. The 1998 series, *King of Queens,* was called a Ralph Kramden remake, with a wife that was a little too bright. *Bless This House* (1995) featured a macho postal worker and feisty wife and also was described as *The Honeymooners* with kids. In 1991 *Roc* featured a not too bright black garbageman with a stereotypic macho attitude and a more educated nurse as wife. In *Grace Under Fire* (1993) the father was an unreliable drunken "good for nothing" who abandoned the family. In the new *Cosby* show (1996), the husband is an unemployed airport worker while his wife co-owns a flower shop and his daughter is a lawyer. *Costello* (1998) was criticized for its crude stereotypes of working-class men. Strong, working wives and mothers ran their families and in some shows, overshadowed their husbands. *Jesse, Thea* and *Grace,* among others, were single mothers who exhibited strength and good character that put their men to shame. Many 1990s shows featured dysfunctional families, but the more serious dysfunctions were blue collar. Alcoholism, spouse abuse, child abandonment or put up for adoption appeared in working-class shows like *Grace*. Divorce and quirky personalities were more typical of middle-class shows [James, 1995].

So, while there were more shows featuring working-class people in the 1990s, the men continued to be stereotyped as not too bright, immature, and contrasted to their more capable and responsible wives or adult female relatives. With few exceptions the working-class male leads were failures in their masculine role. They were portrayed with traits stereotypically applied to women or children. They were in other words de-masculinized. Undercutting their status as men in turn confirmed their lower status as working-class, and resolved the contradictory statuses of adult white male on the one hand and working-class on the other. *Plus a change, plus c'est la même chose.*

❧ Middle-Class: From Superdad to Several-Dad Types

The image of the working class contrasts sharply to television's middle-class families. There have been over thirty middle-class series which survived five or more seasons on prime time. There has been more variation of formula among these series than among the working-class series. However the majority reversed the pattern of working-class series. Middle-class fathers were rarely portrayed as buffoons. By characterizing them successfully fulfilling their roles as fathers and husbands gender confirmed class status. Status hierarchies remained intact. When a middle-class series rarely used the fool as a source of humor, it was usually the wife; the husband was the mature, sensible one. In most cases the middle-class fool of a wife did not get involved in crazy schemes, but simply was there to offer punch lines indicating how dumb and lacking in common sense she was.

But in many middle-class series the parents were a superb team. Both were intelligent, sensible and mature. They, especially the father, were calm and affable, in stark contrast to the hysteria which typified the slapstick comedy of the working-class series. In these series the situation was typically a problem involving one of the children. The parents, seldom perplexed, guide the child through a solution, providing a moral lesson along the way. The parents were calm and rational in the face of all problems. Childishness was confined to children. In the 1950s and 1960s the parents were invariably right and reasonable, almost serene as they watched amused with their children's antics and struggles. Like gods they descend to help. Through the 1970s and 1980s the parents became increasingly fallible, making mistakes, getting upset—but not to the hysterical degree of the working-class series. They allow their children to speak to them much more as equals than those in the earlier series. Yet they remain unflappable and ultimately retain their roles as guides and models to their children. They co-opt the high ground by admitting their mistakes and summarizing the moral lesson for their children, and the audience.

❧ The 1950s

While the classic working-class buffoon was being aired in the 1950s the middle class was represented by such successful series as *The George Burns and Grace Allen Show, The Stu Erwin Show, I Love Lucy, The Adventures of Ozzie and Harriet, The Danny Thomas Show, Father Knows Best, Leave it to Beaver* and *December Bride. Father Knows Best* is of course the archetype of its title, the completely self-assured and successful father, admired by his wife and children, the ideal of 1950s middle-class masculinity. Father Jim Anderson was always calm, reasonable, and ready with the answers. When the children forgot his birthday, his wife Margaret got upset. Jim, unfazed, admonished her for getting angry. This calm, rational unemotional approach in which the parent has all the answers is typical of these super-parents series.

The parents in *The Adventures of Ozzie and Harriet, The Danny Thomas Show* and *Leave it to Beaver* were similarly in charge. Ozzie Nelson, who wrote the scripts for *Ozzie and Harriet,* expressed his own concepts of family and childrearing in the show, portraying himself and Harriet as relaxed, but also making clear the morality that was expected [Joslyn & Pendleton, 1973]. Episodes depicted the boys learning, with their parents' guidance, to be respectful and considerate of others. The alternate title to *The Danny Thomas Show, Make Room for Daddy,* made clear who was important in this family. In *Leave it to Beaver,* the parents, while sometimes surprised by their little boy, had things well in hand.

I Love Lucy—and her various reincarnations, *Here's Lucy,* etc.—was the singular example of the woman as buffoon, with the husband as the mature, sensible and patient one. Lucy reversed the gender roles of *Riley* and *The Honeymooners.* Gracie Allen of *The Burns and Allen Show* was the prototype of the dizzy blonde, interjecting inane statements in her husband, George's conversation. In *December Bride* the mother-in-law played the scatterbrain. One of the rare exceptions to the rule, *The Stu Erwin Show* was a middle-class version of the bumbling father, a high school principal who couldn't do anything right at home. The show at one point was titled *Trouble with Father.* So, while the fool was a common character in these 1950s middle-class series, it usually was a woman.

◉ The 1960s

In the working-class vacuum of the 1960s the middle class reigned with *The Donna Reed Show, The Dick Van Dyke Show, Petticoat Junction, Bewitched, Green Acres, My Three Sons* and *Family Affair. The Donna Reed Show, My Three Sons* and *Family Affair* were classic super-parent series. In each the parents were calm and rational. Donna Reed was the 1960s equivalent to the super-parents on *Father Knows Best.* It was nicknamed "Mother Knows Best," but the father, a pediatrician, was not ineffectual; he merely let his wife take primary care of the children. The same traditional division of labor was a continuing theme in *My Three Sons,* the difficulty an all male household had with domestic matters. Steve, the widowed father, an engineer, however clearly is more than an adequate in helping his sons grow up, despite minor mishaps at home. His success as a man is further attested by a continual stream of women attracted to him while he is engrossed in his fatherly role. *Family Affair* revived the *Bachelor Father* formula, a prosperous bachelor who inherits children and becomes a devoted father. *The Dick Van Dyke Show* had no children, but it too reinforced traditional gender roles; the wife Laura typically asked the questions or posed the problem and husband Dick provided the answer.

Petticoat Junction and Green Acres were part of a rural nostalgia period of 1960s television. Both were set in the same rural town and shared characters. Petticoat Junction featured three teen-age daughters in feminine petticoats. Green Acres featured a stereotypic "dumb blonde" wife, ala Gracie Allen, opposite a successful husband who gave up his Manhattan law practice life to be a gentleman farmer. In Bewitched, Samantha, the wife was a competent witch often tempted to use her powers to get her way or help her husband's career, but wanted to abandon witchcraft to please her husband, Darrin. Darrin was sometimes befuddled by the supernatural shenanigans, but depicted as a competent advertising executive.

❂ The 1970s

When Archie Bunker and Fred Sanford expounded their wisdom for the 1970s the spokespersons for the middle class were The Brady Bunch, Happy Days, The Jeffersons, The Bob Newhart Show, Maude and One Day at a Time. All but One Day at a Time—a single mother with two teen-age girls who doesn't have all the answers—feature a husband. This was the one period when the proportions of domestic situation comedies featuring professional heads of house significantly dropped. The changed nature of situation comedy also is evident in these series, which exhibit a new irreverence toward professionals. Happy Days and The Brady Bunch followed tradition, but others diverged. The Bob Newhart Show featured a psychologist who hesitated, had self-doubts, and often was caught in his own words. His office mate, a dentist was a schemer; and his neighbor, Howard a divorced airplane pilot and a buffoon. Maude was an outspoken feminist woman whose demands continually exasperated her husband Walter. While Walter was a match for Maude, his friend Arthur, an MD was a bit of a buffoon. George Jefferson, the husband in The Jeffersons who owned a dry cleaning chain, had features of the classic working-class buffoon, loud mouth, endless schemes, although he was not portrayed as dumb—or lovable. His attitude is "explained" by the show in terms of his "background." He was only recently affluent and thus had not acquired the manners of the middle class. Not coincidentally he was black. In none of these series that deviated from the calm, competent middle-class man, however were there any young children to witness their limitations, as there were in several working-class series.

The *Brady Bunch* maintained the super-parent tradition of *Father Knows Best*. The parents, Mike and Carol had the answers to all of their children's questions. When vacationing at the Grand Canyon they explained the canyon and the traditions of the local Hopi tribe as if they were trained guides. They consistently approached problems calmly and rationally, even in an episode in which one of the children is lost. In another episode where the other children vote to exclude Peter, the middle boy from a singing group in hopes of a recording contract, mom calmly reasons why people are more important than money. In *Happy Days* the father, Howard Cunningham, was the reasonable and sensible father, while the mother, Marion, added a touch of the dizzy woman as contrast. Fonzie, a working-class rebel whom the kids admired and women found irresistible, typically supported the father's moral authority.

❧ The 1980s

The successful middle-class series of the 1980s represent a minor revival of the super-parent tradition: *Benson, Gimme a Break, Newhart, Family Ties, Kate & Allie, Who's the Boss, The Hogan Family, Cosby Show, Growing Pains, Wonder Years,* and *Empty Nest*. The classic middle-class father appears in *Cosby, Hogan, Family Ties, Growing Pains. The Cosby Show* is a throwback to the 1950s; while Heathcliff Huxtable jokes around with his children he also makes it clear who's the boss. *Growing Pains, Family Ties* and to a lesser degree, *The Hogan Family* feature more fallible parents. In one episode of *Growing Pains* the parents insist that their daughter plead guilty to a charge of resisting arrest to avoid a trial. The daughter says that's not honest and refuses. The judge respects her and let's her off. The parents however regain the high ground by approving her behavior and summarizing the lesson.

The operating theme of *Who's the Boss* is the gender reversal between Angela, the mother as the boss and Tony as the housekeeper. But, as the title suggests, Angela, the head of the house, is inadequate as the boss. Here we have a double message. Tony, portrayed as ethnic blue collar in origin, is a wiser parent and better housekeeper than the middle-class advertising executive, Angela. This class reversal however is veiled by a simultaneous gender reversal. Angela is a failure as housewife, while Tony succeeds. Even Harry of *Empty Nest,* who becomes flustered dealing with his own personal problems, still provides sound advice to his grown daughters.

While these fathers exhibit foibles and flaws absent in Jim Anderson, they are nonetheless fathers who know best. They dispense words of wisdom to help the children through the dilemmas of growing up. Other series diverge from tradition. The father in *Wonder Years,* Jack, whose occupation is unidentified but who wears a suit, tie and briefcase to work, is singularly uninvolved in his family. He's not a buffoon and he's not de-masculinized. He simply is tuned out; his advice to the kids is "do what your mother said." *Gimme a Break* and *Benson* present middle-class fathers who are bettered at parenting by their black servants. *Gimme a Break*'s widower is a competent police captain but ineffective father; his black maid bails him out when he gets himself into a domestic jam. Benson, who began as a black butler, regularly rescues his boss who is a buffoon as governor and father. Benson was successively was promoted to budget director, lieutenant governor and in the last episode was a candidate for governor.

❂ The 1990s

Unlike working-class characters of the 1990s who continued to be true to stereotype, middle-class series came in all forms and sizes. One show featured a fired soap opera actor ex-husband, another a con-artist who moves in with his successful lawyer sister, another a hyper party planner on her third husband, and another a suspended pro athlete moves in with his professor brother. There were four black middle-class families and one mixed race couple.

But there continued to be plenty of warm and fuzzy middle-class families, including shows with off-beat parents. *Harts of the Wests, Something Wilder, Tony Danza Show, Gregory Hines Show* featured wholesome families. The *American Dreamer* was a single father who gives up the big time as TV correspondent to move to a small town and quiet life to raise his kids. *7th Heaven* was a *Father Knows Best* revival. *Something So Right* was called the *Brady Bunch* with taboos; and *Cleghorne* was called a dysfunctional *Family Ties;* and *Parenthood* was likened to *Thirtysomething*. Some may have been quirky, sassy and a bit dysfunctional, but these families were still warm and comforting inside, with competent parents.

The biggest hits of the 1990s were all middle-class series, *Home Improvement, Mad About You,* and *Everybody Loves Raymond*. The men in these are not fathers who know best, but nor are they buffoons like those of working-class series. Tim of *Home Improvement* is star of his own successful TV show. At home, unlike the *Brady Bunch,* the focus is on the antics of the father rather than the children. But his antics involve his asserting his own independence and macho masculinity, rather than making a fool of himself. *Mad About You* is about the little annoyances and knots of relationships. It has been described as *Seinfeld* for young marrieds. Both partners are professionals with promising careers; both work together to sort out their differences; both are mature and intelligent adults. *Everybody Loves Raymond* is a little closer to the working-class form: Raymond's brother is a policeman, jealous of Raymond and his parents' exhibit some of the manners of a stereotypic ethnic New Yorkers. Raymond is a sportswriter, but clueless in dealing with his wife and helpless in confronting the interference of his parents. He is perennially perplexed about relationships. Yet clueless is not buffoon, and Raymond is professionally successful and is not bested by his children, as in many working-class series. So, while the 1990s has continued the trend to show middle-class people as imperfect and show a wide variety of types, the variety itself avoided the stereotyping in working-class series.

❧ Conclusion

While there have been variations and exceptions across five and half decades of television the stock character of the ineffectual, even buffoonish working-class man has persisted as the dominant image. In the prime-time tapestry he is contrasted to consistently-competent working-class wives and children and middle-class fathers, a composite image in which working-class men are de-masculinized and their gender status is inverted. The persistence of the working-class male stereotype is contrasted to the changes in depictions of middle-class families. While they too were stereotypically perfect in the 1950s and 1960s, from the 1970s on the depictions of middle-class progressively broadened to include a wide range of character types and situations, supplanting any stereotypic imagery with variety.

❧ ❧ ❧

Questions

1. Describe how class is coded in gender terms.

2. List specific information about the author's sample, procedures, and measures used to analyze the sitcoms.

3. Compare and contrast the characterizations of working class and middle class men? How has each changed across time?

4. Discuss how the 1990s working class characters differed from previous years.

5. Apply the historical analysis to newer shows not on the list such as *The Osbournes*. Does the argument hold up? Assess the role of cable television and lesser-known networks such as UPN and the WB that target market to audiences. Does the author's argument hold up?

◎ Bibliography

Baron, A. "Questions of Gender: Deskilling and De-masculinization in the U.S. Printing Industry, 1830–1915." *Gender and History* 1 (Summer 1989): 178–199.

Braverman, H. *Labor and Monopoly Capital*. New York: Monthly Review, 1974.

Brooks, T. & E. Marsh. *The Complete Directory to Prime Time Network TV Shows*. 7th edition. New York: Ballantine, 1999.

Butsch, R. & L. Glennon. "Families on TV: Where Was the Working Class?". *Televisions* 7, 2/3 (1980):11–12.

———. "Social Class: Frequency Trends in Domestic Situation Comedy, 1946–1978." *Journal of Broadcasting* 27 (Winter 1983): 77–81.

Cantor, M. "Popular Culture and the Portrayal of Women: Content and Control." In *Analyzing Gender: A Handbook of Social Science research*. Edited by Beth Hess & Myra Marx Ferree. Newbury Park, Ca: Sage, 1987, 190–215.

———. "Prime-Time Fathers: A Study In Change and Continuity." *Critical Studies in Mass Communication* 7 (1990): 275–285.

Craig, S., ed. *Mediated males: Men, Masculinity and the Media*. Beverly Hills: Sage, 1992.

Davis, N. "Women on Top." In *Society and Culture in Early Modern France*. Stanford: Stanford University Press, 1975, 124–151.

DeFleur, M. "Occupational Roles as Presented an Television." *Public Opinion Quarterly* 28 (Spring 1964): 57–74.

Ferguson, M. "Images of Power and the Feminine Fallacy." *Critical Studies in Mass Communication* 7 (September 1990): 215–230.

Feuer, J. "Genre Study and Television." In *Channels of Discourse*. Edited by R. C. Allen. Chapel Hill: University of North Carolina Press, 1987, 113–133.

"From the Old Country." *Time* (February 26, 1951): 86.

Gerbner, G. "Violence in Television Drama: Trends and Symbolic Functions." In *Television and Social Behavior*. Edited by George Comstock and Eli Rubinstein. Volume I. Washington, D.C.: U.S. Department of Health Education and Welfare, 1972, 28–187.

Glennon, L. & R. Butsch. "The Family as Portrayed on Television, 1946–1978." In *Television and Behavior: Ten Years of Scientific Progress and Implications for the Eighties*. Edited by D. Pearl, L. Bouthilet & J. Lazar. Volume II, Technical Reviews. Washington, D.C.: U.S. Department of Health and Human Services, 1982, 264–271.

Gray, H. "Television and the New Black Man: Black Male Images in Prime Time Situation Comedy." *Media Culture and Society* 8 (April 1986): 223–242.

Greenberg, B., K. Simmons, L. Hogan, & C. Atkin. "The Demography of Fictional TV Characters." In *Life on Television: Content Analyses of U.S. TV Drama*. Edited by B. Greenberg. Norwood, NJ: Ablex, 1980, 35–46.

Hall, S. & P. Whanel. *The Popular Arts*. London: Hutchinson, 1964.

Hanke, R. "Hegemonic Masculinity in *Thirtysomething*." *Critical Studies in Mass Communication* 7 (1990): 231–248.

Heilbron, L. *Domesticating Social Change: The Situation Comedy As Social History*. Ph.D. dissertation, University of California, Berkeley, 1986.

Horowitz, S. "Sitcom Domesticus: A Species Endangered by Social Change." In *Television: A Critical View*. Edited by H. Newcomb. 4th edition. New York: Oxford University Press, 1987, 106–111.

Joslyn, J. & J. Pendleton. "The Adventures of Ozzie and Harriet." *Journal of Popular Culture* 7, 1 (1973): 23–41.

Klapp, O. *Heroes, Villains and Fools*. Englewood Cliff, NJ: Prentice Hall, 1962.

Lipsitz, G. "The Meaning of Memory: Family, Class and Ethnicity in Early Network Television Programs." *Cultural Anthropology* 1, 4 (1986): 355–387.

Miller, M. C. "Deride and Conquer." In *Watching Television*. Edited by T. Gitlin. New York: Pantheon, 1986, 183–228.

Olson, B. & W. Douglas. "The Family on Television: Evaluation of Gender Roles in Situation Comedy." *Sex Roles* 36, 5–6 (March 1997): 409–427

Schutz, A. *The Phenomenology of the Social World*. Chicago: Northwestern University Press, 1967.

Scott, J. *Gender and the Politics of History*. New York: Columbia University Press, 1988.

Seggar, J. & P. Wheeler. "World of Work on TV." *Journal of Broadcasting* 17 (Spring 1973): 201–214.

Smythe, D. "Reality as Presented by Television." *Public Opinion Quarterly* 18 (Summer 1954):143–156.

Steenland, S. "Content Analysis of the Image of Women on Television." In *Women and Media: Content, Careers and Criticism.* Edited by C.M. Lont. Belmont CA: Wadsworth, 1995.

Taylor, E. *Prime Time Families.* Berkeley: University of California Press, 1989.

Thomas, S. & B. Callahan. "Allocating Happiness: TV Families and Social Class." *Journal of Communication* 32, 3 (1982):184–190.

Tuchman, G., A. Daniels & J. Benet. *Hearth and Home: Images of Women in the Mass Media.* New York: Oxford University Press, 1978.

U.S. Commission on Civil Rights. *Window Dressing on the Set.* Washington, DC: U.S. Government Printing Office, 1977.

Vidmar, N. & M. Rokeach. "Archie Bunker's Bigotry: A Study in Selective Perception and Exposure." *Journal of Communication* 24, 1(1974): 36–47.

The Saints and the Roughnecks

WILLIAM J. CHAMBLISS

*In this article, William Chambliss examines gang behavior in
two groups of high school boys, the Saints and the
Roughnecks. Though they engaged in similar behaviors,
including drinking, theft, and vandalism, these two groups
elicited different reactions from teachers and police. As you
read the article, pay attention to the attributes and characteristics of the individual gang members, as well as the overall
gangs themselves. Think about how these attributes might
explain the contrasting responses each gang experienced from
the surrounding community.*

*E*ight promising young men—children of good, stable, white
upper-middle-class families, active in school affairs, good pre-
college students—were some of the most delinquent boys at Hanibal
High School. While community residents and parents knew that
these boys occasionally sowed a few wild oats, they were totally
unaware that sowing wild oats completely occupied the daily routine
of these young men. The Saints were constantly occupied with truancy, drinking, wild driving, petty theft and vandalism. Yet not one
was officially arrested for any misdeed during the two years I
observed them.

This record was particularly surprising in light of my observations during the same two years of another gang of Hanibal High
School students, six lower-class white boys known as the

"The Saints and the Roughnecks," by William J. Chambliss, reprinted from *Society*,
Vol. 11, No. 1, November/December 1973. pp. 24–31.

Roughnecks. The Roughnecks were constantly in trouble with police and community even though their rate of delinquency was about equal with that of the Saints. What was the cause of this disparity? the result? The following consideration of activities, social class and community perceptions of both gangs may provide some answers.

❂ The Saints from Monday to Friday

The Saints' principal daily concern was with getting out of school as early as possible. The boys managed to get out of school with minimum danger that they would be accused of playing hookey through an elaborate procedure for obtaining "legitimate" release from class. The most common procedure was for one boy to obtain the release of another by fabricating a meeting of some committee, program or recognized club. Charles might raise his hand in his 9:00 chemistry class and asked to be excused—a euphemism for going to the bathroom. Charles would go to Ed's math class and inform the teacher that Ed was needed for a 9:30 rehearsal of the drama club play. The math teacher would recognize Ed and Charles as "good students" involved in numerous school activities and would permit Ed to leave at 9:30. Charles would return to his class, and Ed would go to Tom's English class to obtain his release. Tom would engineer Charles' escape. The strategy would continue until as many of the Saints as possible were freed. After a stealthy trip to the car (which had been parked in a strategic spot), the boys were off for a day of fun.

Over the two years I observed the Saints, this pattern was repeated nearly every day. There were variations on the theme, but in one form or another, the boys used this procedure for getting out of class and then off the school grounds. Rarely did all eight of the Saints manage to leave school at the same time. The average number avoiding school on the days I observed them was five.

Having escaped from the concrete corridors the boys usually went either to a pool hall on the other (lower-class) side of town or to a cafe in the suburbs. Both places were out of the way of people the boys were likely to know (family or school officials), and both provided a source of entertainment. The pool hall entertainment was the generally rough atmosphere, the occasional hustler, the sometimes drunk proprietor and, of course, the game of pool. The cafe's entertainment was provided by the owner. The boys would "accidentally" knock a glass on the floor or spill cola on the counter—not all the time, but enough to be sporting. They would also bend spoons, put salt in sugar bowls and generally tease whoever was working in the cafe. The owner had opened the cafe recently and was dependent on the boys' business which was, in fact, substantial since between the horsing around and the teasing they bought food and drinks.

◉ The Saints on Weekends

On weekends the automobile was even more critical than during the week, for on weekends the Saints went to Big Town—a large city with a population of over a million 25 miles from Hanibal. Every Friday and Saturday night most of the Saint would meet between 8:00 and 8:30 and would go into Big Town. Big Town activities included drinking heavily in taverns or nightclubs, driving drunkenly through the streets, and committing acts of vandalism and playing pranks.

By midnight on Fridays and Saturdays the Saints were usually thoroughly high, and one or two of them were often so drunk they had to be carried to the cars. Then the boys drove around town, calling obscenities to women and girls; occasionally trying (unsuccessfully so far as I could tell) to pick girls up; and driving recklessly through red lights and at high speeds with their lights out. Occasionally they played "chicken." One boy would climb out the back window of the car and across the roof to the driver's side of the car while the car was moving at high speed (between 40 and 50 miles an hour); then the driver would move over and the boy who had just crawled across the car roof would take the driver's seat.

Searching for "fair game" for a prank was the boys' principal activity after they left the tavern. The boys would drive alongside a foot patrolman and ask directions to some street. If the policeman leaned on the car in the course of answering the question, the driver would speed away, causing him to lose his balance. The Saints were careful to play this prank only in an area where they were not going to spend much time and where they could quickly disappear around a corner to avoid having their license plate number taken.

Construction sites and road repair areas were the special province of the Saints' mischief. A soon-to-be repaired hole in the road inevitably invited the Saints to remove lanterns and wooden barricades and put them in the car, leaving the hole unprotected. The boys would find a safe vantage point and wait for an unsuspecting motorist to drive into the hole. Often, though not always, the boys would go up to the motorist and commiserate with him about the dreadful way the city protected its citizenry.

Leaving the scene of the open hole and the motorist, the boys would then go searching for an appropriate place to erect the stolen barricade. An "appropriate place" was often a spot on a highway near a curve in the road where the barricade would not be seen by an oncoming motorist. They boys would wait to watch an unsuspecting motorist attempt to stop and (usually) crash into the wooden barricade. With saintly bearing the boys might offer help and understanding. . . .

Abandoned houses, especially if they were located in out-of-the-way places, were fair game for destruction and spontaneous vandalism. The boys would break windows, remove furniture to the yard and tear it apart, urinate on the walls and scrawl obscenities inside.

Through all the pranks, drinking and reckless driving the boys managed miraculously to avoid being stopped by police. Only twice in two years was I aware that they had been stopped by a Big City policeman. Once was for speeding (which they did every time they drove whether they were drunk or sober), and the driver managed to convince the policemen that it was simply an error. The second time they were stopped they had just left a nightclub and were walking through an alley. Aaron stopped to urinate and the boys began making obscene remarks. A foot patrolman came into the alley, lectured the boys and sent them home. Before the boys got to the car one began talking in a loud voice again. The policeman, who had followed them down the alley, arrested this boy for disturbing the peace and took him to the police station where the other Saints gathered. After paying a $5.00 fine, and with the assurance that they would be no permanent record of the arrest, the boy was released.

The boys had a spirit of frivolity and fun about their escapades. They did not view what they were engaged in as "delinquency," though it surely was by any reasonable definition of that word. They simply viewed themselves as having a little fun and who, they would ask, was really hurt by it? The answer had to be no one, although this fact remains one of the most difficult things to explain about the gang's behavior. Unlikely though it seems, in two years of drinking, driving, carousing and vandalism no one was seriously injured as a result of the Saints' activities.

◉ The Saints in School

The Saints were highly successful in school. The average grade for the group was "B," with two of the boys having close to a straight "A" average. Almost all of the boys were popular and many of them held offices in the school. One of the boys was vice-president of the student body one year. Six of the boys played on athletic teams.

At the end of their senior year, the student body selected ten seniors for special recognition as the "school wheels"; four of the ten were Saints. Teachers and school officials saw no problem with any of these boys and anticipated that they would all "make something of themselves."

How the boys managed to maintain this impression is surprising in view of their actual behavior while in school. Their technique for covering truancy was so successful that teachers did not even realize that the boys were absent from school much of the time. Occasionally, of course, the system would backfire and then the boy was on his own. A boy who was caught would be most contrite, would plead guilty and ask for mercy. He inevitably got the mercy he sought.

Cheating on examinations was rampant, even to the point of orally communicating answers to exams as well as looking at one another's papers. Since none of the group studied, and since they were primarily dependent on one another for help, it is surprising that grades were so high. Teachers contributed to the deception in their admitted inclination to give these boys (and presumably others like them) the benefit of the doubt. When asked how the boys did in school, and when pressed on specific examinations, teachers might admit that they were disappointed in John's performance, but would quickly add that they "knew that he was capable of doing better," so John was given a higher grade than he had actually earned. How often this happened is impossible to know. During the time that I observed the group, I never saw any of the boys take homework home. Teachers may have been "understanding" very regularly.

One exception to the gang's generally good performance was Jerry, who had a "C" average in his junior year, experienced disaster the next year and failed to graduate. Jerry had always been a little more nonchalant than the others about the liberties he took in school. Rather than wait for someone to come get him from class, he would offer his own excuse and leave. Although he probably did not miss any more classes than most of the others in the group, he did not take the requisite pains to cover his absences. Jerry was the only Saint whom I ever heard talk back to a teacher. Although teachers often called him a "cut up" or a "smart kid," they never referred to him as a troublemaker or as a kid headed for trouble. It seems likely, then, that Jerry's failure his senior year and his mediocre performance his junior year were consequences of his not playing the game the proper way (possibly because he was disturbed by his parents' divorce). His teachers regarded him as "immature" and not quite ready to get out of high school.

◉ The Police and the Saints

The local police saw the Saints as good boys who were among the leaders of the youth in the community. Rarely, the boys might be stopped in town for speeding or for running a stop sign. When this happened the boys were always polite, contrite and pled for mercy. As in school, they received the mercy they asked for. None ever received a ticket or was taken in to the precinct by the local police.

The situation in Big City, where the boys engaged in most of their delinquency, was only slightly different. The police there did not know the boys at all, although occasionally the boys were stopped by a patrolman. Once they were caught taking a lantern from a construction site. Another time they were stopped for running a stop sign, and on several occasions they were stopped for speeding. Their behavior was as before: contrite, polite and penitent. The urban police, like the local police, accepted their demeanor as sincere. More important, the urban police were convinced that these were good boys just out for a lark.

◉ The Roughnecks

Hanibal townspeople never perceived the Saints' high level of delinquency. The Saints were good boys who just went in for an occasional prank. After all, they were well dressed, well mannered and had nice cars. The Roughnecks were a different story. Although the two gangs of boys were the same age, and both groups engaged in an equal amount of wild-oat sowing, everyone agreed that the not-so-well-dressed, not-so-well-mannered, not-so-rich boys were heading for trouble. Townspeople would say, "You can see the gang members at the drugstore, night after night, leaning against the storefront (sometimes drunk) or slouching around inside buying cokes, reading magazines, and probably stealing old Mr. Wall blind. When they are outside and girls walk by, even respectable girls, theses boys make suggestive remarks. Sometimes their remarks are downright lewd."

From the community's viewpoint, the real indication that these kids were in for trouble was that they were constantly involved with the police. Some of them had been picked up for stealing, mostly small stuff, of course, "but still it's stealing small stuff that leads to big time crimes." "Too bad," people said. "Too bad that these boys couldn't behave like the other kids in town; stay out of trouble, be polite to adults, and look to their future."

The community's impression of the degree to which this group of six boys (ranging in age from 16 to 19) engaged in delinquency was somewhat distorted. In some ways the gang was more delinquent than the community thought; in other ways they were less.

The fighting activities of the group were fairly readily and accurately perceived by almost everyone. At least once a month, the boys would get into some sort of fight, although most fights were scraps between members of the group or involved only one member of the group and some peripheral hanger-on. Only three times in the period of observation did the group fight together: once against a gang from across town, once against two blacks and once against a group of boys from another school. For the first two fights the group went out "looking for trouble"—and they found it both times. The third fight followed a football game and began spontaneously with an argument on the football field between one of the Roughnecks and a member of the opposition's football team. . . .

More serious than fighting, had the community been aware of it, was theft. Although almost everyone was aware that the boys occasionally stole things, they did not realize the extent of the activity. Petty stealing was a frequent event for the Roughnecks. Sometimes they stole as a group and coordinated their efforts; other times they stole in pairs. Rarely did they steal alone.

The thefts ranged from very small things like paperback books, comics and ballpoint pens to expensive items like watches. The nature of the thefts varied from time to time. The gang would go through a period of systematically shoplifting items from automobiles or school lockers. Types of thievery varied with the whim of the gang. Some forms of thievery were more profitable than others, but all thefts were for profit, not just thrills.

Roughnecks siphoned gasoline from cars as often as they had access to an automobile, which was not very often. Unlike the Saints, who owned their own cars, the Roughnecks would have to borrow their parents' cars, an event which occurred only eight or nine times a year. The boys claimed to have stolen cars for joy rides from time to time. . . .

The Roughnecks, then, engaged mainly in three types of delinquency: theft, drinking and fighting. Although community members perceived that this gang of kids was delinquent, they mistakenly believed that their illegal activities were primarily drinking, fighting and being a nuisance by passersby. Drinking was limited among the gang members, although it did occur, and theft was much more prevalent than anyone realized. . . .

The community's perception of drinking as prevalent stemmed from the fact that it was the most obvious delinquency the boys engaged in. When one of the boys had been drinking, even a causal observer seeing him on the corner would suspect that he was high.

There was a high level of mutual distrust and dislike between the Roughnecks and the police. The boys felt very strongly that the police were unfair and corrupt. Some evidence existed that the boys were correct in their perception.

The main source of the boys' dislike for the police undoubtedly stemmed from the fact that the police would sporadically harass the group. From the standpoint of the boys, these acts of occasional enforcement of the law were whimsical and uncalled for. It made no sense to them, for example, that the police would come to the corner occasionally and threaten them with arrest for loitering when the night before the boys had been out siphoning gasoline from cars and the police had been nowhere in sight. To the boys, the police were stupid on the one hand, for not being where they should have been and catching the boys in a serious offense, and unfair on the other hand, for trumping up "loitering" charges against them.

From the viewpoint of the police, the situation was quite different. They knew, with all the confidence necessary to be a policeman, that these boys were engaged in criminal activities. They knew this partly from occasionally catching them, mostly from circumstantial evidence ("the boys were around when those tires were slashed"), and partly because the police shared the view of the community in general that this was a bad bunch of boys. The best the police could hope to do was to be sensitive to the fact that these boys were engaged in illegal acts and arrest them whenever there was some evidence that they had been involved. Whether or not the boys had in fact committed a particular act in a particular way was not especially important. The police had a broader view: their job was to stamp out these kids' crimes; the tactics were not as important as the end result.

Over the period that the group was under observation, each member was arrested at least once. Several of the boys were arrested a number of times and spent at least one night in jail. While most were never taken to court, two of the boys were sentenced to six months' incarceration in boys' schools.

● The Roughnecks in School

The Roughnecks' behavior in school was not particularly disruptive. During school hours they did not all hang around together, but tended instead to spend most of their time with one or two other members of the gang who were their special buddies. Although every member of the gang attempted to avoid school as much as possible, they were not particularly successful and most of them attended school with surprising regularity. They considered school a burden—something to be gotten through with a minimum of conflict. If they were "bugged" by a particular teacher, it could lead to trouble. One of the boys, Al, once threatened to beat up a teacher and, according to the other boys, the teacher hid under a desk to escape him.

Teachers saw the boys the way the general community did, as heading for trouble, as being uninterested in making something of themselves. Some were also seen as being incapable of meeting the academic standards of the school. Most of the teachers expressed concern for this group of boys and were willing to pass them despite poor performance, in the belief that failing them would only aggravate the problem.

The group of boys had a grade point average just slightly above "C." No one in the group failed either grade, and no one had better than a "C" average. They were very consistent in their achievement or, at least, the teachers were consistent in their perception of the boys' achievement.

Two of the boys were good football players. Herb was acknowledged to be the best player in the school and Jack was almost as good. Both boys were criticized for their failure to abide by training rules, for refusing to come to practice as often as they should, and for not playing their best during practice. What they lacked in sportsmanship they made up for in skill, apparently, and played every game no matter how poorly they had performed in practice or how many practice sessions they had missed.

◉ Two Questions

Why did the community, the school and the police react to the Saints as though they were good, upstanding, nondelinquent youths with bright futures but to the Roughnecks as though they were tough, young criminals who were headed for trouble? Why did the Roughnecks and the Saints in fact have quite different careers after high school—careers which, by and large, lived up to the expectations of the community?

The most obvious explanation for the differences in the community's and law enforcement agencies' reactions to the two gangs is that one group of boys was "more delinquent" than the other. Which group *was* more delinquent? The answer to this question will determine in part how we explain the differential responses to these groups by the members of the community and, particularly, by law enforcement and school officials.

In sheer number of illegal acts, the Saint were the more delinquent. They were truant from school for at least part of the day almost every day of the week. In addition, their drinking and vandalism occurred with surprising regularity. The Roughnecks, in contrast, engaged sporadically in delinquent episodes. While these episodes were frequent, they certainly did not occur on a daily or even a weekly basis.

The difference in frequency of offenses was probably caused by the Roughnecks' inability to obtain liquor and to manipulate legitimate excuses from school. Since the Roughnecks had less money than the Saints, and teachers carefully supervised their school activities, the Roughnecks' hearts may have been as black as the Saints', but their misdeeds were not nearly as frequent.

There are really no clear-cut criteria by which to measure qualitative differences in antisocial behavior. The most important dimension of the difference is generally referred to as the "seriousness" of the offenses.

If seriousness encompasses the relative economic costs of delinquent acts, then some assessment can be made. The Roughnecks probably stole an average of about $5.00 worth of goods a week. Some weeks the figure was considerably higher, but these times must be balanced against long periods when almost nothing was stolen.

The Saints were more continuously engaged in delinquency but their acts were not for the most part costly to property. Only their vandalism and occasional theft of gasoline would so qualify. Perhaps once or twice a month they would siphon a tankful of gas. The other costly items were street signs, construction lanterns and the like. All of these acts combined probably did not quite average $5.00 a week, partly because much of the stolen equipment was abandoned and presumably could be recovered. The difference in cost of stolen property between the two groups was trivial, but the Roughnecks probably had a slightly more expensive set of activities than did the Saints.

Another meaning of seriousness is the potential threat of physical harm to members of the community and to the boys themselves. The Roughnecks were more prone to physical violence; they not only welcomed an opportunity to fight; they went seeking it. In addition, they fought among themselves frequently. Although the fighting never included deadly weapons, it was still a menace, however, minor, to the physical safety of those involved.

The Saints never fought. They avoided physical conflict both inside and outside the group. At the same time, though, the Saints frequently endangered their own and other people's lives. They did so almost every time they drove a car, especially if they had been drinking. Sober, their driving was risky; under the influence of alcohol, it was horrendous. In addition, the Saints endangered the lives of others with their pranks. Street excavations left unmarked were a very serious hazard.

Evaluating the relative seriousness of the two gangs' activities is difficult. The community reacted as though the behavior of the Roughnecks was a problem, and they reacted as though the behavior of the Saint was not. But the members of the community were ignorant of the array of delinquent acts that characterized the Saints' behavior. Although concerned citizens were unaware of much of the Roughnecks' behavior as well, they were much better informed about the Roughnecks' involvement in delinquency than they were about the Saints".

◉ Visibility

Differential treatment of the two gangs resulted in part because one gang was infinitely more visible than the other. This differential visibility was a direct function of the economic standing of the families. The Saints had access to automobiles and were able to remove themselves from the sight of the community. In as routine a decision as to where to go to have a milkshake after school, the Saints stayed away from the mainstream of community life. Lacking transportation, the Roughnecks could not make it to the edge of town. The center of town was the only practical place for them to meet since their home were scattered throughout the town and any noncentral meeting place put an undue hardship on some members. Through necessity the Roughnecks congregated in a crowded area where everyone in the community passed frequently, including teachers and law enforcement officers They could easily see the Roughnecks hanging around the drugstore.

The Roughnecks, of course, made themselves even more visible by making remarks to passersby and by occasionally getting into fights on the corner. Meanwhile, just as regularly, the Saints were either at the cafe on one edge of town or in the pool hall at the other edge of town. Without any particular realization that they were making themselves inconspicuous, the Saints were able to hide their time-wasting. Not only were they removed from the mainstream of traffic, but they were almost always inside a building.

On their escapades the Saints were also relatively invisible, since they left Hanibal and travelled to Big City. Here, too, they were mobile, roaming the city, rarely going to the same area twice.

◉ Demeanor

To the notion of visibility must be added the difference in the responses of group members to outside intervention with their activities. If one of the Saints was confronted with an accusing policeman, even if he felt he was truly innocent of a wrongdoing, his demeanor was apologetic and penitent. A Roughneck's attitude was almost the polar opposite. When confronted with a threatening adult authority, even one who tried to be pleasant, the Roughneck's hostility and disdain were clearly observable. Sometimes he might attempt to put up a veneer of respect, but it was thin and was not accepted as sincere by the authority.

School was no different from the community at large. The Saints could manipulate the system by feigning compliance with the school norms. The availability of cars at school meant that once free from the immediate sight of the teacher, the boys could disappear rapidly. And this escape was well enough planned that no administrator or teacher was nearby when the boys left. A Roughneck who wished to escape for a few hours was in a bind. If it were possible to get free from class, downtown was still a mile away, and even if he arrived there, he was still very visible. Truancy for the Roughnecks meant almost certain detection, while the Saints enjoyed almost complete immunity from sanctions.

◎ Bias

Community members were not aware of the transgressions of the Saints. Even if the Saints had been less discreet, their favorite delinquencies would have been perceived as less serious than those of the Roughnecks.

In the eyes of the police and school officials, a boy who drinks in an alley and stands intoxicated on the street corner is committing a more serious offense than is a boy who drinks to inebriation in a nightclub or a tavern and drives around afterwards in a car. Similarly, a boy who steals a wallet from a store will be viewed as having committed a more serious offense than a boy who steals a lantern from a construction site.

Perceptual bias also operates with respect to the demeanor of the boys in the two groups when they are confronted by adults. It is not simply that adults dislike the posture affected by boys of the Roughneck ilk; more important is the conviction that the posture adopted by the Roughnecks is an indication of their devotion and commitment to deviance as a way of life. The posture becomes a cue, just as the type of the offense is a cue, to the degree to which the known transgressions are indicators of the youths' potential for other problems.

Visibility, demeanor and bias are surface variables which explain the day-to-day operations of the police. Why do these surface variables operate as they do? Why did the police choose to disregard the Saints' delinquencies while breathing down the backs of the Roughnecks?

The answer lies in the class structure of American society and the control of legal institutions by those at the top of the class structure. Obviously, no representative of the upper class drew up the operational chart for the police which led them to look in the ghettoes and on streetcorners—which led them to see the demeanor of lower-class youth as troublesome and that of upper-middle-class youth as tolerable. Rather, the procedure simply developed from experience—experience with irate and influential upper-middle-class parents insisting that their son's vandalism was simply a prank and his drunkenness only a momentary "sowing of wild oats"—experience with cooperative or indifferent, powerless, lower-class parents who acquiesced to the laws definition of their son's behavior.

❂ Adult Careers of the Saints and the Roughnecks

The community's confidence in the potential of the Saints and the Roughnecks apparently was justified. If anything, the community members underestimated the degree to which these youngster would turn out "good" or "bad."

Seven of the eight members of the Saint went on to college immediately after high school. Five of the boys graduated from college in four years. The sixth one finished college after two years in the army, and the seventh spent four years in the air force before returning to college and receiving a B.A. degree. Of these seven college graduates, three went on for advanced degrees. One finished law school and is now active in state politics, one finished medical school and is practicing near Hanibal, and one boy is now working for a Ph.D. The other four college graduates entered submanagerial, managerial or executive training positions with larger firms.

The only Saint who did not complete college was Jerry. Jerry had failed to graduate from high school with the other Saints. During his second senior year, after the other Saints had gone on to college, Jerry began to hang around with what several teachers described as a "rough crowd"—the gang that was heir apparent to the Roughnecks. At the end of his second senior year, when he did graduate from high school, Jerry took a job as a used-car salesman, got married and quickly had a child. Although he made several abortive attempts to go to college by attending night school, when I last saw him (ten years after high school) Jerry was unemployed and had been living on unemployment for almost a year. His wife worked as a waitress.

Some of the Roughnecks have lived up to community expectations. A number of them were headed for trouble. A few were not.

Jack and Herb were the athletes among the Roughnecks and their athletic prowess paid off handsomely. Both boys received unsolicited athletic scholarships to college. After Herb received his scholarship (near the end of his senior year), he apparently did an about-face. His demeanor became very similar to that of the Saints. Although he remained a member in good standing of the Roughnecks, he stopped participating in most activities and did not hang on the corner as often.

Jack did not change. If anything, he became more prone to fighting. He even made excuses for accepting the scholarship. He told the other gang members that the school had guaranteed him a "C" average if he would come to play football—an idea that seems far-fetched, even in this day of highly competitive recruiting.

During the summer after graduation from high school, Jack attempted suicide by jumping from a tall building. The jump would certainly have killed most people trying it, but Jack survived. He entered college in the fall and played four years of football. He and Herb graduated in four years, and both are teaching and coaching in high schools. They are married and have stable families. If anything, Jack appears to have a more prestigious position in the community than does Herb, though both are well respected and secure in their positions.

Two of the boys never finished high school. Tommy left at the end of his junior year and went to another state. That summer he was arrested and placed on probation on a manslaughter charge. Three years later he was arrested for murder; he pleaded guilty to second degree murder and is serving a 30-year sentence in the state penitentiary.

Al, the other boy who did not finish high school, also left the state in his senior year. He is serving a life sentence in a state penitentiary for first degree murder.

Wes is a small-time gambler. He finished high school and "bummed around." After several years he made contact with a bookmaker who employed him as a runner. Later he acquired his own area and has been working it ever since. His position among the bookmakers is almost identical to the position he had in the gang; he is always around but no one is really aware of him. He makes no trouble and he does not get into any. Steady, reliable, capable of keeping his mouth closed, he plays the game by the rules, even though the game is an illegal one.

That leaves only Ron. Some of his former friends reported that they had heard he was "driving a truck up north," but no one could provide any concrete information.

❂ Reinforcement

The community responded to the Roughnecks as boys in trouble, and the boys agreed with the perception. Their pattern of deviancy was reinforced, and breaking away from it became increasingly unlikely. Once the boys acquired an image of themselves as deviants, they elected new friends who affirmed that self-image. As that self-conception became more firmly entrenched, they also became willing to try new and more extreme deviances. With their growing alienation came freer expression of disrespect and hostility for representatives of the legitimate society. This disrespect increased the community's negativism, perpetuating the entire process of commitment to deviance. Lack of a commitment to deviance works the same way. In either case, the process will perpetuate itself unless some event (like a scholarship to college or a sudden failure) external to the established relationship intervenes. For two of the Roughnecks (Herb and Jack), receiving college athletic scholarships created new relations and culminated in a break with the established pattern of deviance. In the case of one of the Saints (Jerry), his parents' divorce and his failing to graduate from high school changed some of his other relations. Being held back in school for a year and losing his place among the Saints had sufficient impact on Jerry to alter his self-image and virtually to assure that he would not go on to college as his peers did. Although the experiments of life can rarely be reversed, it seems likely in view of the behavior of the other boys who did not enjoy this special treatment by the school that Jerry, too, would have "become something" had he graduated as anticipated. For Herb and Jack outside intervention worked to their advantage; for Jerry it was his undoing.

Selective perception and labelling—finding, processing and punishing some kinds of criminality and not others—means that visible, poor, nonmobile, outspoken, undiplomatic "tough" kids will be noticed, whether their actions are seriously delinquent or not. Other kids, who have established a reputation for being bright (even though underachieving), disciplined and involved in respectable activities, who are mobile and monied, will be invisible when they deviate from sanctioned activities. They'll sow their wild oats—perhaps even wider and thicker than their lower-class cohorts—but they won't be noticed. When it's time to leave adolescence most will follow the expected path, settling into the ways of the middle class, remembering fondly the delinquent but unnoticed fling of their youth. The Roughnecks and others like them may turn around, too. It is more likely that their noticeable deviance will have been so reinforced by police and community that their lives will be effectively channelled into careers consistent with their adolescent background.

◉ ◉ ◉

Questions

1. What role did affluence play in the responses of teachers and police to the Saints' and Roughnecks' behavior?

2. To what degree did the labels applied to these boys affect their later lives? How might you separate the effect of the label from the effect of social class?

3. To what degree did the Saints' mobility, as well as the visibility of their behavior, contribute to the treatment and labeling they received? How might teachers and police have responded differently to the two gangs if the only difference between them was socioeconomic status?

The Way We Weren't: The Myth and Reality of the "Traditional" Family

STEPHANIE COONTZ

Many politicians and religious leaders have urged a return to the "traditional" family. However, historian Stephanie Coontz argues that this supposed "traditional" family is actually mythological. In this article, she provides snapshots of family life from colonial to present times. By doing so, she reveals that none of these family structures protected people from inequalities based on race, class, gender, or interpersonal conflict.

. . .

◎ Colonial Families

American families always have been diverse, and the male breadwinner-female homemaker, nuclear ideal that most people associate with "the" traditional family has predominated for only a small portion of our history. In colonial America, several types of families coexisted or competed. Native American kinship systems subordinated the nuclear family to a much larger network of marital alliances and kin obligations, ensuring that no single family was forced to go it alone.

Wealthy settler families from Europe, by contrast, formed independent households that pulled in labor from poorer neighbors and relatives, building their extended family solidarities on the backs of truncated families among indentured servants, slaves, and the poor. Even wealthy families, though, often were disrupted by death; a majority of colonial Americans probably spent some time in a stepfamily. Meanwhile, African Americans, denied the legal protection of marriage and parenthood, built extensive kinship networks and obligations through fictive kin ties, ritual co-parenting or godparenting, adoption of orphans, and complex naming patterns designed to preserve family links across space and time.

The dominant family values of colonial days left no room for sentimentalizing childhood. Colonial mothers, for example, spent far less time doing child care than do modern working women, typically delegating this task to servants or older siblings. Among white families, patriarchal authority was so absolute that disobedience by wife or child was seen as a small form of treason, theoretically punishable by death, and family relations were based on power, not love.

◉ The Nineteenth-Century Family

With the emergence of a wage-labor system and a national market in the first third of the nineteenth century, white middle-class families became less patriarchal and more child-centered. The ideal of the male breadwinner and the nurturing mother now appeared. But the emergence of domesticity for middle-class women and children depended on its absence among the immigrant, working class, and African American women or children who worked as servants, grew the cotton, or toiled in the textile mills to free middle-class wives from the chores that had occupied their time previously.

Even in the minority of nineteenth-century families who could afford domesticity, though, emotional arrangements were quite different from nostalgic images of "traditional" families. Rigid insistence on separate spheres for men and women made male-female relations extremely stilted, so that women commonly turned to other women, not their husbands, for their most intimate relations. The idea that all of one's passionate feelings should go toward a member of the opposite sex was a twentieth-century invention—closely associated with the emergence of a mass consumer society and promulgated by the very film industry that "traditionalists" now blame for undermining such values.

❂ Early Twentieth-Century Families

Throughout the nineteenth century, at least as much divergence and disruption in the experience of family life existed as does today, even though divorce and unwed motherhood were less common. Indeed, couples who marry today have a better chance of celebrating a fortieth wedding anniversary than at any previous time in history. The life cycles of nineteenth-century youth (in job entry, completion of schooling, age at marriage, and establishment of separate residence) were far more diverse than they became in the early twentieth-century. At the turn of the century a higher proportion of people remained single for their entire lives than at any period since. Not until the 1920s did a bare majority of children come to live in a male breadwinner-female homemaker family, and even at the height of this family form in the 1950s, only 60% of American children spent their entire childhoods in such a family.

From about 1900 to the 1920s, the growth of mass production and emergence of a public policy aimed at establishing a family wage led to new ideas about family self-sufficiency, especially in the white middle class and a privileged sector of the working class. The resulting families lost their organic connection to intermediary units in society such as local shops, neighborhood work cultures and churches, ethnic associations, and mutual-aid organizations.

As families related more directly to the state, the market, and the mass media, they also developed a new cult of privacy, along with heightened expectations about the family's role in fostering individual fulfillment. New family values stressed the early independence of children and the romantic coupling of husband and wife, repudiating the intense same-sex ties and mother-infant bonding of earlier years as unhealthy. From this family we get the idea that women are sexual, that youth is attractive, and that marriage should be the center of our emotional fulfillment.

Even aside from its lack of relevance to the lives of most immigrants, Mexican Americans, African Americans, rural families, and the urban poor, big contradictions existed between image and reality in the middle-class family ideal of the early twentieth century. This is the period when many Americans first accepted the idea that the family should be sacred from outside intervention; yet the development of the private, self-sufficient family depended on state intervention in the economy, government regulation of parent-child relations, and state-directed destruction of class and community institutions that hindered the development of family privacy. Acceptance of a youth and leisure culture sanctioned early marriage and raised expectations about the quality of married life, but also introduced new tensions between the generations and new conflicts between husband and wife over what were adequate levels of financial and emotional support.

The nineteenth-century middle-class ideal of the family as a refuge from the world of work was surprisingly modest compared with emerging twentieth-century demands that the family provide a whole alternative world of satisfaction and intimacy to that of work and neighborhood. Where a family succeeded in doing so, people might find pleasures in the home never before imagined. But the new ideals also increased the possibilities for failure: America has had the highest divorce rate in the world since the turn of the century.

In the 1920s, these contradictions created a sense of foreboding about "the future of the family" that was every bit as widespread and intense as today's. Social scientists and popular commentators of the time hearkened back to the "good old days," bemoaning the sexual revolution, the fragility of nuclear family ties, the cult of youthful romance, the decline of respect for grandparents, and the threat of the

"New Woman." But such criticism was sidetracked by the stock-market crash, the Great Depression of the 1930s, and the advent of World War II.

Domestic violence escalated during the Depression, while murder rates were as high in the 1930s as in the 1980s. Divorce rates fell, but desertion increased and fertility plummeted. The war stimulated a marriage boom, but by the late 1940s one in every three marriages was ending in divorce.

☻ The 1950s Family

At the end of the 1940s, after the hardships of the Depression and war, many Americans revived the nuclear family ideals that had so disturbed commentators during the 1920s. The unprecedented post-war prosperity allowed young families to achieve consumer satisfactions and socioeconomic mobility that would have been inconceivable in earlier days. The 1950s family that resulted from these economic and cultural trends, however, was hardly "traditional." Indeed it is best seen as a historical aberration. For the first time in 100 years, divorce rates dropped, fertility soared, the gap between men's and women's job and educational prospects widened (making middle-class women more dependent on marriage), and the age of marriage fell—to the point that teenage birth rates were almost double what they are today.

Admirers of these very *nontraditional* 1950s family forms and values point out that household arrangements and gender roles were less diverse in the 1950s than today, and marriages more stable. But this was partly because diversity was ruthlessly suppressed and partly because economic and political support systems for socially-sanctioned families were far more generous than they are today. Real wages rose more in any single year of the 1950s than they did in the entire decade of the 1980s; the average thirty-year-old man could buy a median-priced home on 15 to 18% of his income. The government funded public investment, home ownership, and job creation at a rate more than triple that of the past two decades, while 40% of young men were eligible for veteran's benefits. Forming and maintaining families was far easier than it is today.

Yet the stability of these 1950s families did not guarantee good outcomes for their members. Even though most births occurred within wedlock, almost a third of American children lived in poverty during the 1950s, a higher figure than today. More than 50% of black married-couple families were poor. Women were often refused the right to serve on juries, sign contracts, take out credit cards in their own names, or establish legal residence. Wife-battering rates were low, but that was because wife-beating was seldom counted as a crime. Most victims of incest, such as Miss America of 1958, kept the secret of their fathers' abuse until the 1970s or 1980s, when the women's movement became powerful enough to offer them the support denied them in the 1950s.

❧ The Post-1950s Family

In the 1960s, the civil rights, antiwar, and women's liberation movements exposed the racial, economic, and sexual injustices that had been papered over by the Ozzie and Harriet images on television. Their activism made older kinds of public and private oppression unacceptable and helped create the incomplete, flawed, but much-needed reforms of the Great Society. Contrary to the big lie of the past decade that such programs caused our current family dilemmas, those antipoverty and social justice reforms helped overcome many of the family problems that prevailed in the 1950s.

In 1964, after 14 years of unrivaled family stability and economic prosperity, the poverty rate was still 19%; in 1969, after five years of civil rights activism, the rebirth of feminism, and the institution of nontraditional if relatively modest government welfare programs, it was down to 12%, a low that has not been seen again since the social welfare cutbacks began in the late 1970s. In 1965, 20% of American children still lived in poverty; within five years, that had fallen to 15%. Infant mortality was cut in half between 1965 and 1980. The gap in nutrition between low-income Americans and other

Americans narrowed significantly, as a direct result of food stamp and school lunch programs. In 1963, 20% of Americans living below the poverty line had *never* been examined by a physician; by 1970 this was true of only 8% of the poor.

Since 1973, however, real wages have been falling for most Americans. Attempts to counter this through tax revolts and spending freezes have led to drastic cutbacks in government investment programs. Corporations also spend far less on research and job creation than they did in the 1950s and 1960s, though the average compensation to executives has soared. The gap between rich and poor, according to the April 17, 1995, *New York Times,* is higher in the United States than in any other industrial nation.

☙ Family Stress

These inequities are not driven by changes in family forms, contrary to ideologues who persist in confusing correlations with causes; but they certainly exacerbate such changes, and they tend to bring out the worst in *all* families. The result has been an accumulation of stresses on families, alongside some important expansions of personal options. Working couples with children try to balance three full-time jobs, as employers and schools cling to policies that assume every employee has a "wife" at home to take care of family matters. Divorce and remarriage have allowed many adults and children to escape from toxic family environments, yet our lack of social support networks and failure to forge new values for sustaining intergenerational obligations have let many children fall through the cracks in the process.

Meanwhile, young people find it harder and harder to form or sustain families. According to an Associated Press report of April 25, 1995, the median income of men aged 25 to 34 fell by 26% between 1972 and 1994, while the proportion of such men with earnings below the poverty level for a family of four more than doubled to 32%. The figures are even worse for African American and Latino men. Poor individuals are twice as likely to divorce as more affluent ones, three to four times less likely to marry in the first place, and five to seven times more likely to have a child out of wedlock.

As conservatives insist, there is a moral crisis as well as an economic one in modern America: a pervasive sense of social alienation, new levels of violence, and a decreasing willingness to make sacrifices for others. But romanticizing "traditional" families and gender roles will not produce the changes in job structures, work policies, child care, medical practice, educational preparation, political discourse, and gender inequities that would permit families to develop moral and ethical systems relevant to 1990s realities.

America needs more than a revival of the narrow family obligations of the 1950s, whose (greatly exaggerated) protection for white, middle-class children was achieved only at tremendous cost to the women in those families and to all those who could not or would not aspire to the Ozzie and Harriet ideal. We need a concern for children that goes beyond the question of whether a mother is waiting with cookies when her kids come home from school. We need a moral language that allows us to address something besides people's sexual habits. We need to build values and social institutions that can reconcile people's needs for independence with their equally important rights to dependence, and surely we must reject older solutions that involved balancing these needs on the backs of women. We will not find our answers in nostalgia for a mythical "traditional family."

◉ ◉ ◉

Questions

1. Describe how children and childhood were perceived in colonial times. How does this perception compare to our view of children today? What changes in society caused us to change our perspective?

2. If you were a white female, in which historical period would you choose to live? Which historical period would you select if you were African American? Explain why you made these choices.

3. According to Coontz, what puts stress on families today? What can we do to relieve some of this stress?

4. Suppose that an editorial appearing in your local newspaper called for a return to the traditional family values of the 1950s as a way to save the family. Write a letter to the editor explaining why this plea is neither feasible nor desirable.

Final Note on a Case of Extreme Isolation

KINGSLEY DAVIS
Princeton University

Kingsley Davis's work is a classic examination of early social-ization and the effect of delayed human contact. In this piece, he briefly reviews the story of a girl named Anna, who was vir-tually isolated from all human contact and affection until she was six years old. Davis then compares Anna's life history and subsequent development to that of another young girl who experienced similar circumstances. Davis concludes that socialization can occur at various stages of the lifecourse, a finding that stands in stark contrast to a more traditional psy-chological explanation.

. . .

S arly in 1940 there appeared in this *Journal* an account of a girl called Anna.[1] She had been deprived of normal contact and had received a minimum of human care for almost the whole of her first six years of life. At that time observations were not complete and the report had a tentative character. Now, however, the girl is dead, and, with more information available,[2] it is possible to give a fuller and more definitive description of the case from a sociological point of view.

Anna's death, caused by hemorrhagic jaundice, occurred on August 6, 1942. Having been born on March 1 or 6,[3] 1932, she was approximately ten and a half years of age when she died. The previ-

---

"Final Note on a Case of Extreme Isolation," by Kingsley Davis, reprinted from *American Journal of Sociology*, vol. 52, 1947. pp. 432–447.

ous report covered her development up to the age of almost eight years; the present one recapitulates the earlier period on the basis of new evidence and then covers the last two and a half years of life.

❧ Early History

The first few days and weeks of Anna's life were complicated by frequent changes of domicile. It will be recalled that she was an illegitimate child, the second such child born to her mother, and that her grandfather, a widowed farmer in whose house her mother lived, strongly disapproved of this new evidence of the mother's indiscretion. This fact led to the baby's being shifted about.

Two weeks after being born in a nurse's private home, Anna was brought to the family farm, but the grandfather's antagonism was so great that she was shortly taken to the house of one of her mother's friends. At this time a local minister became interested in her and took her to his house with an idea of possible adoption. He decided against adoption, however, when he discovered that she had vaginitis. The infant was then taken to a children's home in the nearest large city. This agency found that at the age of only three weeks she was already in a miserable condition, being "terribly galled and otherwise in very bad shape." It did not regard her as a likely subject for adoption but took her in for a while anyway, hoping to benefit her. After Anna had spent nearly eight weeks in this place, the agency notified her mother to come to get her. The mother responded by sending a man and his wife to the children's home with a view to their adopting Anna, but they made such a poor impression on the agency that permission was refused. Later the mother came herself and took the child out of the home and then gave her to this couple. It was in the home of this pair that a social worker found the girl a short time thereafter. The social worker went to the mother's home and pleaded with Anna's grandfather to allow the mother to bring the child home. In spite of threats, he refused. The child, by then more than four months old, was taken to another children's home in a nearby town.

A medical examination at this time revealed that she had impetigo, vaginitis, umbilical hernia, and a skin rash.

Anna remained in this second children's home for nearly three weeks, at the end of which time she was transferred to a private foster home. Since, however, the grandfather would not, and the mother could not, pay for the child's care, she was finally taken back as a last resort to the grandfather's house (at the age of five and a half months). There she remained, kept on the second floor in an attic-like room because her mother hesitated to incur the grandfather's wrath by bringing her downstairs.

The mother, a sturdy woman weighing about 180 pounds, did a man's work on the farm. She engaged in heavy work such as milking cows and tending hogs and had little time for her children. Sometimes she went out at night, in which case Anna was left entirely without attention. Ordinarily, it seems, Anna received only enough care to keep her barely alive. She appears to have been seldom moved from one position to another. Her clothing and bedding were filthy. She apparently had no instruction, no friendly attention.

It is little wonder that, when finally found and removed from the room in the grandfather's house at the age of nearly six years, the child could not talk, walk, or do anything that showed intelligence. . . .

Anna's condition when found, and her subsequent improvement, have been described in the previous report. It now remains to say what happened to her after that.

❂ Later History

In 1939, nearly two years after being discovered, Anna had progressed, as previously reported, to the point where she could walk, understand simple commands, feed herself, achieve some neatness, remember people, etc. But she still did not speak, and though she was much more like a normal infant of something over one year of age in mentality, she was far from normal for her age.

On August 30, 1939, she was taken to a private home for retarded children, leaving the country home where she had been for more than a year and a half. In her new setting she made some further progress, but not a great deal. In a report of an examination made November 6 of the same year, the head of the institution pictured the child as follows:

> Anna walks about aimlessly, makes periodic rhythmic motions of her hands, and, at intervals, makes guttural and sucking noises. She regards her hands as if she had seen them for the first time. It was impossible to hold her attention for more than a few seconds at a time—not because of distraction due to external stimuli but because of her inability to concentrate. She ignored the task in hand to gaze vacantly about the room. Speech is entirely lacking. Numerous unsuccessful attempts have been made with her in the hope of developing initial sounds. I do not believe that this failure is due to negativism or deafness but that she is not sufficiently developed to accept speech at this time. . . . The prognosis is not favorable. . . .

More than five months later, on April 25, 1940, a clinical psychologist, the late Professor Francis N. Maxfield, examined Anna and reported the following: large for her age; hearing "entirely normal," vision apparently normal; able to climb stairs; speech in the "babbling stage" and "promise for developing intelligible speech later seems to be good." He said further that "on the Merrill-Palmer scale she made a mental score of 19 months. On the Vineland social maturity scale she made a score of 23 months."[4]

. . . Professor Maxwell gave it as his opinion at that time that Anna would eventually "attain an adult mental level of six or seven years."[5]

The school for retarded children, on July 1, 1941, reported that Anna had reached 46 inches in height and weighed 60 pounds. She could bounce and catch a ball and was said to conform to group socialization, though as a follower rather than a leader. Toilet habits were firmly established. Food habits were normal, except that she still used a spoon as her sole implement. She could dress herself except for fastening her clothes. Most remarkable of all, she had finally begun to develop speech. She was characterized as being at about the two-year level in this regard. She could call attendants by name and bring in one when she was asked to. She had few complete sentences to express her wants. The report concluded that there was nothing peculiar about her, except that she was feeble-minded—"probably congenital in type."[6]

A final report from the school, made on June 22, 1942, and evidently the last report before the girl's death, pictured only a slight advance over that given above. It said that Anna could follow directions, string beads, identify a few colors, build with blocks, and differentiate between attractive and unattractive pictures. She had a good sense of rhythm and loved a doll. She talked mainly in phrases but would repeat words and try to carry on a conversation. She was clean about clothing. She habitually washed her hands and brushed her teeth. She would try to help other children. She walked well and could run fairly well, though clumsily. Although easily excited, she had a pleasant disposition.

❧ Interpretation

Such was Anna's condition just before her death. It may seem as if she had not made much progress, but one must remember the condition in which she had been found. One must recall that she had no glimmering of speech, absolutely no ability to walk, no sense of gesture, not the least capacity to feed herself even when the food was put in front of her, and no comprehension of cleanliness. She was so apathetic that it was hard to tell whether or not she could hear. And all this at the age of nearly six years. Compared with this condition, her capacities at the time of her death seem striking indeed, though they do not amount to much more than a two-and-a-half-year mental level. One conclusion therefore seems safe, namely, that her isolation prevented a considerable amount of mental development that was undoubtedly part of her capacity. Just what her original capacity was, of course, is hard to say; but her development after her period of confinement (including the ability to walk and run, to play, dress, fit into a social situation, and, above all, to speak) shows that she had at least this much capacity—capacity that never could have been realized in her original condition of isolation.

A further question is this: What would she have been like if she had received a normal upbringing from the moment of birth? A definitive answer would have been impossible in any case, but even an approximate answer is made difficult by her early death. If one assumes, as was tentatively surmised in the previous report, that it is "almost impossible for any child to learn to speak, think, and act like a normal person after a long period of early isolation," it seems likely that Anna might have had a normal or near-normal capacity, genetically speaking. On the other hand, it was pointed out that Anna represented "a marginal case, [because] she was discovered before she had reached six years of age," an age "young enough to allow for some plasticity."[7] While admitting, then, that Anna's isolation *may* have been the major cause (and was certainly a minor cause) of her lack of rapid mental progress during the four and a half years following her rescue from neglect, it is necessary to entertain the hypothesis that she was congenitally deficient.

In connection with this hypothesis, one suggestive though by no means conclusive circumstance needs consideration, namely, the mentality of Anna's forebears. Information on this subject is easier to obtain, as one might guess, on the mother's than on the father's side. Anna's maternal grandmother, for example, is said to have been college educated and wished to have her children receive a good education, but her husband, Anna's stern grandfather, apparently a shrewd, hard-driving, calculating farmowner, was so penurious that her ambitions in this direction were thwarted. Under the circumstances her daughter (Anna's mother) managed, despite having to do hard work on the farm, to complete the eighth grade in a country school. Even so, however, the daughter was evidently not very smart. "A schoolmate of [Anna's mother] stated that she was retarded in school work;

was very gullible at this age; and that her morals even at this time were discussed by other students." Two tests administered to her on March 4, 1938, when she was thirty-two years of age, showed that she was mentally deficient. On the Stanford Revision of the Binet-Simon Scale her performance was equivalent to that of a child of eight years, giving her an I.Q. of 50 and indicating mental deficiency of "middle-grade moron type."[8]

As to the identity of Anna's father, the most persistent theory holds that he was an old man about seventy-four years of age at the time of the girl's birth. If he was the one, there is no indication of mental or other biological deficiency, whatever one may think of his morals. However, someone else may actually have been the father.

To sum up: Anna's heredity is the kind that *might* have given rise to innate mental deficiency, though not necessarily.

☺ Comparison with Another Case

Perhaps more to the point than speculations about Anna's ancestry would be a case for comparison. If a child could be discovered who had been isolated about the same length of time as Anna but had achieved a much quicker recovery and a greater mental development, it would be a stronger indication that Anna was deficient to start with.

Such a case does exist. It is the case of a girl found at about the same time as Anna and under strikingly similar circumstances. . . .

Born apparently one month later than Anna, the girl in question, who has been given the pseudonym Isabelle, was discovered in November, 1938, nine months after the discovery of Anna. At the time she was found she was approximately six and a half years of age. Like Anna, she was an illegitimate child and had been kept in seclusion for that reason. Her mother was a deaf-mute, having become so at the age of two, and it appears that she and Isabelle had spent most of their time together in a dark room shut off from the rest of the mother's family. As a result Isabelle had no chance to develop speech; when she communicated with her mother, it was by means of gestures. . . . Her behavior toward strangers, especially men, was almost that of a wild animal, manifesting much fear and hostility. In lieu of speech she made only a strange croaking sound. In many ways she acted like an infant. . . . At first it was even hard to tell whether or not she could hear, so unused were her senses. Many of her actions resembled those of deaf children.

It is small wonder that, once it was established that she could hear, specialists working with her believed her to be feeble-minded. . . .

In spite of this interpretation, the individuals in charge of Isabelle launched a systematic and skillful program of training. It seemed hopeless at first. The approach had to be through pantomime and dramatization, suitable to an infant. It required one week of intensive effort before she even made her first attempt to vocalization. Gradually she began to respond, however, and, after the first hurdles had at last been overcome, a curious thing happened. She went through the usual stages of learning characteristic of the years from one to six not only in proper succession but far more rapidly than normal. In a little over two months after her first vocalization she was putting sentences together. Nine months after that she could identify words and sentences on the printed page, could write well, could add to ten, and could retell a story after hearing it. Seven months beyond this point she had a vocabulary of 1,500–2,000 words and was asking complicated questions. Starting from an educational level of between one and three years (depending on what aspect one considers), she had reached a normal level by the time she was eight and a half years old. In short, she covered in two years the stages of learning that ordinarily require six. . . . [9]

When the writer saw Isabelle a year and a half after her discovery, she gave him the impression of being a very bright, cheerful, energetic little girl. She spoke well, walked and ran without trouble, and sang with gusto and accuracy. Today she is over fourteen years old and has passed the sixth grade in a public school. Her teachers say she participates in all school activities as normally as other children. . . .

Clearly the history of Isabelle's development is different from that of Anna's. In both cases there was an exceedingly low, or rather blank, intellectual level to begin with. In both cases it seemed that the girl might be congenitally feeble minded. In both a considerably higher level was reached later on. But the Ohio girl achieved a normal mentality within two years, whereas Anna was still marked inadequate at the end of four and a half years. This difference in achievement may suggest that Anna had less initial capacity. But an alternative hypothesis is possible.

One should remember that Anna never received the prolonged and expert attention that Isabelle received. The result of such attention, in the case of the Ohio girl, was to give her speech at an early stage, and her subsequent rapid development seems to have been a consequence of that. "Until Isabelle's speech and language development, she had all the characteristics of a feeble-minded child." Had Anna, who, from the standpoint of psychometric tests and early history, closely resembled this girl at the start, been given a mastery of speech at an earlier point by intensive training, her subsequent development might have been much more rapid. . . .

Consideration of Isabelle's case serves to show, as Anna's case does not clearly show, that isolation up to the age of six, with failure to acquire any form of speech and hence failure to grasp nearly the whole world of cultural meaning, does not preclude the subsequent acquisition of these. Indeed, there seems to be a process of accelerated recovery in which the child goes through the mental stages at a more rapid rate than would be the case in normal development. Just what would be the maximum age at which a person could remain isolated and still retain the capacity for full cultural acquisition is hard to say. Almost certainly it would not be as high as age fifteen; it might possibly be as low as age ten. Undoubtedly various individuals would differ considerably as to the exact age.

Anna's not an ideal case for showing the effects of extreme isolation, partly because she was possible deficient to begin with, partly because she did not receive the best training available, and partly because she did not live long enough. Nevertheless, her case is instructive when placed in the record with numerous cases of extreme isolation. This and the previous article about her are meant to place her in the record. It is to be hoped that other cases will be described in the scientific literature as they are discovered (as unfortunately they will be), for only in these rare cases of extreme isolation is it possible "to observe *concretely separated* two factors in the development of human personality which are always otherwise only analytically separated, the biogenic and the sociogenic factors."[10]

Endnotes

[1]Davis, K. (1940, January). Extreme social isolation of a child, *American Journal of Sociology, 45,* 554–565.

[2]Sincere appreciation is due to the officials in the Department of Welfare, Commonwealth of Pennsylvania, for their kind co-operation in making available the records concerning Anna and discussing the case frankly with the writer. . . .

[3]The records are not clear as to which day.

[4]Letter to one of the state officials in charge of the case.

[5]*Ibid.*

[6]Progress report of the school.

[7]Davis, *op. cit.,* p. 564.

[8]The facts set forth here as to Anna's ancestry are taken chiefly from a report of mental tests administered to Anna's mother by psychologists at a state hospital where she was taken for this purpose after the discovery of Anna's seclusion. This excellent report was not available to the writer when the previous paper on Anna was published.

[9]Mason, M. K. (1942). Learning to speak after six and one-half years of silence, *Journal of Speech Disorders, 7,* 295–304.

[10]Singh & Zingg, *op cit.,* pp. xxi–xxii, in a foreword by the writer.

Questions

1. How did the early experiences of the two young girls in the article differ prior to their discovery? How were they alike?

2. How did the two girls' experiences differ after their discovery? In other words, were there systematic differences in their training and education? If so, what were they, and how could these differences have affected the girls?

3. Anna had very little exposure to any human contact, while Isabelle likely had some contact with her mother, who was a deaf mute. To what degree could the developmental differences between Anna and Isabelle have stemmed from differences in mental ability? To what degree could these differences be explained by the varied contact that the girls had with other human beings?

Tattooing and Civilizing Processes: Body Modification as Self-control*

MICHAEL ATKINSON, McMaster University

Based on the results of his ethnographic research, Michael Atkinson claims that tattooing in Canada is a social paradox and an odd combination of cultural values about the body and its display. He further claims that tattoos allow the owners to modify their bodies as a means of "doing" social identity.

North America is experiencing what some call a second "tattoo renaissance" (DeMello, 2000). As part of this revolution in the popular cultural significance of tattooed flesh, tattooing is ascending to unprecedented levels of popularity among a vast array of social groups. Once a long-standing symbol of the North American underclass, this "body project" (Shilling, 1993) is now a floating signifier of a full panorama of social statuses, roles and identities. The tattoo is blossoming as a polysemic symbol of Canadian culture, and is actively inserted into the identity politics of a melange of actors. More so than in any previous era, tattoos are, as Hebdige (1979) might describe, "pregnant" with cultural significance.

Sociologists and other academics, however, almost invariably describe tattooing as cultural deviance (Atkinson, 2003a; DeMello, 2000; Copes and Forsyth, 1993; Irwin, 2000). Studies of tattooing

*This study was funded in part by the Social Sciences and Humanities Research Council of Canada. The author would like to think Marilyn Porter and the reviewers for their helpful comments on an earlier draft of this article. This manuscript was first submitted in May 2003 and accepted in March 2004. Contact: atkinsm@mcmaster.ca.

Reprinted from *Canadian Review of Sociology & Anthropology* 41, no. 2 (2004), by permission of Canadian Review of Sociology and Anthropology.

among the mentally challenged (Ceniceros, 1998; Measey, 1972), prisoners (Kent, 1997; Seaton, 1987), gang members (Rubin, 1988), and deviant youth subcultures (Atkinson, 2002), represent the tattoo as a badge of dislocated, ostracized, and disenfranchised communities. Apart from anthropological analyses of tattooing in Japanese, Melanesian, African, and Polynesian cultures (Gell, 1993; Kaplan and Dubro, 1986; Kitamura and Kitamura, 2001; Mascia-Lees and Sharpe, 1992), few social scientific studies portray tattooing as either rational or pro-social. Even comprehensive historical (Caplan, 2000; Gilbert, 2000) or ethnographic (DeMello, 2000; Irwin, 2000; Vail, 1999) analyses of the practice selectively link tattooed bodies to stigmatized populations. Tattooing is decoded as esoterically normative within the boundaries of historically marginal groups, as its profanity well represents group members' feelings of difference and exclusion. It is deciphered, in Cohen's (1955) terminology, as a deviant "collective solution" to sentiments of social inferiority.

While tattooing is by no means widely respected in Western cultures, its one-dimensional depiction as uncontested deviance is sociologically myopic (see DeMello, 1995; Fisher, 2002; Friedman, 1996; Gallick, 1996). A majority of empirical analyses of tattooing fail to consider how the body project symbolizes conformity to prevailing cultural body idiom, or expectations of affective control upheld throughout Western nations. Even fewer juxtapose the booming popularity of tattooing against cultural prescriptions to engage in a style of body work underpinned by the impetus to display one's "individualism" to others. Theorists regularly ignore whether tattooing may be a part of what White and Young (1997) refer to as the established "middle-class body ascetic," or what Monaghan (2001) describes as "vibrant physicality."

In this paper, the tattooing projects of selected Canadians are inspected as acts of compliance to "established" (Elias and Scotson, 1965) codes of bodily control and display. While tattooing is not the pinnacle of normative behaviour in Canada, the self-expressed meanings of Canadians' tattooing projects smack with compliance to a diffuse cultural imperative to engage in disciplined body work. Through a theoretical framework provided by figurational sociology (Elias, 1983; 1994; 1996), contemporary sensibilities about tattooed skin are interpreted as an extension of long-term civilizing processes.

◉ Theoretical Underpinnings

Mainstay social-psychological interpretations of tattooing revolve around a construction of tattoo enthusiasm as inherently pathological (Gittleson and Wallfn, 1973; Grumet, 1983; Houghton et al., 1996; Howell et al., 1971; Newman, 1982). Social psychologists typically contend that a tattooed body is the manifestation of a mind fraught with disorder. Furthermore, they suggest wearers cannot conform to dominant social norms, values and beliefs as a result of developmental or cognitive defect (see Williams, 1998). If we accept classic social psychological interpretations of tattooing offered by Gittleson et al. (1969), Goldstein (1979), Lombroso-Ferrero (1972), Measey (1972) and Pollak and McKenna (1945), tattooing predicts more serious deviance; as individuals who brutally mutilate their bodies in such a barbaric way cannot contain other "primitive" or contra-normative impulses.

In related medical and epidemiological research, tattooing is attributed to youth impetuousness and irrationality (Armstrong, 1994; 1995; Armstrong and McConnell, 1994; Armstrong and Pace-Murphy, 1997; Armstrong et al., 2000; Grief and Hewitt, 1998; Gurke and Armstrong, 1997; Houghton et al., 1996; Martin, 1997). Tattooing indicates immaturity among "at-risk youth" and is correlated with other forms of self-harm such as physical aggressiveness, promiscuity, substance abuse and suicide (Braithwaite et al., 2001; Korn, 1996; Roberts and Ryan, 2002). Accordingly, enthusiasts exhibit a paucity of foresight in their behaviours, prefer physical expression over cognitive or verbal, and demonstrate feelings of social inferiority through unhygienic and physically dangerous patterns of action (see Frederick and Bradley, 2000). To voluntarily inflict pain on one's body and mar the skin with everlasting symbols of impurity is described as overtly antisocial (see Gottfredson and Hirschi, 1990; Loimer and Werner, 1992). Such interpretations ring with Judeo-Christian understandings of the body as a sacred "home," and legitimate Western-scientific theories about tattoo enthusiasm prevalent since the turn of the 19th century (see Atkinson, 2003a).

Sociological analyses of tattooing produce a slightly broader spectrum of interpretation than psychological-medical. Yet despite Sanders' (1989) and DeMello's (2000) path-breaking analyses of tattooing as a contextual and negotiated signifier of identity, sociological statements on the cultural use of tattoos in North America ultimately (re)produce a conceptualization of the practice as contra-normative. The symbiotic relationship between tattooing and illegal behaviour (or otherwise unconventional lifestyles) still dominates in sociological research. Sociologists prefer to study the subversive subcultural uses of tattooing among groups such as prisoners (Kent, 1997; Seaton; 1987) and youth gangs (Govenar, 1988). Examinations of everyday life in tattoo studios equally "verify" the disreputable nature of North American tattooing cultures (Burchett and Leighton, 1958; McCabe, 1997; St. Clair and Govenar, 1981; Steward, 1990; Webb, 1979). Tattooing is deconstructed as a signifying practice that purposefully embraces and promulgates images of Otherness. It is postulated to be part of what Willis (1978) calls a "homology" of deviant style, that is, a set of complementary group practices coalescing around a shared set of outsider ideologies, activities and representational preferences.

With apparent irreverence to Klesse's (1999), Myers' (1997), Mifflin's (1997), Rosenblatt's (1997), and Atkinson's (2002; 2003a) claims that non-mainstream forms of body modification foster cultural bonds, few examine tattoos as pro-social markers. The nature of tattooing as a normative practice is rarely considered, because both the pathology of the act and actor is assumed. Reflective of this ongoing tradition of interpretation, there presently exists a giant schism between social scientific interpretations of tattooing and contemporary sensibilities about the act circulated by Canadian practitioners. The dominant manner of analysing tattoos in academic research may, however, be challenged by exploring several of the sensitizing principles of figurational sociology (Elias, 1994; 1996).

⊙ Method

Data utilized in this paper stem from a three-year, participant observation-based study of tattoo enthusiasm in Canada.[1] During the research, I spent three years "hanging out" (Willis, 1980) with tattoo artists and their clients in Calgary and Toronto. Through the research process, I interacted with hundreds of tattoo enthusiasts and eventually interviewed 92 of them. I met participants in a variety of social contexts, but first encountered a majority of them at tattoo studios in Calgary. Some of the enthusiasts were return patrons to the Calgary studios, while others were tattooing neophytes. I also met selected interviewees through friendship networks cultivated during the participant-observation phases of the research (i.e., during the first two years of field work). A smaller number of interviewees were students or friends of mine at a university in Canada (see Atkinson, 2003a).

The nature of my participation in tattooing considerably influenced the sampling process. As a person who immersed himself in a tattoo-enthusiast role and as a researcher who spent copious amounts of time hanging around with tattoo enthusiasts, I interacted with a substantial diversity of individuals during the field work process. At first, I interacted with a core group of enthusiasts in Calgary, but progressively "branched out" by hanging around with their tattooed friends in various social locales. By tactically "doing nothing" (Atkinson and Shaffir, 2003) with them in everyday life (i.e., going to restaurants, running routine errands, watching television, sitting in tattoo studios, or simply "shooting the breeze" over drinks), I casually inquired about their tattooing experiences, perspectives, and stories. In spending leisure time with tattoo enthusiasts, initial insights into the complex motivations for and meaning structures attributed to tattoo projects developed. The sampling process utilized in the research is therefore best described as a pastiche of convenience, snowball, and theoretical sampling.

The number of field interviews conducted in this research totalled 92, including 27 tattoo artists and 65 clients. The average age of the artists interviewed is 25, with an overall range in age from 20 to 55. While men and women are more or less equally represented among tattoo enthusiasts in Canada (Atkinson, 2003a; Atkinson and Young, 2001), only four (15%) of the artists I interviewed in this study are women. Eighteen (67%) of the artists have working-class family backgrounds and nine (33%) have middle-class family backgrounds, as measured by Blishen's (1967) socio-economic index. Twenty of the artists have completed a high-school degree (74%), and four (15%) have received either a post-secondary degree or at least one year of college/university education. All of the artists interviewed are White, with the exception of one Asian-Canadian artist. Twenty of the artists (74%) are single, while three have spouses (11%) and four are divorced (15%). Two (7%) of the artists have one child, and three (11%) of the artists have two children. The income of the artists interviewed in this study averages from $500–$3,000 per week. The artists have a range of professional experience/employment in the business of tattooing from eight months to 35 years, with an average of six years. Each of the artists has tattoos varying in size, location and in the amount of the body surface covered by the work.

Comparatively, the average age of the clients interviewed is 24, with an overall range in age from 18 to 50. Forty of the clients (62%) are women and 25 (38%) are men. Sixteen (25%) of the clients interviewed have working-class backgrounds, with 41 (63%) located in the middle class, and eight in the upper class (12%). Of all the clients interviewed, 51 (78%) have some form of employment, with an average group income of approximately CAD$24,000. Clients in the sample are more educated than artists, with 42 (64%) of them holding a post-secondary degree or at least one year of university education. Fifty-three (82%) of the clients interviewed are White, eight (12%) Asian-Canadian, and four (6%) Afro-Canadian. Forty-nine (75%) are single, 13 (20%) have a spouse/partner and three (5%) are divorced. Twelve (18%) of the clients have children: five have one child, three have two children, and four have three or more children.

A majority of the clients, 41 (63%), had one tattoo at the time of the interview. Seven (11%) clients have two tattoos, two of the clients (3%) have three tattoos, and 15 clients (23%) have three or more tattoos. Clients' experience with tattooing is varied, with the age of entry into the practice ranging from 14 to 48 (with a mean of 22). Fifty-six (86%) of the clients received their first tattoo in either Calgary or Toronto (including nine different studios in Calgary and six different studios in Toronto). Other Canadian cities in which individuals experienced tattooing include Vancouver (B.C.), Victoria (B.C.), Edmonton (Alta.), Lethbridge (Alta.), Regina (Sask.), Winnipeg (Man.), Windsor (Ont.), Kitchener-Waterloo (Ont.), London (Ont.), Montreal (Que.), Quebec City (Que.), Charlottetown (P.E.I.), Halifax (N.S.), and St. John's (N.L.).

I conducted field interviews in a variety of settings, such as my office at the university, coffee shops, pool halls, local restaurants or tattoo studios. In all but a few instances, I avoided using a tape recorder in the sessions. Instead, I created field notes both during and after the interviews and subsequently entered them into computer files. Interviews ranged in length from 45 minutes to four hours. In all cases, pseudonyms are used to protect the participants' identities.

The interview strategy adopted in this research closely followed the prescriptions for open-ended interviewing as outlined by Lofland and Lofland (1995) and Prus (1996), but incorporated Gubrium and Holstein's (1997) suggestions for exploring "layered" narratives through an "active interviewing" process. I required an interview strategy that would elicit free-ranging responses from people about their experiences with tattooing, including, of course, whether they view tattooing as deviant, different, rebellious or risk-taking. As a result, the interviews became narrative explorations of how people decide to become tattooed, experience tattooing, and rely upon a series of "interpretive resources" (Gubrium and Holstein, 1997) when telling stories about their tattoos.

As an elicitation technique, I often introduced academic interpretations of tattooing into the interviews. Academic constructions of tattoos sparked concern and frustration among enthusiasts because they feel academics grossly misinterpret the cultural relevance of tattoos in North America. Individuals, feeling particularly eager to address problems of academic interpretation, adopted a teacher's role and lectured me at great length about the tattooing process. Interviews evolved into collaborative sessions addressing the ascendance of the body project in Canada and the interpretive vantage points from which people give meaning to tattoos. Exploring what Ronai (1992) refers to as "multi-layered accounts" of social experience, I subsequently inspected how people assign social meaning to their tattoos and how motivations for, experiences with, and constructions of tattooing are intersubjectively defined. Needless to say, the bulk of social scientific interpretations of tattooing resembled little of what I learned through field work with enthusiasts.

◉ Tattooing and the "Civilized" Habitus

Ethnographic data collected on Canadian tattoo enthusiasm in this study suggest that tattooing is routinely undertaken as: *i) a rational form of identity expression; and ii) a conservative gesture of conformity to dominant norms of self-restraint.* Viewed from this perspective, the tattooed body is both a marker of social position in Canada and a symbol of "civilized" individuality therein.[2] Without interrogating the complex relation between the tattoo's status as both, we overlook how the tattooing process may jibe with and homologically fit into "established" (Elias and Scotson, 1965) cultural ideas about communicating the self through avant-garde and individualistic body work. While researchers have laboured to inspect the highly "individualistic" motivations (i.e., psychologically pathological) buttressing tattoo projects (see DeMello, 2000; Steward, 1990), few interpret how one's sense of individualism is a product of cultural membership and position. Divorcing the tattooed body from larger cultural contexts within which it is situated and defined obscures how pervasive body habits may influence personal preferences for tattooing.

Figurational sociologists, for example, argue that body projects like tattooing cannot be understood outside of the "figurations" within which they are produced (Atkinson, 2003a). A "figuration" is a complex matrix of social relationships based on far-ranging individual and group interdependencies that interconnect family, school, workplace, leisure, religious and political spheres. Elias's concept of the figuration is based upon a rather simple idea that individuals are mutually bound to one another through extended networks or "chains" of action:

> The network of interdependencies among human beings is what binds them together. Such interdependencies are the nexus of what is here called the figuration, a structure of mutually oriented and dependent people. Since people are more or less dependent on each other, first by nature and then by social learning, through education, socialization, and socially generated reciprocal needs, they exist, one might venture to say, only as pluralities, only in figurations (1994, p. 214).

Through social interaction processes within figurations, common cultural ways of thinking, or "habituses," are formed (Elias, 1996). A habitus is internalized through socialization processes and becomes a socially learned "second nature" of behaviour (Elias 1983; 1996).

By attending to enthusiasts' tattooing narratives we realize how the practice is a *learned cultural habit* that is dialogical with, and not irreverent to, diffuse body norms within a figuration. As tattoo enthusiast Matthew (22) suggests, "I never thought about getting tattooed until I started hanging around with a lot of people who had them, you know." Modifying the body as a normative act is learned through and reinforced by one's interdependencies with others. As such, we must examine the conditions of social interdependence giving rise to tattooing habits and the character of broader body modification norms "framing" (Goffman, 1974) cultural understandings of tattooing.

Rational Identity Expression

At a very basic level, tattooing projects reinforce and reflect "I-WE" figurational relationships (Elias, 1978; 1991). Tattooing the body represents one's sense of "I" within social circles; starting with quite intimate and mutually identified "WE" groups (e.g., family, friends, peers, or social club members) and extending to WE groups bound by lengthy chains of interdependency (e.g., social classes, religious groups, or fellow lifestyle participants). Carl's (23) words about the multi-WE group significance of his first tattoo help to clarify:

> I can't say my first tattoo represents just this *or* that wherever I go. Of course, as we talked about, I got it right after I graduated [to symbolise the accomplishment]. . . . In a way, I did it to show mom and dad how their faith in me helped me persevere and graduate. Because it is a cross, it also tells Christians I am committed to our religion. . . . And, it looks very masculine in the way it frames the outside of my deltoid.

Carl expresses how his tattoo at once signifies an identity shift to university graduate, his relationship with his parents, identification with other Christians, and understanding of dominant codes of masculinity. Carl begins by describing his tattoo's primary significance as an expression of bonding with his parents, but then articulates how the tattoo's meaning represents other cultural groups and practices. Previous research on tattooing attests to how tattoos mark intimate WE-group perspectives about and experiences with body modification (DeMello, 2000; Sanders, 1989), but limit the study of social influences to proximal group bonds. Even though primary social groups' perspectives about the body are imprinted on individuals, more ubiquitous WE cultural preferences are equally germane. Sandra (29) argues, "It's silly to think your tattoo is always defined the same way. It's even sillier to think a tattoo is defined as meaningful by people immediately around you." Although enthusiasts articulate how close social relationships are intextuated into and confirmed by their tattoos (see DeMello, 2000; Sanders, 1989; Steward, 1990), we should heed Sandra's suggestion and attend to how one's location in a broader matrix of interdependence is deeply embedded in tattoo projects.

By widening our analytical lens and exploring the impact of diffuse cultural habits on body modification attitudes, one may examine how tattoo enthusiasts display an acceptance of established cultural standards to improve, beautify and personalize the body through its invasive manipulation (see Dutton, 1995). In Carl's excerpt above, for example, he mentions how the tattoo makes his body more "masculine," thereby indicating his understanding of the appropriately gendered body. Equally, the vast majority of tattoo enthusiasts interviewed (83, 92%), speak of the power and legitimacy of cultural expectations to perform identity through "aesthetically pleasing" forms of physical manipulation. Despite claims that women are more pressured than men to conform with such cultural body ideals (Balsamo, 1996; Davis, 1997), ethnographic data collected in this study point to the sweeping impact of established constructions of the "body beautiful" on both.

Tattooing is described, for instance, by many enthusiasts as a calculated effort to "fit in with other people and look appealing" (Jill, 34). Tattoos are clearly forms of "social capital" (Bourdieu, 1984) in this respect, and document the social power, accolade and acceptance garnered by manipulating the "natural" body to comply with diffuse figurational norms. Just as cosmetic surgery (Gillespie, 1996), dieting (Lupton, 1996) and exercise (Loland, 2000) empower practitioners by generating culturally revered body shapes (i.e., young, slim, toned and beautiful), tattooing produces aesthetically enhanced and socially acknowledged bodies. Tattooing narratives speak of a cultural pressure to do "something" with the body and make it more physically attractive. Jim's (24) narrative suggests:

An ugly body I can forgive as long as you're trying to look better. Not everyone is beautiful, but if you don't try to enhance yourself, you're lazy. You work at being attractive, it doesn't come naturally. . . . My tattoos get so many compliments, and part of it comes from people's realization of how much effort I put into them. And, since they're art and not just Post-It notes tacked onto my body, I know people admire the way I look. I mean, don't we all treat gorgeous, carefully sculpted bodies better than hideous ones?

Jim explains that building "better looking" bodies (i.e., powerful, beautiful and controlled) is a vehicle for acquiring recognition, admiration, and inclusion within mutually identified WE groups (see Maguire and Mansfield, 1998). Jim does not view tattooed bodies as stark rejections of established WE norms and ideologies in Canada, but rather a fulfilment of the imperative to maintain an outwardly decorated/cultural body. Eve (30) similarly describes:

I see tattooing as crafting your body into a piece of moving art. Look at my arms . . . what is naturally attractive about a blank arm? Place a beautiful piece of art on your arm and it becomes something unique, something coloured, something fluid and moving. . . . I don't think we [Canadians] embrace art like in other cultures. Tattooing might be our generation's call to be aware of artistic bodies.

Conformity to established WE ideals about the body beautiful often involves commodifying the flesh (Falk, 1994; Featherstone, 2000; Miles et al., 1998). Canadians flock in droves to professional "body modificationists" to rework their bodies/selves in a multitude of non-invasive or invasive ways. Fitness experts, dieticians, physical therapists, cosmetic surgeons, aestheticians and personal stylists collectively instruct people to redesign, rehabilitate, reconstruct and extend their bodies through the aid of commercial products and services. Their services allow us to achieve preferred cultural body shapes through precise techniques, and understand the body as something to be individually "worked." The flesh is subjected to a series of rationalized services/products in the burgeoning body industries, and becomes more structured by specific "technologies of the self" (Foucault, 1977). Not surprisingly, tattoo enthusiasts speak of bodies as objects to be rationally modified via the aid of various "flesh artists":

> I see nothing wrong with changing what God gave you. With everything available to us, people are crazy for not taking advantage. I went through plastic surgeries, diets, and exercise programs in the last five years to get my body in the best looking and feeling shape possible. . . . So I thought, hey, a tattoo artist is a kind of aesthetician. He could help make me beautiful, like the doctor who surgically raised my brow, or the trainer who brought out my stomach [muscles] (Rachel, 35).

One might argue that as tattooing is progressively compared to other "professional" body modification industries in Canada (i.e., as respectable, businesslike and regulated), its cultural status is elevated. The tattoo artist Earl (26) explains:

> This isn't the old days. When people come into my studio they can expect to see a professional operation in every aspect. I don't take my art lightly, it's a very personal and intimate act for me. My clients share this seriousness and want to meet someone who is a professional artist when they come in. . . . Making my shop clean, having a strong portfolio, and respecting people as clients and friends are not "extras," these things are everyday practice. People know that . . . they have to know that or they'll find someone else who is a professional.

Enthusiasts' tattooing projects should not be conceived, however, as *explicit* consent to corporeal docility and consumerism. Enthusiasts do not envision the tattooing process as part of what Stu (27) called, "the blind acceptance of Canadians' ideas to look a certain, cookie-cutter way." While a standard cultural imperative to modify/improve the body is evident in many tattoo enthusiasts' narratives, so too is the culturally learned habit of innovatively "customizing" the body in the pursuit of individuality. In social figurations categorized by a high degree of functional and cultural interdependence (Elias, 1978; 1991; 1994), expressing one's sense of *I* to *we* and *they* others via "alternative" body projects is quite common:

> There's something about a tattoo that screams individuality. First, not everyone does it, so it's still tricky [non-mainstream]. Plus, you completely style the way it looks. No one else, probably ever, will look like you afterward. With every person I know running out to buy the spring line at the Gap or get the new "Ross" haircut, I see my tattoos as statements about who I really am. When my friends say, "wow, your tattoo is fantastic," the key word is *your*. They don't say "that tattoo you have is amazing". . . . Most people I know wouldn't *ever* copy someone else's tattoo. The whole point of redesigning your body is to make it your own, so why destroy it by stealing someone else's? (Carl, 26).

Whereas wearing a particular style of clothing, reshaping the muscles through exercise, or styling one's hair are well-received techniques for performing individuality and complying to established gender, ethnic, class and sexual standards of body idiom (see Miles et al., 1998), tattooing projects are considered ideal for literally illustrating individuality. In this process, enthusiasts like Carl tactically poach the tattoo's long-standing status as a symbol of "difference" in Canada, and invert its meaning by attributing pro-social and culturally normative meanings to the practice.

By describing the tattoo's significance as a symbol of individuality, enthusiasts also express a keen understanding of how physical display is monitored and judged as part of everyday life. They claim audiences are watching every physical communiqué offered in social spaces, and therefore one must regulate public behaviour to transmit favourable messages about the self. To them, the display-view-judge process is amplified by the ongoing development of communication, information and surveillance technologies, as well as our new cultural penchant for "on-line" digital voyeurism. Enthusiasts discuss how the "Internet age" encourages a stronger "culture of surveillance" (Foucault, 1977; Pecora, 2002), in which watching bodies move in every conceivable space is normative. Jack (26) explains:

> With people looking at you all the time, it has an impact. When I was a kid, mom always told me not to stare, but I don't think it's a rule anymore. I feel, like, well this is going to sound stupid, if I don't prepare myself to be watched, people will exclude me. . . . We spend so much time on-line looking at the most private and personal parts of life. I'm desensitized and jaded by everything and want to see everything, so I want to show everything. . . . How is tattooing any different? A tattoo is a piece of information about yourself that you put out for other people to download. It says, "I want you to watch me."

Jack's remarks allude to the taken-for-granted process of monitoring body cues in everyday life. The pressure to self-monitor is not seen as an invasive violation of personal rights and freedoms, but simply an off-shoot of participating in progressively high-tech social relationships.

In sum, tattoo enthusiasts' projects of self-redesign are "customized" forms of compliance to established body norms and practices in Western figurations like Canada. Tattoos reflect one's position in social networks of identification and illustrate one's identities and statuses held therein. The marks do not ring with irreverence to others, as they are interpreted by wearers as rational gestures of identity given to be "read" as cultural signs. Tattooing projects also reverberate with a cultural preference to beautify the body through highly individualized body work, especially via the help of service professionals. Enthusiasts ultimately contend that their predilections for tattooing are congruent with established cultural habituses detailing appropriate body use and display.

Affect Management and Conformity

The enthusiasts involved in this study view tattooing projects as communicative acts of conformity to prevailing body idiom in Canada.

Yet they equally believe tattoos speak a language of culturally normative "emotion work." Practically without exception, enthusiasts'
tattooing narratives collected in this study are layered with emotional accounts of social life. In particular, enthusiasts refer to tattooing as
a way of etching controlled representations of emotional experience
onto the body, or managing "problematic" emotions stirred through
social interaction. Many of the enthusiasts with whom I spoke understand their tattoos as "contained" representations of affect, and give
them to be read as such in the process of communicating "desirable"
messages about their selves.[3]

Among some women tattoo enthusiasts, for example, body mark-
ings are replete with strong feelings of sexual desire. Tattoos draw
wanted sexual attention to the body and heighten erotic sensations in
certain contexts of exchange (i.e., in a night club, on a date, within a
leisure scenario, or during intimate sexual interaction). Since
Canadian women have been, at least historically, dissuaded from
participating in tattooing in light of its hypermasculinist image
(Atkinson, 2002; Cohen, 2000; Wroblewski, 1992), marking the
body in this manner may signify sexual independence, freedom and
self-determination; qualities recently popularized by "girl power"
attitudes in Canada. Marie (22) remarks, "My 'Canadian girls kick ass'
tattoo is about being a proud and sexy woman. Girls do kick ass, so
my tattoo, which is right above my ass, lets guys know that I'm pretty
but I'm also very strong." Tattoos in this vein are neither flamboyant
nor large and exist on locations of the body that are concealed in
everyday life. They serve to accentuate the "natural" fleshy curves and
sexy contours of the stereotypically female body:

> When you arrange a tattoo with sex in mind, it gives you con-
> fidence. Men love my tattoos and I feel incredibly attractive
> when men gawk at me . . . . I want people to stare at my tattoos
> [around the hips] and see a confident woman who isn't afraid
> to be herself . . . a woman with sexual feelings . . . . I don't go
> around and sleep with every guy who gets aroused by my
> body. It's enough to know that I could have guys if I wanted.
> That's the real sexual power of a tattoo (Allison, 20).

Rather than expressing sexuality through forms of risk taking (i.e., promiscuity), these women emote sexuality through tattooing in a self-restrained and personally responsible manner.

Enthusiasts also engage in tattooing to manage feelings of grief or sorrow. Elias (1983; 1994), like Sennett (1998), points out that displays of sorrow are regularly "pushed behind the scenes" of social life because they connote shameful instability. If grief is publicly managed in a rehabilitative manner, though, individuals highlight their capacity for self-control. Particularly troubling or wrenching emotional experiences (most usually, the loss of valued bonds with *we* others) and their management structure such tattooing projects. Through a "controlled decontrolling of emotional controls" (Elias and Dunning, 1986), individuals lower their learned emotional guards and vent feelings of detachment from WE others in tattoo projects. Tattoos commemorating a death of a loved one, divorce, exiting from an especially close peer group (e.g., a team, school, or friendship clique), or even national "victimization" (as noted by the spate of post-9/11 tattoos) help illustrate:

> There's a point in your life where you either take the bull by the horns, or sit in your house and be a loser. When I left the [hockey] team, I wanted to be the second kind of guy. It felt like I was dying, having to be away from the guys and not feeling the camaraderie. It was total shit. My friends wanted nothing to do with me because I would piss and moan. So, I withdrew into a shell . . . that's where the tattoo [team logo] comes from. There's only so much you and your family can stand and then you help yourself . . . . I feel empty and depressed some days because I'm not the player I was, but having the tattoo reminds me of happier times. Those memories can't be taken away, and my tattoo shows I was once part of a special group of guys (Shane, 27).

Shane thinks that wallowing in self-pity or angst is counter-productive and emits an undesirable outsider image (i.e., as powerless, dominated or psychologically weak). Tattoo enthusiasts like him prefer to rework the body through tattooing and engage in innovative self-help. To receive personal meaning for Shane, this self-help must be recognized and understood by others.

Although largely misinterpreted in the tattooing literature, feelings of fear and anxiety motivate certain tattooing projects. Bodies are tattooed by some individuals in response to fears produced by a gamut of diseases (e.g., cancer, Alzheimer's and AIDS/HIV), social conditions placing people at risk (e.g., crime, poverty, discrimination, war, terrorism and stratification), and cultural trends restructuring WE/THEY group identification (e.g., gentrification, globalization, fragmentation and secularization). These tattooing projects communicate a sense of self-empowerment, efficacy and restraint in the face of such daunting conditions:

> It's totally understandable to me why tattooing is popular now, when there are a million ways your body can be invaded. How can I hear about rapists, gang-bangers, these fucking corporations who pollute every product we buy, or strangers with disease and not think, hmmm, maybe I should be afraid . . . . After a while you pay attention to how your body works and looks. A weak-looking body is a target . . . . With all the risks I can't control, I put on this armour [tattoos] and show how I won't lie down and be a victim. It's like drawing a line in the sand saying, I might be at risk but you can't cross this line. Right here is where I make my stand (Regina, 29).

By accepting the cultural imperative to perform identity through body work (i.e., including personal response to threat), Regina interprets tattooing as congruent with established figurational ideals about facing one's fears and overcoming them in socially/self-responsible ways.

Where certain tattoo enthusiasts intextuate symbols of social anxiety onto the body, others symbolise "positive" emotions like joy and exuberance through tattoos. Tattooing the body can be a gesture of love, happiness, excitement and belonging for those seeking to display the satisfaction gleaned from involvement in valued WE-groups. Individuals denote the value placed on emotional attachments and publicly announce the importance of such bonds by indelibly inscribing the skin:

> To show my friends and co-workers how much my relationship with my daughter means [through her tattoo] is incredible. We have an extremely close friendship, and having people see the symbol of her [daughter's abstract artwork] on

my back makes me glow. I'm bursting with pride for her and I can't find the words to describe the joy she adds to my life. I'm truly blessed to be her mom, so I try to find every way possible to let the world know . . . . Even when we are apart, I want her to be with me and feel the warmth of togetherness. My tattoo takes those feelings and puts them in this weird bottle I carry around with me (Helen, 45).

For Helen, tattooing is physically exhilarating and well represents the excitement produced by her relationship with her daughter. Elias and Dunning (1986) discuss how the pursuit of these "mimetic" forms of "exciting significance" are common in figurations wherein an elevated level of affective containment and moral regulation is customary. Narrative accounts of the tattooing process indicate how "significantly" body modification projects mark and extend emotions like excitement.

For a small group of the enthusiasts, tattooing projects express "negative" feelings of anger, resentment or aggression. These enthusiasts pursue tattooing projects as mutually identifiable and personally controlled coping mechanisms. Instead of attacking the source of frustration through a physically threatening or malicious act, they design corporeal projects to illustrate their learned capacities for self-restraint. Even though substantial portions of the social-psychological literature depict tattooing as symptomatic of an inability to cope with aggression (i.e., the tattoo is a quintessential mark of aggression or an anger-based lifestyle), enthusiasts articulate how tattooing the body releases anger in a restrained fashion:

The bastards let me go without any notice or decent explanation. I gave them over ten years of loyal, hard work, and I got the shaft. There's a happy story for you. The pricks didn't even have the courtesy to tell me to my face. The p.f.o. ["please fuck off"] papers were sent regular post . . . . They wouldn't allow any tattoos at work, so two weeks after I was canned, I headed down to the shop to do something for myself. Being tattooed restored my self-respect. I felt like walking into the office and punching out my ex-boss, but I channelled the anger. It changed my life because, like three months later, I felt so in control I started up the business I'm running now (Andy, 32).

Enthusiasts like Andy understand why the public display of self-help and personal control receives kudos. According to Andy, Canadians uphold the "keep things to yourself philosophy when things go wrong," but similarly expect people to share success stories of self-help when their circumstances improve. The pressure to contain negative affect is viewed by enthusiasts like him to be a fundamental part of the Canadian habitus. As Andy further describes, "Every time you turn on a television, wimps on talk shows are crying about how miserable their little lives are . . . but, the testimonials always turn around into how they privately overcame life's hardships . . . then we clap."

Unlike Andy, others tattoo their bodies to vent anger and frustration in deliberately confrontational ways. Such tattoo enthusiasts typically find membership in mutually identified outsider groups. Members of the "alternative" youth figuration called Straightedge, for example, illustrate their contempt for mainstream cultures of corporeal excess through selected tattoo projects (Atkinson, 2003b). The Straightedge Evan (24) states:

> Straightedge is a lifestyle that rejects the self-killing shoved down our throats as acceptable; like drinking, screwing without protection, and doing drugs . . . . My "Down for Life" tattoo is an emblem for the lifestyle of discipline I live each day of my life. I won't treat my body like a garbage dump and I want everyone to know how much disgust I feel about others who do. I find it really ironic when people see *me* as the freak of nature. Screw them, they're total hypocrites.

As Evan's story implies, individuals do not tattoo their bodies to manage fleeting sources of frustration, or to temporarily alleviate noxious environmental influences (Atkinson, 2003b). The tattooing process is a permanent gesture exhibiting a critical social commentary about one's "outsider" status and the cultural conditions creating outsider identities in a figuration.

In brief, tattoos are encoded with a broad range of emotions. By inspecting the narratives of Canadian tattoo enthusiasts, we learn how tattooing is not merely an unbridled outcome of uncontrolled emotionality, but simply one stage in the processual social experience of affect. Having internalized established cultural instruction to modify the body and regulate affective display, enthusiasts understand tattooing as a pro-social and rational method of communicating "normative" identity and emotion to others in a figuration.

◉ Discussion

A dominant theme running through Elias's research on long-term social transformation in Western nations is the idea that "early" (i.e., pre-Medieval) social configurations relied on coercion and external force as the main mechanisms of social control. But as functions within social institutions increasingly differentiate and people rely upon others more extensively in daily life, individuals become more attuned to the needs of many actors (Elias, 1994). The predictability and control of personal action is essential in complex social figurations, as individuals acquire more specific, extended and interdependent roles (Elias, 1983; 1994). Personality structures are subsequently altered over the long term such that cultural habits involving high levels of inner containment became part of the collective habitus (Elias, 1991; 1994; 1996).

Persons choosing to act impulsively or irrationally jeopardize their ascribed and achieved social positions in figurations demanding high levels of inner restraint. In step with and predating Goffman's (1959; 1963), Foucault's (1977; 1979), and Bourdieu's (1984) landmark statements on the disciplining of bodies via cultural codes, Elias argued that individuals in Western nations self-regulate all facets of public conduct and self-display because they fear a loss of status accompanying socially unwanted behaviour. To Elias (1994), this represents a "civilizing" change in the functioning of social control. Self-restraint among a vast group of people results when the experience of shame (and a learned compulsion to avoid it) becomes a cornerstone of their shared cultural habitus (Elias, 1994; 1996; Scheff, 2001). In conjunction with the push toward self-control and the notable impact of shame on personality structures, cultural thresholds toward licentious, disgusting, immoral or otherwise lascivious behaviours lower over the course of time (Elias, 1978; 1994).

In outlining the above civilizing processes, Elias (1994) underscores the importance of "bodily control" as a symbol of one's inner pacification. Arguing that the body transforms into a text through which a person performs social distinction, status and affective control, Elias (1983; 1994; 1996) notes how personal control is intentionally inscribed onto the skin. Key to understanding Elias's (1994) analysis of corporeal performance is the notion that bodies are increasingly rationalized over the course of civilizing processes. If affective containment and the daily exhibition of personal control symbolize one's cultural standing and help maintain one's positions, roles and varied social statuses, the inner pacification one "does" through body work significantly shapes one's social identity (Elias, 1983; 1994). Whereas the articulation of control through conversation may illustrate inner pacification, most notable forms of self-restraint are often unspoken corporeal acts of compliance to established body idiom.

Given the ongoing diversification in the cultural uses of tattooing in Canada and some of the sensitizing theoretical principles outlined above, social scientists might recalibrate our understandings of the social interdependencies and affective communications embedded in tattoos. Preferred academic interpretations of the body project hold firmly to a conceptualization of tattoo enthusiasts as impulsive and non-reflexive social misfits who express disdain for conventional body practices (see Armstrong, 1992; Armstrong and Pace-Murphy, 1997; Loimer and Werner, 1992). Despite recent estimates that anywhere from 10%–20% of Canadians have tattoos (Atkinson, 2003a), academics generally deconstruct tattooing as atypical and isolated risk-taking behaviour. However, by letting go of heretofore preferred theoretical constructions of tattooing and actually conversing with tattoo enthusiasts, we begin to appreciate "alternative" empirical lessons about this brand of body modification.

Figurational sociology may help rebuild the decaying analytical bridge between social-psychological constructions of tattooing and everyday interpretations of tattoos that wearers make. Akin to Copes and Forsyth's (1993) analysis of the body project, figurational sociologists point out how popular uses of tattooing reflect a collective sensitivity to the social importance of publicly performed inner restraint and acceptance of established cultural body habits (Atkinson 2003a; 2003b). Enthusiasts' narratives suggest how social interdependencies influence both the desire to become tattooed and the character of tattooing projects. Furthermore, individuals either explicitly or implicitly manage affective expression through their tattoos, thereby transforming the skin into a social billboard of normative emotion work.

Even though Canadian tattoo enthusiasts promulgate pro-social constructions of the act, many do not wish tattooing to achieve *widespread* cultural acceptance. In fearing the tattoo will transform into a vacuous cultural commodity through its common usage (and quickly forgotten as a passé trend), enthusiasts stress how "tattooing is too good for most people" (Kurt, 27). For these people, the historically deviant nature of the practice is alluring, exciting and chic. It is a quasi-normative form of body marking allowing one to customize the self through "alternative" skin art and explore a culturally recognizable sense of "individuality" (Atkinson 2003a; Sanders, 1989).

Contemporary tattooing in Canada is, then, a social paradox and strange amalgam of cultural values about the body and its display. The tattooed body both marks long-term "civilized" cultural preferences to alter the flesh as part of "doing" social identity, and signifies more recent social influences on body modification preferences arising from corporeal commodification, risk processes and technological innovation. In reading the tattooed body as a marker of figurational ebbs and flows, the "micrological" and "macrological" influences on our cultural attitudes regarding tattooed flesh are highlighted. Future social-psychological research on tattooing in Canada and abroad should challenge overly simplistic, ahistorical and stereotypical constructions of the tattooing process, and pursue empirical explanations of the practice grounded in the lived experience of being tattooed.

Endnotes

[1]For a full description of the research methodologies employed in this study see Atkinson (2003a).

[2]Figurational sociology is often defined through the work of Norbert Elias. Elias's work and the bedrock of contemporary "figurational" approaches are moulded by the concept of "civilizing processes." In studying Western figurations like France, England and Germany, Elias notes how individual personalities transform over historical periods such that self-restraint, foresight, and mutual recognition become engrained in everyday cultural habits (a process referred to as "psychogenesis"). As a result, he traces the development of such changes in personalities to broader "social-structural" shifts within figurations, including the formation of courts, an increased division of labour, the pacification of life through a monopolization of violence by the state, and a general increase in social interdependencies (processes collectively referred to as "sociogenesis"). For Elias and figurational sociologists, then, the analysis of how social spaces are "civilized" (read self-controlled) or "de-civilized" (read affectively unrestrained) is a fundamental task.

[3]As outlined elsewhere (Atkinson, 2002) there is a noteworthy correlation between one's gender and the size/amount of one's tattoos. Canadian women tend to receive smaller, more concealable and conservative tattoos in comparison to men. This does not suggest, though, that men more boastfully express inner-restraint or emotion work through tattoo projects. The size, amount and content of one's tattoos should not be haphazardly associated with the strength of one's emotions, ability to manage affect, understanding of established body idiom, or desire to have his/her body read as normative.

References

Armstrong, M. 1994. "Tattoos: A risk-taking art." *Texas Nursing*, Vol. 68, No. 2, pp. 8–9.

Armstrong, M. 1995. "Adolescent tattoos: Educating vs. pontificating." *Pediatric Nursing*, Vol. 21, No. 6, pp. 561–64.

Armstrong, M., Y. Masten and R. Martin. 2000. "Adolescent pregnancy, tattooing, and risk taking." *American Journal of Maternal Child Nursing*, Vol. 25, No. 5, pp. 258–61.

Armstrong, M. and C. McConnell. 1994. "Tattooing in adolescence, more common than you think: The phenomenon and risks." *Journal of School Nursing*, Vol. 10, No. 1. pp. 22–29.

Armstrong, M. and K. Pace-Murphy. 1997. "Tattooing: Another adolescent risk behavior warranting health education." *Applied Nursing Research*, Vol. 10, No. 4, pp. 181–89.

Armstrong, R. 1992. "Tattooing should be regulated." *New England Journal of Medicine*, Vol. 326, No. 3, pp. 207.

Atkinson, M. 2002. "Pretty in ink: Conformity, resistance, and negotiation in women's tattooing." *Sex Roles*, Vol. 47, Nos. 5–6, pp. 219–35.

Atkinson, M. 2003a. *Tattooed: The Sociogenesis of a Body Art*. Toronto: The University of Toronto Press.

Atkinson, M. 2003b. "The civilizing of resistance: Straightedge tattooing." *Deviant Behavior*, Vol. 24, No. 3, pp. 197–220.

Atkinson, M. and W. Shaffir. 2003. "Doing nothing as a strategy in field-work." Paper presented at the Qualitative Analysis Conference. Ottawa, Ont., 22–24 May.

Atkinson, M. and K. Young. 2001. "Flesh journeys: Neo Primitives and the contemporary rediscovery of radical body modification." *Deviant Behavior*, Vol. 22, No. 2, pp. 117–46.

Balsamo, A. 1996. *Technologies of the Gendered Body: Reading Cyborg Women*. Durham: Duke University Press.

Blishen, B. 1967. "A socioeconomic index for occupations in Canada." *The Canadian Review of Sociology and Anthropology*, Vol. 4, No. 1, pp. 41–53.

Bourdieu, P. 1984. *Distinction: A Social Critique of Judgement of Taste*. Cambridge: Harvard University Press.

Braithwaite, R., A. Robillard, T. Woodring, T. Stephens and K. Arriola. 2001. "Tattooing and body piercing among adolescent detainees: Relationship to alcohol and other drug use." *Journal of Substance Abuse*, Vol. 13, No. 1–2, pp. 5–16.

Burchett, G. and P. Leighton. 1958. *Memoirs of a Tattooist*. London: Oldbourne Book Company.

Caplan, J. 2000. *Written on the Body: The Tattoo in European and American History*. Princeton: Princeton University Press.

Carroll, S., R. Riffenburgh, T. Roberts and E. Myhre. 2002. "Tattoos and body piercings as indicators of adolescent risk-taking behaviors." *Pediatrics*, Vol. 109, No. 6, pp. 1021–28.

Cenieeros, S. 1998. "Tattooing, body piercing, and Russian roulette." *Journal of Nervous and Mental Disease*, Vol. 186, No. 8, pp. 199–204.

Cohen, A. 1955. *Delinquent Boys: The Culture of the Gang.* New York: Free Press.

Cohen, T. 2000. *The Tattoo.* London: Greenwich Editions.

Copes, J. and C. Forsyth. 1993. "The tattoo: A social psychological explanation." *International Review of Modern Sociology,* Vol. 23, pp. 83–89.

Davis, K. 1997. "My body is my art: Cosmetic surgery as feminist utopia?" *The European Journal of Women's Studies,* Vol. 4, No. 1, pp. 23–37.

DeMello, M. 1995. "Not just for bikers anymore: Popular representations of American tattooing." *Journal of Popular Culture,* Vol. 29, No. 3. pp. 37–52.

DeMello, M. 2000. *Bodies of Inscription: A Cultural History of the Modern Tattoo Community.* Durham: Duke University Press.

Dutton, K. 1995. *The Perfectible Body: The Western Idea of Physical Development.* London: Cassell.

Elias, N. 1978. *What is Sociology?* London: Hutchinson.

Elias, N. 1983. *The Court Society.* Oxford: Basil Blackwell.

Elias, N. 1991. *The Society of Individuals.* Oxford: Basil Blackwell.

Elias, N. 1994. *The Civilising Process.* Oxford: Basil Blackwell.

Elias, N. 1996. *The Germans: Studies of Power Struggles and the Development of Habitus in the Nineteenth and Twentieth Centuries.* Oxford: Polity Press.

Elias, N. and E. Dunning. 1986. *Quest for Excitement: Sport and Leisure in the Civilizing Process.* Oxford: Basil Blackwell

Elias, N. and J. Seotson. 1965. *The Established and the Outsiders.* London: Sage.

Falk, P. 1994. *The Consuming Body.* London: Sage.

Featherstone, M. 2000. *Body Modification.* London: Sage.

Fisher, J. 2002. "Tattooing the body, making culture." *Body & Society,* Vol. 8, No. 4, pp. 91–107.

Foucault, M. 1977. *Discipline and Punish: The Birth of the Prison.* London: Penguin Books.

Foucault, M. 1979. *The History of Sexuality, Volume 1: An Introduction.* London: Allen Lane/Penguin.

Frederick, C. and K. Bradley. 2000. "A different kind of normal? Psychological and motivational characteristics of young adult tattooers and body piercers." *North American Journal of Psychology,* Vol. 2, No. 2, pp. 379–91.

Friedman, A. 1996. "From subcultural sign to fashion statement: The changing meaning of tattoos." Paper presented at the Popular Culture Association. Las Vegas, Nev., 10–13 April.

Gallick, R. 1996. "The tattoo: An American pop art form" *The Mid-Atlantic Almanac*, Vol. 5, pp. 1–13.

Gell, A. 1993. *Wrapping in Images: Tattooing in Polynesia*. Oxford: Oxford University Press.

Gilbert, S. 2000. *Tattoo History: A Sourcebook*. San Francisco: Juno Publishing.

Gillespie, R. 1996. "Women, the body and brand extension in medicine: Cosmetic surgery and the paradox of choice." *Women and Health*, Vol. 24, No. 4, pp. 69–85.

Gittleson, N. and G. Wallfn. 1973. "The tattooed male patient." *British Journal of Psychiatry*, Vol. 122, No. 568, pp. 295–300.

Gittleson, N., G. Wallfn and K. Dawson-Butterworth. 1969. "The tattooed psychiatric patient." *British Journal of Psychiatry*, Vol. 115, pp. 1249–53.

Goffman, E. 1959. *Presentation of Self in Everyday Life*. Garden City: Doubleday.

Goffman, E. 1963. *Stigma*. Englewood Cliffs: Spectrum.

Goffman, E. 1974. *Frame Analysis*. Cambridge. Harvard University Press.

Goldstein, N. 1979. "Laws and regulations relating to tattoos." *Journal of Dermatologic Surgery and Oncology*, Vol. 5, pp. 913–15.

Gottfredson, M. and T. Hirschi. 1990. *A General Theory of Crime*. Stanford: Stanford University Press.

Govenar, A. 1988. "The variable context of Chicano tattooing." In *Marks of Civilization*. A. Rubin (ed.). Los Angeles: Museum of Cultural History, University of California, pp. 209–17.

Grief, J. and W. Hewitt. 1998. "The living canvass: Health issues in tattooing, body piercing and branding." *Advances for Nurse Practitioners*, Vol. 12, pp. 26–31.

Grumet, G. 1983. "Psychodynamic implications of tattoos." *American Journal of Orthopsychiatry*, Vol. 53, No. 3, pp. 482–92.

Gubrium, J. and J. Holstein. 1997. *The New Language of Qualitative Method*. New York: Oxford University Press.

Gurke, B. and M. Armstrong. 1997. "D-tag: Erasing the tag of gang membership." *Journal of School Nursing*, Vol. 13, No. 2, pp. 13–17.

Hebdige, D. 1979. *Subculture: The Meaning of Style*. New York: Methuen and Company.

Houghton, S., K. Durkin, E. Parry, Y. Turbett and P. Odgers. 1996. "Amateur tattooing practices and beliefs among high school adolescents." *Journal of Adolescent Health*, Vol. 19, No. 6, pp. 420–25.

Howell, R., R. Payne and A. Roe. 1971. "Differences among behavioral variables, personal characteristics, and personality scores of tattooed and non-tattooed prison inmates." *Journal of Research in Crime and Delinquency*, Vol. 8, pp. 32–37.

Irwin, K. 2000. "Negotiating the tattoo." In *Constructions of Deviance*. P. Adler and P. Adler (eds.). Belmont, Calif.: Wadsworth, pp. 469–80.

Kaplan, D. and A. Dubro. 1986. *Yakuza: The Explosive Account of Japan's Criminal Underworld*. Reading, Mass.: Addison-Wesley.

Kent, D. 1997. "Decorative bodies: The significance of convicts' tattoos." *Journal of Australian Studies*, Vol. 53, pp. 78–88.

Kitamura, T. and K. Kitamura. 2001. *Bushido: Legacies of the Japanese Tattoo*. Atglen, Penn.: Schiffer Publishing.

Klesse, C. 1999. "Modern primitivism: Non-mainstream body modification and racialized representation." *Body & Society*, Vol. 5, No. 2–3, pp. 15–38.

Kom, K. 1996. "Body adornment and tattooing: Clinical issues and state regulations." *Physician Assistant*, Vol. 20, No. 5, pp. 85–100.

Lofland, J. and L. Lofland. 1995. *Analysing Social Settings*. Belmont, Calif.: Wadsworth.

Loimer, N. and E. Werner. 1992. "Tattooing and high-risk behaviour among drug addicts." *Medicine and Law*, Vol. 11, No. 3–4, pp. 167–74.

Loland, N. 2000. "The art of concealment in a culture of display: Aerobicizing women's and men's experiences and use of their own bodies." *Sociology of Sport Journal*, Vol. 17, No. 2, pp. 111–29.

Lombroso-Ferrero, G. 1972. *Criminal Man: According to the Classification of Cesare Lombroso*. Montelair, N.J.: Patterson Smith.

Lupton, D. 1996. *Food, the Body, and the Self*. London: Sage.

Maguire, J. and L. Mansfield, 1998. "No-body's perfect: Women, aerobies and the body beautiful." *Sociology of Sport Journal*, Vol. 15, No. 2, pp. 109–37.

Martin, A. 1997. "On teenagers and tattoos." *Journal of the American Academy of Child and Adolescent Psychiatry*, Vol. 36, No. 6, pp. 860–61.

Maseia-Lees, F. and P. Sharpe. 1992. *Tattoo, Torture, Mutilation, and Adornment: The Denaturalization of the Body in Culture and Text.* New York: SUNY Press.

MeCabe, M. 1997. *New York City Tattoo: The Oral History of an Urban Art.* Honolulu: Hardy Marks Publications.

Measey, L. 1972. "The psychiatric and social relevance of tattoos in Royal Navy detainees," *British Journal of Criminology*, Vol. 12, pp. 182–86.

Mifflin, M. 1997. *Bodies of Subversion: A Secret History of Women and Tattoo.* New York: June Books.

Miles, S. D. Cliff and V. Burr. 1998. "Fitting in and sticking out: Consumption, consumer meanings and the construction of young people's identities." *Journal of Youth Studies*, Vol. 1, No. 1, pp. 81–120.

Monaghan, L. 2001. "Looking good, feeling good: The embodied pleasures of vibrant physicality." *Sociology of Health and Illness*, Vol. 23, No. 3, pp. 330–56.

Myers, J. 1997. "Nonmainstream body modification." In *Constructions of Deviance* P. Adler and P. Adler (eds.), Belmont, Calif.: Wadsworth, pp. 516–32.

Newman, G. 1982. "The implication of tattooing in prisoners." *Journal of Clinical Psychiatry*, Vol. 43, pp. 231–34.

Pecora, V. 2002. "The culture of surveillance." *Qualitative Sociology*, Vol. 25, No. 3, pp. 345–58.

Pollak, O. and E. McKenna. 1945. "Tattooed psychotic patients." *American Journal of Psychiatry*, Vol. 101, pp. 673–74.

Prus, R. 1996. *Symbolic Interaction and Ethnographic Research: Intersubjectivity and the Study of Human Lived Experience.* Albany: SUNY Press.

Roberts, T. and S. Ryan. 2002. "Tattooing and high-risk behavior in adolescents." *Pediatrics*, Vol. 110, No. 6, pp. 1058–63.

Ronai, C. 1992. "The reflexive self through narrative: A night in the life of an exotic dancer/researcher." In *Investigating Subjectivity: Research on Lived Experience.* C. Ellis and M. Flaherty (eds.), Newbury Park, Calif.: Sage, pp. 102–24.

Rosenblatt, D. 1997. "The antisocial skin: Structure, resistance, and "modern primitive" adornment in the United States." *Cultural Anthropology*, Vol. 12, No. 3, pp. 287–334.

Rubin, A. 1988. *Marks of Civilization: Artistic Transformations of the Human Body*. Los Angeles: Museum of Cultural History, University of California.

Sanders, C. 1989. *Customizing the Body: The Art and Culture of Tattooing*. Philadelphia: Temple University Press.

Scheff, T. 2001. "Unpacking the civilizing process: Interdependence and shame." In *Norbert Elias and Human Interdependencies*. T. Salumets (ed.), Montreal and Kingston: McGill-Queen's University Press, pp. 99–115.

Seaton, E. 1987. "Profaned bodies and purloined looks: The prisoner's tattoo and the researcher's gaze." *Journal of Communication Inquiry*, Vol. 11, No. 2, pp. 17–25.

Sennett, R. 1998. *The Corrosion of Character*. New York: Norton.

Shilling, C. 1993. *The Body and Social Theory*. London: Sage.

St. Clair, L. and A. Govenar. 1981. *Stoney Knows How: Life as a Tattoo Artist*. Lexington: University of Kentucky Press.

Steward, S. 1990. *Bad Boys and Tough Tattoos: A Social History of the Tattoo with Gangs. Sailors, and Street Corner Punks*. New York: The Haworth Press.

Vail, A. 1999. "Tattoos are like potato chips . . . you can't have just one: The process of becoming and being a collector." *Deviant Behavior*, Vol. 20, No. 3, pp. 253–73.

Webb, S. 1979. *Pushing Ink: The Fine Art of Tattooing*. New York: McGraw-Hill.

White, P. and K. Young. 1997. "Health and the New Age Ascetic." In *Taking Sport Seriously: Social Issues in Canadian Sport*. P. Donnelly (ed.), Toronto: Thompson, pp. 106–10.

Williams, K. 1998. "Tattoos, scars, body adornment and dishevelment in an acute psychiatric population." *Psychiatric Bulletin*, Vol. 22, pp. 94–96.

Willis, P. 1978. *Profane Culture*, London: Routledge and Kegan Paul.

Willis, P. 1980. "Notes on method." In *Culture, Media, Language*, S. Hall (ed.), London: Hutchinson, pp. 88–96.

Wroblewski, C. 1992. *Tattooed Women*. London: Virgin Publishing.

❂ ❂ ❂

Questions

1. Is tattooing a form of deviance? Explain why or why not.

2. Explain how Atkinson collected the data for this article. What other research methods could he have used?

3. According to the article, why do people get tattoos?

4. What is a "figuration"? How is it important to understanding tattoos?

5. Do you have a tattoo? If so, why did you get one? Does your explanation fit with Atkinson's?